SEARCH *FOR*
THE MEANING
OF LIFE

OTHER BOOKS
BY WILLIGIS JÄGER

Contemplation
A Christian Path

The Way to Contemplation
Encountering God Today

SEARCH *FOR* *THE* MEANING *OF* LIFE

Essays and
Reflections
on the
Mystical
Experience

Willigis Jäger

TRIUMPH™ BOOKS
Liguori, Missouri

Published by Triumph™ Books
Liguori, Missouri 63057-9999
An Imprint of Liguori Publications

Library of Congress Cataloging-in-Publication Data

Jäger, Willigis.
　　[Suche nach dem Sinn des Lebens. English]
　　Search for the meaning of life ; essays and reflections on the mystical experience / Willigis Jäger. — 1st ed.
　　　　p. cm.
　　Translation of: Suche nach dem Sinn des Lebens.
　　ISBN 0-89243-774-X
　　1. Mysticism. 2. Mysticism—Catholic Church. 3. Catholic Church-Doctrines. I. Title.
BV5082.2.J3413 1995
248.2'2—dc20　　　　　　　　　　　　　　　　　　　94-40337
　　　　　　　　　　　　　　　　　　　　　　　　　　　　　CIP

CONTENTS

TRANSLATOR'S FOREWORD

Even readers well-versed in Catholic spirituality will be surprised by this collection of lectures and talks on mysticism by the German Benedictine, Fr. Willigis Jäger. Although Fr. Jäger's thinking is anchored in the work of such traditional writers as John Cassian, Meister Eckhart, and John of the Cross, that tradition is itself quite radical and offers a great deal of scope for personal interpretation.

Fr. Jäger is a mystical theologian, as his writing clearly demonstrates. For example, while a dogmatic theologian will talk about "objective" truths, Father Jäger, as a mystical theologian, is more attuned to subjective experience. Whereas the dogmatic theologian sees the Fall as the cause of death and the legacy of original sin, a mystical theologian views it more as an image of the universal human tragedy of "being cast out into the loneliness of the ego." While dogmatic theology stresses the enormous distance between God and humans, mystical theology boldly dreams of union and even fusion with God.

This is what Fr. Jäger offers in *Search for the Meaning of Life*. Mysticism, as Father Jäger shows, is not sloppily emotional, but clear-eyed and clearheaded. It is open to all the sciences, whether psychology, cosmology, or physics; it is also open to other religions, especially Buddhism (Fr. Jäger is an expert in Zen), Hinduism, and Islam. It is intensely pragmatic, a skill one learns through patient, carefully monitored exercises. And, as the many testimonials from ordinary laypeople who have taken Fr. Jäger's courses confirm, it *works*.

The reader is invited to bear in mind that this is a translation from the original German text. It is also a collection, as mentioned before, of lectures and talks. Thus the movement of the text will occasionally appear irregular and certain content will be repetitious. These minor intricacies, however, simply enrich the authentic wealth of wisdom and experience Fr. Jäger shares with his audience. Readers who can leave behind the baggage of their orthodox preconceptions will find in this book an exhilarating and enlightening journey.

PETER HEINEGG

PART I

LECTURES

INTRODUCTION

Why these lectures? Didn't the *Tao te Ching* say long ago, "The one who knows doesn't speak; the one who speaks doesn't know"? But in a Zen didactic poem we read: "With the intention of attracting the blind, Buddha let playful words spring from his golden mouth."[1] The word is what lures us onto the path, until we notice that *IT* can't be found there.

In addition, many Christians today are looking for guidance in their contemplative prayer. They often turn to Hinduism and Buddhism because they get practically no help at all from Christianity. In fact, as in the past, they are often warned, even in monasteries and by the Church's institutions, about the dangers of contemplative prayer.

I'd like to begin with a fantasy. According to the latest scientific findings, the universe has been in existence for around seventeen billion years. If we compress these seventeen billion years into a single year so that each month equals a little over a billion years, we get an interesting picture.

Through the momentum of the mysterious primordial explosion, matter expanded against its own gravity and in the process began to cool. In a tiny fraction of the first second of January 1, matter comes into being: the elementary particles, and immediately after that, the simplest atomic nuclei, hydrogen and helium. Before the end of January, matter and radiation become uncoupled, and the galaxies emerge.

Around the middle of August, our solar system forms from a collapsing cloud of gas and dust. Earth witnesses the arrival of the first complicated chemical, followed by biological structures. The oldest rocks on the earth's surface go back to the middle of September.

The beginning of October marks the birth of fossil algae. In the course of two months, an enormous variety of plant and animal species begins growing in the waters.

On December 19, the plants colonize the continents. By the twentieth the land masses are covered with forests, and life begins creating an oxygen-rich atmosphere. On the twenty-second and twenty-third fish evolve into four-footed amphibians and conquer the moist surface of the earth. They in turn evolve into the reptiles on the twenty-fourth. On the twenty-fifth the first warm-blooded creatures come into existence. Late in the evening of the twenty-fifth, the first mammals appear alongside the dominant saurians. On the night of the thirtieth, the Alps begin to fold upward.

On the night of the thirty-first (on the last day, in other words) humans branch off from their ancestral apes. The Neanderthals live five minutes before midnight, and seventeen seconds before twelve Jesus Christ is born. One-half second before twelve the technological age commences.[2]

American scientists claim to have discovered a cosmos that does not derive from the above-described Big Bang. Evidently, cosmic systems come and go without beginning or end.

THE SIGNIFICANCE OF HUMAN LIFE

In the cosmic context, what does the birth and life of the human Jesus mean (in the last "seventeen seconds" of the universe)? How has the Divine Reality revealed itself in other galaxies? Doesn't it always and everywhere reveal itself in everything that takes on form? Isn't it the structural principle of evolution? Do we really have to look for it outside of evolution?

What does redemption mean, or the resurrection of the body? In a million years humans will have distanced themselves from today's human being, just as we have from the apes. So, as what species will we be resurrected?

What do eighty years of human life mean in the face of the billions of years the cosmos has been in existence?

What does time mean? What does eternity?

What is the meaning of human systems of thought, of dogmatic declarations?

How long can we go on talking about God as if the rest of the universe revolved around the Earth?

In the course of cosmic evolution, mind has no doubt developed a thousandfold in other galaxies as well. Indeed, mind is the primal matter from which everything is made. Why do we have to separate them into a dualism?

OBSOLETE OR UP-TO-DATE UNDERSTANDING OF THE WORLD AND RELIGION

Mysticism has always tried to look through and beyond these questions. Just as science and transpersonal psychology do today, the mystic school has always spoken of spaces in consciousness that allow us to get a more comprehensive experience of reality. Atomic scientist Gary Zukav writes: "Do not be surprised if physics curricula in the twenty-first century include classes in meditation."[3] By meditation he means a transrational experience. Humanity and the cosmos are more than our intellectual consciousness can prove. *Ratio* (reason), the mystics tell us, is a prison.

In the final analysis, how I formulate my experience of Ultimate Reality depends upon whether my understanding of the self and the world is anthropological or cosmic. People who consider the human species the center of cosmic events will always run into trouble when they try to describe mystical experience. Reason must cling to the notion of a preeminently personal structure because it has no other way of interpreting the world. By contrast, mystical experience transcends such grand personal structures. It is transparent; it moves beyond dualistic opposition; it is more comprehensive than reason and differs from it in kind and not just degree. Reason can't understand that, and so neither can it accept it. Reason senses that behind mystical experience there is a dissolution of the person and the danger of its own structure being eliminated. Anyone who can't deal with an experience transcending human reason will always have problems with mysticism. Such people will be inclined to suspect even "authentic gnosis."

REDOGMATIZATION OF MYSTICAL EXPERIENCE

Because our Christian faith is interpreted rationally, the experience of Christian mystics has always been redogmatized, which ultimately means repersonalized. Not a few Christian theologians maintain that a personal understanding of the world and faith is *the* new achievement that won Christianity a place among the world's religions. But against the background of continual advances in the sciences and especially psychology, this personalistic bias is looking increasingly problematic. Interpretation of Jesus' life and teaching has not kept pace with scientific findings. Ultimate Reality is transpersonal and beyond the concept of God, cherished by the traditional theistic religions, which lack the cosmic and holistic perspective. The way a contemporary thinking person understands the world sharply diverges from the theologian's interpretation.

Basically, we have yet to overcome the so-called ontological dualism between God and creation, although that is precisely what Jesus aimed at overcoming. "I am the vine, you are the branches" (John 15:5); "I do not call you servants any longer,…but I have called you friends" (John 15:15); "…that they may all be one. As you, Father, are in me and I am in you, may they also be in us, so that the world may believe that you have sent me" (John 17:21). Finally, Jesus strove to bring us to the same consciousness that filled him. In contemplation we strive for the consciousness that Christ had.

More and more people are managing to complete the rational domain of experience through transpersonal possibilities. The esoteric paths of the great religions are proving to be a valuable help in this effort.

THANKS TO ALL WHO HAVE ENRICHED ME

The following lectures contain not only my own experiences and realizations but the thoughts and experiences of many other men and women. At times I could not determine whose literary property I was transcribing and who was the author of a given thought. I have learned valuable things in many private conversations and in some books as well. I therefore extend my most heartfelt thanks to all those who have contributed to the making of these pieces.

CHAPTER 1

SEARCH FOR THE
MEANING OF LIFE

E veryday human consciousness may be compared to a passenger on a ship. The passenger can see only as far as the horizon. But what lies beyond the horizon is greater and mightier by far than everything in front of it. Our ego-consciousness recognizes only the reality accessible to reason and the senses. What lies beyond this capacity for knowledge, however, is far greater and more powerful.

"Just as a hand held in front of your eyes conceals the tallest mountain, so our little earthly life conceals the vision of the manifold lights and wonders that deeply enrich our world. And those who can pull that little earthly life from in front of their eyes, the way one pulls away a hand, will see the powerful splendor of inner worlds."[1]

The field of perception open to ego-consciousness is a limited one. We find ourselves in a cosmic system whose real dimensions lie "beyond the horizon," incomprehensible to our ego. On the one side, matter disappears into the subatomic realm in fields of force. On the macrocosmic side, matter slips away into the "black hole." Matter has nothing solid or constant about it. It is porous; it arises and passes away from our senses and our understanding. We can split matter; when we do, however, it no longer breaks down into smaller parts, but is transformed into energy. And energy can once again appear anew as particles, as matter.

7

The previous scientific world picture, based on Newtonian physics, declared axiomatically that all the phenomena in the cosmos are to be explained solely through material causes. This principle, however, is no longer tenable. The foundations of matter are nonmaterial in nature. The constant element in the universe is not statics but dynamics. And the continuity of our life lies not in what we are now, but in the core of our being, which goes with us through all the forms of our existence.

COSMIC DIMENSIONS

In our solar system, the Milky Way, there are about one hundred billion (10^{11}) shining stars. With our technical equipment we can make out around a hundred million (10^8) such solar systems. We have no idea how many such systems lie beyond our reach. Thus we are faced with a many-dimensional world, but we can take in only some of its dimensions.

Hans Peter Dürr once proposed the following example in a lecture: Vis-à-vis the universe we are like an illiterate person looking at a magnificent poem. Since we can't read or write, we scan the whole thing carefully and note that some letters are continuously repeated. So we begin to count these signs, to organize and catalog them. In the end, we know that the piece of paper contains so many A's, B's and C's, and so on. We are proud of our research, but we haven't the slightest understanding of the poem.

The universe, which came into being an unthinkable number of light-years ago and which will likely go on endlessly (since the downfall of worlds and the emergence of new worlds is an essential structural principle of this universe), baffles our understanding, much as the meaning of the poem baffles the illiterate. The universe has obviously been organized in a nonrational way. Rationality is only one "computer program," and God has many such programs.

Apart from humans, are there intelligent beings in the universe? Most scientists consider it probable that the cosmos contains civilizations similar to the one on our earth.

Harlow Shapley alerts us: "Of all the stars in the universe perhaps only every thousandth star has planets. Let's make the very conservative assumption that only every thousandth planetary system has a planet with temperatures capable of sustaining life. Let us further assume that only one of a thousand of these is big enough to have an atmosphere. Among these remaining planets, let's choose again only one out of a thousand and assume that these planets also have a chemical composition favorable to the generation of life. According to our calculations, this would mean that of every thousand billion stars there would be exactly one with a viable planet. And then how many viable planets would there be? In that case there would still be a hundred million viable planets in the cosmos. A hundred million planets like the earth."

So we are by no means as unique as we might think. Perhaps other creatures have become much more highly developed. Perhaps we are not the "crown of creation" after all.

THE MEANING OF OUR LIFE

As human beings, we ask ourselves "What can life, which may last eighty years, possibly mean, when measured against these tremendous expanses of time? What do eighty years of life mean on the scale of billions? What does a day mean, or an hour? What importance does a war have, waged on this speck of dust called earth? In this context, how important is an insult that bowls us over?"

For the mystic, meaningfulness comes about in the experience of timelessness. In mystical experience the time factor does not exist. There is no omega point toward which everything is aimed, only alpha and omega together. In the West we are accustomed to thinking linearly. By contrast, mystics experience things holistically. Mystical experience resembles an encounter with a sphere. If we grasp the entire sphere, everything is simultaneous. We must grasp the entire sphere from this point, where we are standing. That is heaven, that is the beatific vision. Mystical experience is experiencing everything simultaneously. Zen tells us that Nirvana is not a distant point, but the experience of coming and going, of being born and dying, as continual reality. Being born and dying are the carrying on of God's life.

Against this background, why do we take ourselves and our lives so seriously? Why do we make so much of a fuss about it? Because our ego constricts us, it dramatizes events, it blows them up into burdensome monstrosities that cause us to live in terror. If the lightning flash of a nuclear holocaust made the earth uninhabitable for several million years, that would have no special significance for the evolution of the cosmos.

That sort of thing happens all the time in the universe. Galaxies come and go. And there are surely millions of stars on which intelligent life exists. Those who see the world from the mystical perspective experience it as a bubble on a torrential river. The little dust particle of earth hangs insignificantly amid billions of other constellations in the infinite sweep of the cosmos, which has been in existence for billions of years.

What does this instant mean in the face of those billions of light-years? What does a human life mean, lasting but a few decades? From that point of view, all personal problems, all the problems of *Homo sapiens* (the species that for a couple of hundred thousand years has had the knack of self-reflection) take on a completely different look. This new perspective gives us a feeling of cheerfulness and ease. This is the cheerfulness of Jesus when he speaks of the sparrows on the roof and the lilies of the field.

This point of view may mislead some people into twiddling their thumbs and retreating into contemplation. But all religions have branded such behavior as a false response. Our existence *does* have a unique significance. Such as we are, we are the way the Divine Reality expresses itself. We are the unique and unmistakable revelation of the divine Life.

We should not understand our existence as something that puts in an appearance for eighty years and then gets definitively frozen into what we call heaven or the vision of God. God is not static; God is rest and dynamic. Experiencing this dynamic in becoming and passing away is heaven. It is the experience of the overflowing "Godhead" that Eckhart speaks of when he says that God is a resting-in-himself and a standing-fast, "but in addition a certain boiling up and giving-birth-to-himself, which glows in itself and overflows itself and boils over, a light that entirely penetrates itself in the light and into the light."[2]

THE UNIVERSE AS GOD'S SELF-REVELATION

We tend to think of God's revelation (revelation of the ultimate truth) as something we have already been told. God caused a prophet to experience something and, in turn, the prophet shaped that experience into words and proclaimed it to everybody else. We assume that the same is true of Jesus.

But mysticism in both the East and West understands revelation to mean *experience*. The Divine reveals itself to humans directly and much more intensely in the happening of the moment. Then, in that moment, human beings find the real presence of God. Only then can we live the experience of God. By way of reason, mystics can only know *about* God. Of this God, Eckhart says, "Once the thought is gone, God is gone too."

I have often used the example of the branch and the tree. When the branch experiences itself as a branch, perceives the other branches around it, and hears about the trunk and the roots, it experiences itself, so to speak, in ego-consciousness. But when it experiences from within, then it experiences itself as a tree. Then it learns what it really is.

The same thing happens with human beings. So long as we know God only by way of reason, our knowledge is paltry stuff. But if we experience from within, if we become aware who we really are—*that* is a holistic experience.

Mystics experience a multidimensional world. If they try to grasp this world in abstract conceptual language, they can only stammer. That doesn't mean they can't make any sort of statement; mystics have always framed their experiences in words and images. But they know that these are not dogmas to be absolutized, but are windows that point to the light that illumines them.

> A man in a rapture
> once saw a fellow
> who boasted of being one with God.
> He looked at him and asked,
> "God, why is Pharaoh condemned to burn,
> For crying out, 'I am God!'
> While Hallaj was transported to heaven
> for crying the same thing—'I am God!'?"
> Then the man heard a voice,
> "When he cried out those words,
> Pharaoh thought only of himself,
> He had forgotten Me.
> But when Hallaj cried out,
> He had forgotten himself,
> And thought only of me.
> Therefore in Pharaoh's mouth
> 'I am' proved a curse to him,
> But in Hallaj 'I am'
> Was the work of my grace."[3]

THE SPIRITUAL NEED IN HUMANS

Today many people have a sense that life is more than what the level of everyday consciousness can offer. They suspect that there are spaces of cosmic proportions inaccessible to the intellect and the senses. They intuitively grasp that only from this source can their own lives and even the life of the entire cosmos derive their meaning. They sense that their lives could be richer and fuller. They are dissatisfied, and dissatisfaction is a sign that our needs are not being met.

When people repress their needs, they get sick. This rule, that applies to the psychological level, holds true on the spiritual level as well. The spiritual is a part of human nature. Here, too, needs can be repressed; for example, the need to interpret the meaning of our life or the need not to have to die. This repression leads to traumatic disturbances and blockages. Transpersonal psychology calls this "metapathology," in other words, the sickness that lies behind normal psychic illness.

C.G. Jung said that he never had a patient over thirty-five whose actual problem wasn't a "religious" one. Up until the midpoint of life, people are outwardly directed and project their hopes for salvation onto the outside world. The search for a partner, sexuality, power, money, career, and so on, conceals the deeper longing for meaning and ultimate fulfillment. "Everyone gets sick, in the first instance, because he or she has lost what living religions have at all times provided their believers with. And no one is really cured unless he again finds his religious attitude—something that has nothing to do with a specific creed or belonging to a church."[4]

It's a good thing to get a sense of your fundamental religious needs and to find a "doctor" to help you still this hunger. An authentic therapist tries to open up to the individual the path to his or her salvation. Such ways of salvation are admittedly very different, but they have one thing in common: they lead through confrontation, through dire need, through fear, through dying and death.

Most people try to do this with religion, and many succeed in finding a path into spiritual depths. But some are dissatisfied with traditional religion, often maintaining that religion itself blocks their personal development. Such persons, therefore, look for a path without the "needless ballast" of religion.

Others say that they have been miseducated by their parents or other authorities so that today, as adults, they suffer from a childhood gone

12

wrong. But it does little good to shift our wretchedness onto the shoulders of others. Life is given to us so we may grow and mature, so we may set out on our journey when we have become weary with the flatness of our superficial consciousness. This weariness is a decisive motive for launching people on their way. After all, we actually have everything—or almost everything—that we need for life.

But why aren't we satisfied? Why do so many people find that even long and intensive psychotherapy doesn't bring inner peace? Why do we look for more than a balanced psychophysical state of comfort? Fortunately, this kind of dissatisfaction and mental trauma serves to fuel our quest, a quest that leads us beyond the limits of our psychophysical existence. We are driven to learn who we really are. We want to know the ultimate meaning of life. It is *divine restlessness* that drives us on. Thus Augustine says, "Our heart is restless till it rests in Thee."

The quest for the meaning of life, the search for our true essence, or—as we Christians usually say—for God, is part of the basic principle of evolution. Actually it isn't a search at all. Rather the Divine is unfolding in us and through us. The Divine comes to consciousness in us. We think that as human beings we are on a quest for God. But we're not the ones searching for the Ultimate Reality. Rather it is the Ultimate Reality that causes the dissatisfied yearning and the search in us. God is the seeker. God awakens in us. We ourselves can't *do* anything; we can only let go so the Divine can unfold itself. We can only "get out of God's way," as Eckhart says. The essential nature reveals itself if only we don't prevent it. And if there is a redemption, then we are redeemed from being possessed by our ego so that our real selves can spread their wings.

THE MEANING OF BEING HUMAN

What is the meaning of the cosmos? What is the meaning of a tree, of an animal, of a person? Eckhart would have said that they exist *sunder warumbe*, without a why. And the poet Angelus Silesius (1624-77) writes, "The rose is without a Why, she blooms because she blooms. / She heeds not herself, nor asks / where she'll be seen in our rooms." Does our existence have any more solid foundation? Why not bloom and fade like a flower? We cannot seek the meaning of our existence outside itself. It must be based on existence itself. This act of our life is utterly precious. We have possibilities that other kinds of phenomena don't.

Why are we on earth? That was the first question in the old catechisms. The answer was, "We are on earth to know God, to love him, to serve him, and then to live with him forever." I can still subscribe to that today, but my reading of it is entirely different from the one I got from my religion teacher.

Our ego-consciousness prevents us from experiencing our true being. We don't know who we are. And we *can't know* who we really are. We can only *experience* it. Our ego-consciousness cuts us off from the experience of Being, not from Being itself. But if we are cut off from the experience of the divine Being, then it has no influence on our life. A merely philosophical, theological, ritual, and sacramental encounter with true Being cannot fully unleash its power. All the expressive forms of religion are designed to lead us to a deeper experience of the Divine.

THE MEANING OF OUR LIFE

The meaning of our life is to experience the divinity of ourselves and of all creatures. When mystics speak of the Divine in human beings, they sometimes say: "I am God." It's easy to mistake this for pantheism. But the mystic does not cease being human; rather, this human form is an expression of God. Wherever Christian mysticism has not been pressed through the sieve of dogmatic theology, it speaks out as clearly on this point as Eastern mysticism does. Thus John of the Cross says, "Our awakening is an awakening of God, and our rising is a rising of God."[5]

God, the Ultimate Reality, knows no inside and no outside. The wave is not *outside* the sea. The wave *is* the sea, but then again it *is not* the sea. Eastern mystics call this the "not-two." If you look at the ocean from above, there are thousands of waves, but the view from the depths shows only ocean.

By way of clarification, the example of a ruler is often cited. One side of the ruler displays the units of measurement, the other side is blank. Both sides, however, constitute the ruler. Both sides, together, are experienced as one thing. In the same way, human beings don't stop being human when they experience God, but they experience their human form of existence as a form of God. "The wave experiences itself as the sea." Once we get there, we experience the unity of all waves with the sea, and thus the connectedness of all living beings with one another through the divine sea or divine life.

We have no way of putting into words, of course, what this experience ultimately is. It could well be the return to identity with God, what Tauler calls the "foundation." It is Eckhart's "godhead," Teresa's "interior castle," and Zen's "essential nature."

From this perspective there is no form that would *not* be an expression of God. If instead of *God's life*, we use the word *energy*, we might draw an analogy to H_2O. H_2O can be organized in various ways: as water, as steam, and as ice. In the same way, divine Life can reveal itself and be experienced in quite different forms. Religious life is a way of being bound into the Divine. That doesn't mean the same thing as submission to moral rules, truths of faith, or rituals. It is rather what Eckhart has in mind when he says that we should get out of God's way so that God can be in us.

That would mean that it is our high responsibility to cultivate all our mental, psychic, and sensory powers to help the Divine unfold in us and to experience it in its unfolding. God is the sole Reality, always present in all things. We are a sport (*Spielform*) of the Divine. We are the God symphony. We are the dance of God the dancer, and dying is as much a part of this dance as being born.

DYING AND LIVING

Our real problem as humans is the certainty that we must die. The life that we have can't be held onto. Sooner or later it will come to an end. We can't avoid going under. We constantly fight off this realization and have developed all sorts of mechanisms that help us to repress death. But everything that has been repressed returns, even if behind a different mask. We know about death, but we can't bear this knowledge. Yet in the final analysis, the noise of our ego-consciousness can't drown out our fear of death. One day death will annihilate us. The crucial point is whether we see it as a stage of development or as a terrifying evil. Believers who make this fundamental discovery loose all fear of death. They know that life cannot die. Only a form of life can die. That is the basis of all experience and the realization of all the mystics.

Dying and rising are part of the structural principle of creation, but our ego resists this process of becoming and passing away. It clings to the form. It wants to hold tight to this form of existence. It embraces a husk and forgets the contents. It's as if we are bewitched. The Hindus call this great enchantress Maya.

Why doesn't this realization about life spread around the globe like wildfire? Why don't we simply shake off death? Because—and I am the only one who can experience this—I have to go through the experience of dying. I have to let go of everything I want to cling to. Mystical death is the death of the ego, but we clutch this ego feverishly. We Westerners have become so identified with our ego that we equate it with life itself. We would like to eternalize this ego, but that seems to be humanity's original sin: we thought that with our ego we could "be like God." Yet this ego is nothing but the intersection of our psychic powers, which gives us the illusion of autonomy. This is the illusion, pure and simple, that must be abandoned. The ego is only a little disk swimming on the surface of our total consciousness. It is only one organ of total consciousness. But it acts as if it were the actual commander, and so it's in constant conflict with the depth of our being. The activity of this apparently autonomous ego, and the egocentricity that it gives rise to, is the real sickness of our time, especially in the West. Some have called it "ego-neurosis."

People who can't let go of their egos, who can't die, who can't look death in the eye, can't live either. Granted, many men and women have grown restless and are in the process of reorienting themselves. But the path of letting the ego die—which is the path of mysticism—is not taken by many, and still fewer take it to the end. Why? Because fear comes before dying.

People who suffer within themselves are not ipso facto capable of entering upon a mystical path. Only a strong ego can let go. As the saying goes, "You have to be somebody before you can be nobody." Some people find that it's better to start out by doing something to strengthen their ego before taking up the mystical path—or at least to seek therapy at the same time.

The encounter with the meaning of life is the most important task we have to accomplish in the years after midlife. Ultimately, this means that we have to get oriented toward maturing and dying. Dying is the price we pay for enhanced life. Without death there is no resurrection to a more comprehensive existence.

But dying has to be learned. We really have to let go of our physical body and our ego-bound existence. Anyone who has practiced letting go in this life will carry it over as a basic tendency into the next. So the essential thing is to change our fundamental patterns, structures, and tendencies in a positive direction. They are a sort of net that we have to reweave, untie, or patch. That is the homework assignment of our life.

Now we can't just voluntarily alter this basic pattern, of course. Rather, everything depends upon letting ourselves be transformed from within. We do not change ourselves, but the Divine unfolds its power in us. Thus letting go means simply taking back our own tendencies so that the Divine can release its full power. We learn to die in order to live. Death is the most important event in our life.

When we die, we will not feel that we are dying. Our life goes on. Reports of near-death experiences tell us that there is an understanding and an experience outside everyday consciousness. What the individual perceives "there" is often described in esoteric writings as the "astral body." We Christians prefer the word *soul*, although both expressions don't refer to the exact same thing. Thus when we die we will step out of our body. Death is only a separation of our deeper identity from this physical body. Only the form dies, not the life. Life gives the billion forms of phenomena their existence—and takes it back again. Our true existence is not static, but dynamic, and this dynamic pattern flows into increasingly new forms. Thus our true identity lies in the flow of life. We have no life of our own. Everything that exists is the sparkle of the Divine. We don't live our own life, but the life of God.

EXPERIENCE OF THE ULTIMATE REALITY

There are various paths for approaching the Numinous or, better, there are different ways of letting go so that the Divine can blossom in us.

There is the *path of the intellect*. We can engage in thinking about God and the world. This is the origin of philosophy, of metaphysics, and of theology.

There is the *path of religion*. The path of cult, ritual, ceremony, the sacraments, and—something usually tied in with these—the path of the study of sacred Scriptures, namely the parables, symbols, and myths that lie concealed beneath the pages of the Bible and point to its essential message. The parables, symbols, and myths of the holy books are like glass windows. They are irradiated by the light behind them. The light itself is something we can't see. We can recognize it only in reflections. Thus it shines forth, as it were, in these windows of parable or myth.

The light, that has no structure itself and can never be grasped, gets its color and structure from the glass window. It's important that we don't take these windows for the Ultimate Reality. They are only a lighting up of that reality in this particular form. We have to look behind the windows.

Best of all, we can follow the *esoteric paths* of the great religions: the path of contemplation (Christianity), the path of Zen and Vipassana (Buddhism), yoga (Hinduism), Tibetan forms of meditation, or Sufism (Islam).

After long practice with these paths, enough progress can be made so that all physical, psychic, and intellectual "motors" within us turn off. We are there in a purely receptive mode. God is a filled emptiness. The goal is not ecstasy (even though that is the view of some Christian mystics and, above all, non-mystics). Rather, the goal is to experience reality as a whole. Our knowing does not follow a linear development that leaves everything behind it, but resembles a pattern of spherical expansion until nothing is left concealed. Every individual thing can become a gateway to the whole. It is a holistic knowing. Everything is open to transcendence. Everything can trigger and express Ultimate Reality. Everything is holy. There is nothing that might not be a "sacrament," the symbolic outside of that Reality.

People returning from such an experience find their hearts full of love for one and all. They can say, "Everything is good the way it is, including suffering and misfortune." Mystics will put themselves at the service of their fellow human beings to help them out of the confinement of their egos.

HUMAN LONELINESS

Human beings evolved out of preconsciousness into ego-consciousness. In so doing they became aware of their limits, their powerlessness, their isolation, and their loneliness.

This feeling of separation is the real source of anxiety in men and women. People live in insecurity, cut off, incapable of interpreting their lives on their own. Once man ate from the "tree of knowledge" and developed into a "spirit bearer," he was able to distinguish between good and evil. It was at that very moment when he realized he was naked, separated, lonely, someone who has not yet learned to stand on his own two feet to find his foundation in himself. From that time on people have had an inborn longing to overcome their loneliness, to transform their separateness into security and all-oneness.

C.G. Jung surely had a much clearer view of humans than Freud and Adler when he argued that the religious longing of men and women is a far stronger propelling force than sexuality and the drive for power. This religious longing is the primal longing for home.

PROJECTIONS ON THINGS AND PERSONS

There are many illusory solutions to the problem of loneliness: sex, drugs, alcohol, diversion. But the tragic fact is that as soon as the effect of the chosen method wears off, the illusion of oneness and security disappears, and the desperation is deeper than before.

Separateness prompts the desire for love and tenderness. Thus the individual looks for fulfillment, in the first instance, from the outside. The child naturally projects this longing onto his or her mother and father. The young man projects it onto the girl he loves, and girl onto the young man. But sooner or later people notice that their partner can't fulfill their illusory expectations.

Such projections can take on every conceivable form: a home of one's own, a new car, a better job, a higher salary, the next vacation. Thus some people are blind enough to spend their entire lives being taken in by their projections, without ever knowing what hit them.

Projections are a natural and valuable kind of psychic energy. They are an essential part of our humanity. But it's important to see through them in time so we can figure out what our fantasies and projections are ultimately trying to express. Sexual fantasies, for example, are for the most part simply a longing to overcome separateness, to achieve wholeness. Hence we should not simply cut off and banish our sexual fantasies when they grow strong. Besides, they often lie outside our conscious control. Christianity has surely erred in advising people to run away from fantasies as quickly as possible, or worse yet, by rating them as fundamentally evil.

PROJECTIONS ON GOD

Once we recognize that we can't find fulfillment in things and other people, we begin to look for fulfillment from God: God is the Father whom

I can love, from whom I can beg forgiveness, whom I must fear. God is the Father whose child I am. God consoles me like a child when I cry out to him. He loves me when I am good, punishes me when I am bad.

Projecting the fulfillment of our longing onto a God who exists somewhere, watches us, directs us, and loves us is generally the last projection we engage in. Thus in the human imagination, God becomes a judging power, an authority checking up on our behavior, a superperson capable of giving or withholding grace. This kind of piety predominates in most religions.

Breakdown of Projections
in the Experience of the Nameless One

It is a decisive step when the individual in contemplation suddenly finds this God vanishing out of sight, or simply crumbling into pieces. This experience can at first give rise to great uncertainty. The Father's hand is withdrawn, loneliness and a sense of lostness turn into a kind of abyss.

Mystics from all religions know about this stage and advise us from the outset not to cling tightly to any image of God. What we can say about God has only a symbolic character. Symbols are open to the whole gamut of reality. We may be dependent on these symbols, since what is conscious can become conscious only through an "opposite number." But we must not press images and pictures too hard and think that God is like this or that. Thus John of the Cross writes that through images of God, man debases him:

> For the creatures, whether terrestrial or celestial, and all distinct images and kinds of knowledge, both natural and supernatural, that can be apprehended by the faculties of the soul, however lofty they be in this life, have no comparison or proportion with the Being of God, since God falls within no genus and no species, as they do.... Wherefore, he that encumbers his memory and the other faculties of the soul with that which he can comprehend cannot esteem God, neither feel concerning Him, as he ought."[6]

One can find in religions an idolatry that is worse than idol-worship—namely the worship of concepts and intellectual constructs of God.

Concepts and dogmas are only windows onto reality. Such windows can be triangular or rectangular or round. One can look through them to grasp some aspect of the Divine, but one may not say "God is triangular"; "God is rectangular"; "God is round."

When Moses asked God's name and got no answer, he thought the Hebrews would not believe him because he couldn't call God by name. So God told him, "I AM the-one-who-is-there" or "I AM WHO I AM" or "I am the one who is on hand." God isn't something that has a specific form or a name. God is the Nameless One who is in all things. Whence the commandment to make no images of God and not to take God's name in vain. This is to help people free themselves from ideas about God. This no doubt also explains the need felt by negative theology to deny God any positive qualities at all. Ultimately, we can only say what God is *not*. Everything that we utter is only helpless stuttering. That's why Eckhart says "Keep silent and don't gape after God, for by gaping after him, you are lying, you are committing sin."[7] And in another passage: "Hence I beg God that he relieve me of God."[8]

ALL THINGS TASTE OF GOD

Grasping the Ultimate Reality is not an intellectual achievement; it is possible only in experience. Let me cite Eckhart:

> A man ought not to have a God who is just a product of his thought, nor should be he satisfied with that, because if the thought disappeared, God too would disappear. But one ought to have a God who is present, a God who is far above the notions of men and of all created things. That God does not disappear, if a man does not willfully turn away from God.
>
> The man who has God essentially present to him grasps God divinely, and to him God shines in all things; for everything tastes to him of God, and God forms himself for the man out of all things.
>
> A man cannot learn this by running away, by shunning things and shutting himself up in an external solitude, but he must practice a solitude of the spirit, wherever or with whomever he is. He must learn to break through things and to grasp God in them and to form him in himself powerfully in an essential manner.
>
> Whoever has God in this way (i.e., in Being) takes God divinely, and to him all things taste like God, and God's image will become visible from all things.
>
> Because he alone has God and looks to God alone, and all things become pure God to him. Such a person bears God in all his ac-

tions and in all places, and all the deeds of this person are done by God alone. For the one who is the cause of the deed, to him the deed belongs more really and truly than to him who carries it out.

Man should comprehend God in all things and should accustom his soul to finding God present at all times. For whoever is to be right has to have one of two things happen: Either he must learn to grasp and hold God in deeds, or he must let go of all deeds. And for all his works man must grasp God in all things."[9]

When Eckhart says that all things "become pure God" to him, he refers to what the East calls "the void." God, who has neither shape nor form, can be experienced only in forms. The Void, God (better Godhead), and nonform can be intellectually distinguished from shape and form. But in reality they can only appear together, just as the dance and the dancer can only appear together. The dance can be distinguished from the dancer, but they can't make their way onto the stage unless they are together. Music can be distinguished from musical instruments, but both can exist only when they're together. "All things taste of God" comes down to saying that "emptiness is form." It is what remains in experience when all projections fade away.

John of the Cross puts it this way:

> And although it is true that the soul is now able to see that these things are distinct from God, inasmuch as they have a created being, and it sees them in Him, with their force, root, and strength, it knows equally that God, in His own Being, is all these things, in an infinite and pre-eminent way, to such a point that it understands them better in His Being than in themselves. And this is the great delight of this awakening: to know the creatures through God and not God through the creatures; to know the effects through their cause and not the cause through the effects; for the latter knowledge is secondary and this other is essential."[10]

God, in his essence, is in all these created things. Emptiness is form. This world is the way the Divine expresses itself. God as our "opposite number" has become the God in everything. Thus authentic mysticism leads us back into the world.

Chapter 2

Science and Mysticism

We are much more than our intellectual reflections, much more than our ego-consciousness. There are inner spaces, levels, and worlds that have cosmic dimensions and that transcend all rational knowledge. There is a metaexperience (mystical experience) that is far more comprehensive than anything our intellect and senses can grasp.

Measured against the findings of such experience, science is a gigantic undertaking of ignorance. To be sure, nothing is harder to transcend than scientific results, convictions, and systems. They are the stubbornest enemies of any comprehensive knowledge because anything that leads us beyond the established truths of science and is no longer immediately demonstrable will be rejected, put down by many of our contemporaries as irrational. Certainly, scientific discoveries are undoubtedly of the greatest importance, but we must completely and thoroughly question them.

For example, the old theories about human brain activity no longer add up. Sir John Carew Eccles, a scientist who won a Nobel prize for brain research, tells us that the brain is not the cause of its convolutions. That is, our brain is not the producer of energies but only the receiver that picks up impulses and transposes them into data that our ego-consciousness can then comprehend. The energies themselves come from a realm inaccessible to measurement, from a purely spiritual level that can only be experienced.

Pressing forward into high states of consciousness that lie beyond our rational capacity seems to be of the utmost importance for the survival of the human race.[1] More and more people are realizing that they have to follow their intuition and do something about deepening their experience of life. But in our society it still takes a certain amount of courage—not to say a bit of foolishness—to set out on such a path. And yet some have already recognized that it is dangerous for us to go on trying to live while cut off from our true self.

ELECTROMAGNETIC FIELDS

There are structures and processes of energy that lie at the root of all forms of life and matter. The structures of energy are invisible fields of force that organize the visible universe. Nowadays quantum physics no longer regards quarks (the smallest known elements in nature) as solid building blocks but as fields of force. They present the universe as a dynamic web. What we take to be solid matter is an electromagnetic field of varying density. Teilhard de Chardin says, "Concretely speaking, there is no matter and spirit; rather there exists only matter that is becoming spirit. The stuff of the universe is spirit-matter." So there aren't two kinds of laws: matter and mind. Rather, there is a single continuous law for both matter and mind. Matter is the domain of space in which the field is extremely dense. Einstein says, "In this new physics there is no place for both field and matter; because field is the only reality."

FIELDS OF LIFE

For forty years, scientist Harold Burr studied the electromagnetic fields that ultimately govern all life. These fields can be measured and checked. Burr tells us that the wonders of nature are neither a feat of complex chemistry nor a mechanical sequence of physiological events, but that behind them lies the ordering power of magnetic fields.

> Such fields are intangible and invisible but measurable. Iron filings scattered on a piece of paper and held over a magnet orient themselves according to the pattern of the lines of force created by this magnetic field. If the filings are mixed up and strewn out on the paper again, they will form the same pattern as before if they're held above the magnet.

The micromagnetic fields produce a similar effect, but the process is much more nuanced. Burr calls them life fields (L-fields).

> The L-fields shape all life. Research tells us that the protein molecules of our bodies—their major constituents—are renewed every six months. After half-a-year we are no longer the same. It is only thanks to the controlling L-fields that our fellow humans can still recognize us as our old selves.[2]

WE'RE NOT MONADS

For many years scientists observed an elm and a maple tree with a voltameter. The data revealed that the L-field is altered by daylight, darkness, moon cycles, and sunspots. These influences are felt even more strongly in the complex L-field of human beings.

Thus we are part of the universe and not monads. These life-fields transcend the laws of chemistry and physics. They impose intrinsic order upon the atoms and molecules of our bodies. After death this order breaks down, and our bodies decompose in keeping with other laws. In the final analysis, the L-fields are what call forms into existence. We are not a mere sequence of physicochemical events. We are in the first instance a metastructure, which in turn shapes our bodies and our psyches. The transcendent organization of the L-fields is responsible for the composition and flow of our existence. The more open we become to these metainfluences, the better we can grasp the whole and develop all the possibilities of our existence.

MORPHOGENETIC FIELDS

Hitherto physics and biology, indeed all of science, have been committed to a mechanistic paradigm. It was assumed that our universe follows certain timeless, unchangeable laws. In the last few decades, however, this assumption has been shattered. How do the various forms of life come about? Why and how does a living creature develop out of an egg? How does a plant develop from a seed? Biology attempted to explain the emergence of forms mechanistically, through purely chemical and physical interactions and processes. But by that route we can only experience *what* happens. The mechanistic viewpoint couldn't, and still can't, tell us where the ultimate foundation lies. For example, why do our arms and legs emerge in precisely this specific form? Chemical substances and reactions don't explain the form that grows out of them. Merely analyzing the stones, mortar, and wood of a building tells an architect nothing about its peculiar structure. An entirely different building could have been constructed with the same bricks, the same mortar, and the same wood.

Organisms have invisible fields that determine their forms. The development of an egg, therefore, is not governed by chemical processes but by metafields that can be neither seen nor measured. If, for example, the egg of a dragonfly is tied off in the middle, out of the tied-off half comes forth not a part of the organism but the whole dragonfly. If one cuts off a piece of willow and sticks it into the ground, a new willow comes forth. The part can produce a new whole. The whole, as everyone knows, is more than the sum of its parts. The morphogenetic field is not destroyed, it is present in every part. Morphogenetic fields are what Rupert Sheldrake calls the metastructures that ultimately shape living creatures. He writes:

> Morphogenetic fields shape and direct the entire animate and inanimate creation. And although the fields are free of matter and energy, they still have an effect on space and time, and can even be changed over space and time. If a member of a biological species acquires a new behavior, its morphogenetic field will be altered. If it retains its new behavior long enough, the morphic resonance will set up a reciprocal effect among all the members of the whole species. The morphogenetic fields are the actual cause of the order, regularity, and constancy of the universe—but they can also admit wholly new modes and forms of behavior.[3]

Thus we are not primarily physiological and biological creatures, but beings with a fundamentally spiritual structure.

But morphogenetic fields are not limited to the organism as a whole. Even molecules and atoms have them, so that a body is composed of various morphogenetic structures. What we call the universe is really nothing more than the comprehensive morphogenetic structure of all existing things.

CONSEQUENCES

As a result of the worldwide influence that these fields have, it seems reasonable to assume that even our sitting in Zen or our contemplation has a strong influence on these metastructures. In other words, we can change humanity, society, and the world by our sitting and changing ourselves. Anyone who enters upon one of the esoteric paths of the great religions is performing the actual work of changing consciousness in our world.

Mystics have always been clear on this point. The silent prayer of the men and women who betake themselves into the presence of God is far stronger and far more powerful than many words. Such persons are, as it were, connecting themselves to God's field of force and becoming conductors of energy to others. We have to learn to become open to this divine source of energy, to which every one of us is linked.

God works by means of the order of his creation; creation and redemption are not structured differently. Everything is laid down in the original plan. If we press forward into the metastructure of humanity and further still into what we call the divine life in us, we transform the world—not through our own strength but through the strength of the Divine to which we open ourselves. Then it works in us and through us. The more it can act without interruption, the more we can let God in (Meister Eckhart would say, the more we get out of God's way), and the stronger the effect. God would like to take shape in us and in the world. That, no doubt, is what we mean when we speak of our being made in God's image and likeness.

Both Zen and Christian contemplation are about opening up in all directions. It's as if we build up consciousness and, indeed, it is something like an accumulation of consciousness. When many people open up in the same direction, a powerful force develops. Then there can be what is called a leap of consciousness: other men and women are influenced by us without ever coming into physical contact with us. Why shouldn't the Divine work on us in this way—as a metastructure of our world? It is by means of these fields, one imagines, that what we Christians call grace comes into effective play.

Chapter 3

TRANSPERSONAL EXPERIENCE

The universe seems to have begun in an unconscious state. Consciousness evidently unfolded in the course of millions of years and will continue to unfold. In the human species a peak has been reached that makes possible a kind of experience that transcends all comprehension. We call this experience transpersonal or mystical. We might think of it as a fourth dimension of consciousness.

Human consciousness can look behind the activities of its everyday mode. It can become one with the foundation out of which all things come into being. Human beings can go beyond their personal consciousness and become aware of a cosmic unity that in traditional religious language we call God, the Absolute, or the Numinous. This is evidently the Ground of Being for all humans. So long as we are cut off from this foundation, we can give our lives no meaning. This is the meaning of salvation or redemption: overcoming the illusory separateness that our ego-consciousness is always falling victim to.

We must do our part, however; we have to open ourselves up and grow into the next dimension of consciousness. The mind returns to itself in the evolution of consciousness. Our intellectual consciousness is only an intermediary stage. The path of contemplation, of Zen or yoga, is designed to help us grow into this next level of consciousness. Religions, too, must transcend their intellectual-dogmatic part and lead men and women into the experience of the transpersonal Divine.

The story of humanity is the story of the evolution from the amoeba to the reptile through the ape to man. This is obviously a movement from lower to higher, and at the same time an unfolding of our consciousness and—bound up with that—our religious self-understanding. We humans stepped out of a premental time period into the Age of Mind. In between the two lies the age of magical and mythical consciousness. Why shouldn't evolution continue? Why shouldn't it be true, as some saints and mystics have imagined, that humanity's next stage of development lies in transcendental consciousness?

We seem to find ourselves, as it were, in the middle of our journey toward full and complete humanness—and it is precisely at this point that we face special danger. No longer animals, we have nevertheless yet to reach full maturity, namely that mystical dimension of consciousness in which the future of humanity evidently lies. Till we get there, we are in a rather tragic stage, as the situation of today's world shows.

LEVELS OF CONSCIOUSNESS

Mystics embody the highest level that persons can reach within a religion. They are thus something like the goal of religious life and, I daresay, at the same time the goal of evolution, the goal of the humanization process. More and more people seem to be nearing and even arriving at this goal.

Hence the times demand that Western religions deal with the question of mysticism. While in the East mystical experience has always been the center and goal of religion, mystical tendencies in the West were not free to develop, and thus they often established themselves outside of the organized churches and denominations.

On the whole, scholars today distinguish four levels of consciousness:[1]

Prerational stage (prepersonal): This is the stage of bodily and sense perception, of emotions, of simple pictorial and symbolic knowledge, of mythical ideas without any clear rational knowledge.

Rational stage (personal): This refers to the level of the ego, of everyday consciousness, of clear rational ideas and logical mental procedures. The highest range on this level constitutes the healthy, well-balanced per-

30

sonality that has integrated persona and shadow. This is also the level of the theological encounter with God.

Transpersonal stage: This level is divided into two parts. The first is the fine-grained material level where things like parapsychological phenomena, visions, prophecy, and the gift of tongues occur. This level is connected to the personal stage. The eye of the seer is slowly opened. Some things experienced here are called paranormal and hence are not automatically accessible to every individual. But the "seeing" is not yet formless, radically transcending images. The insights are rather experienced within quite specific structures and symbols. Then there is the causal level. Here it becomes possible to experience oneness with the object of one's religion: the personal God, Purusha, Brahman, Yahweh, Allah.

Cosmic consciousness: This level is characterized by the terms *Void, Godhead, Sunyata, Tathagata, ground.* Here one experiences pure being, the source from which all things flow. It is the level that necessarily precedes everything that can come into existence. Here the mystic finds that being is nothing but what emerges from it: "Emptiness is form, form is emptiness." Nature and supernature are not-two. In Zen this is the level on which the enlightened person returns to the marketplace. All things are one, and yet they remain separate from one another. Consciousness is experienced as the actual process of the world, which excludes nothing. This experience doesn't change the world, only one's view of the world. But since a new view of the world changes one's personality, it does, in fact, change the world.

Names for the Ultimate Reality

Individual religions have various names for the esoteric paths that can bring us step by step to these experiences. In Mahayana Buddhism, there are the paths of the Tibetans or the way of Zen (Shikantaza-Koan). In Hinduism, there are the different forms of yoga. In Islam, there is Sufism. In Judaism, there is the teaching of the Cabala. In Christianity, there is contemplation. All of these can lead people to the ultimate level, to cosmic consciousness, to the "beatific vision." But a companion-advisor is needed, someone who has actually traveled the route before.

Religion is based on God's revelation. This revelation has two aspects:

it occurs in the pure consciousness of the individual and it is formless, prelinguistic, and precultural. The revelation experienced in pure consciousness forever remains the same, whence the phrase *perennial philosophy* coined by Leibnitz. Since the experience of the Ultimate Reality cannot be adequately expressed, people have to take pains to experience it personally. Religious language and rites are designed to be guides and companions on the way.

Revelation is like music. One can grasp music only by listening to it. To be communicated textually, it has to be written down as a score. The formal language and cult of a religion are like the score. The contents of revelation are like the music. Although a score can be "written" in quite different systems of notation, the music remains the same. In the same way, the contents of revelation experienced in mysticism always remain the same. The "music" always and forever sounds the same. Despite all the wars of religion, the true sages have always known about this unity of experience. All scores are registers of the same music.

Thus all religions have their deepest source in mystical experience. The point of departure, to which the sages have given various names, is proverbial, formless, without symbols or words. Shape, form, word, symbol, parable, and doctrine come afterward. When the contents of revelation are expressed in religious form or cultic language, they take on the language and expressive mode of the people in question. Thus religions necessarily have to be different because peoples, customs, and times are different. Even in the so-called revelatory religions (Judaism, Christianity, and Islam), revelation occurs in pre-linguistic space. Why should it be otherwise with Jesus, who we believe to be fully human? Even his verbalization of God's message had to be set down in a distinct form if he wished to reach people.

How enlightened persons phrase their experience depends upon their degree of education, their religion, and the culture and time period in which they live. Thus in the fifth century B.C. Parmenides verbalized his experience in a completely different fashion from Plotinus who lived seven hundred years later. And a Zen master from the classical Zen period in China sounds utterly unlike Patanjali and the Upanishads or Meister Eckhart and John of the Cross. They all come from the same experience of Being, but because of the differences of time, culture, education, and religious allegiance, they articulated the experience quite differently.

The experience in pure consciousness takes on concrete form in underlying layers of consciousness. For example, Moses first had his experience of illumination at the burning bush. Only then came his question of how to name what he had experienced. He finally called it, "I AM WHO I AM" (Exodus 3:14).

Jesus, who always lived in essential unity with the Ultimate Reality, refers to the reality he experienced as "Father," "the kingdom of God," or "eternal life." He withdrew for whole nights at a time into the experience of oneness with the Divine. When he came down from the mountain, he gave men and women the Our Father, the beatitudes, and his parables. But these were already formulations of his experience of oneness. In his farewell discourses, he makes this point by saying, "Whoever has seen me has seen the Father" (John 14:9), or "Before Abraham was, I am" (John 8:58).

RELIGION AND SACRED SCRIPTURES

The writings of the mystics and sacred Scripture can be read and understood on quite different levels. I think one clear example of this is Jesus' conversation with the Samaritan woman (John 4:5). He spoke for some time about the water of life, while the woman continued to think about the natural well water. Jesus took this opportunity to point out that God isn't something one can worship on this mountain or any other: "God is spirit, and those who worship him must worship in spirit and truth" (John 4:24).

When Jesus spoke of the Father, he didn't mean a fatherly superego, but the masses to whom he spoke had no understanding of what he really had in mind. He wanted to point to God, who is not graspable through the senses or the intellect, but who can only be experienced. Yet for most of Jesus' listeners, God or "Father" was the superego that loved and punished, blessed and condemned.

People who believe that the Absolute is a kind of great Father who watches over all like a shepherd over his flock are practicing the religion of petitioners. Their goal is simply to get the blessing and protection of that God and to offer him gratitude and veneration in exchange. They try to live according to what they take to be God's law, and for that effort they hope to receive the reward of eternal life. This sort of religion pursues the goal of being redeemed—from pain, suffering, evil, and ultimately even death.

Angelus Silesius and Eckhart, to name only two, understood Scripture on a completely different level. They interpreted it from the standpoint of their religious experience. Thus Angelus Silesius writes: "Whoever pleads with God for gifts, / Is in a very bad way. / He worships not his Maker, / But the creature of a day." Eckhart says:

> You lower the infinite God to a milch cow, which one prizes for milk and cheese, for one's own profit. *Isti faciunt capram de Deo, pascunt eum foliis verborum. Item faciunt Deum histrionem, dant sibi vetres et viles vestes suas.* These people make God into a nanny goat. They feed him with word-leaves. In the same way they make God into an actor, to whom they give their old and worn out clothes.[2]

> I tell you truly: As long as you do your deeds for the sake of the Kingdom of Heaven or God, or your eternal bliss, (in other words) for external motives, then things are really not right with you. You may indeed be accepted, but that is *not* the best, for truly if someone thinks to get more of God in inwardness, devotion, sweet ecstasy, and special graces than by the hearth or in the stable, that is no different from taking God, wrapping him up in a cloak, and shoving him under a bench. For whoever seeks God in a (particular) way is taking the path and missing God, who is hidden in the path. But whoever seeks God without a path will grasp him as he is in himself; and such a person lives with the Son, who is life itself.[3]

Such examples shouldn't mislead us into despising oral prayer. Eckhart was a priest and religious. He surely said Mass and prayed the canonical hours. As long as we are human, we will address and celebrate the Divine. And the only way we can do that is with words, images, ceremonies, and rites. But as we do so, it's important to remain aware that these are only the "fingers" that point to the moon. It looks as if only a small handful of people are called to withdraw into a space devoid of liturgy.

Thus sacred Scripture and religion as a whole are the expression of deep mystical experience, and conversely, it is the task of religion to awaken the individual to such an experience.

MYSTICAL EXPERIENCE

The mystical experience is perfect and fulfilling, timeless and incommunicable, and is an awakening of God. Each deserves careful attention.

Perfect and Fulfilling

Mystical consciousness could be described as a region of experience in which everything is the way it is and, as such, is perfect. In such consciousness, we are neither happy nor unhappy, neither satisfied nor dissatisfied, neither merry nor sad. Being merry would, by definition, be something less, as would being sad. Acceptance and love already belong to a subordinate region. There is no bliss, no happiness here, in the sense of a feeling. By comparison, all other levels of consciousness appear relative, while this condition is self-contained, perfect, and filled to the bursting point. The other states of consciousness are preliminary and unfulfilled.

In this mode of consciousness form and formlessness are one. It is the fulfillment of all our longings. There is no subject and object, but only Being. Here we experience our divine origin and are inclined to say, "I am God." This saying has nothing to do with arrogance. Rather, it is buoyed up by an enormous humility and accompanied by the need to help all living creatures reach this same experience. This is the basis of Buddhism's first vow: "The number of living creatures is countless. I pledge to save them all."

In mystical consciousness we realize that our ego-understanding of this world is only like a view of the sky through a tube: a very limited view indeed. Our conceptual understanding of the cosmos, however scientific it may be, is pathetically incomplete. From this perspective, science is constricting. Gradually, however, it is beginning to unfold and to incorporate mystical consciousness into the purview of its research. Scientists have noted that the world can no longer be explained with Newtonian and Cartesian categories alone.

With our religious systems we make a great deal of cosmic noise, and we think that will get us to God. But compared with great mystical experience, our prayers and thoughts of God are nothing more than a boiling over in the tiny test tube of the ego.

There is a very serious danger here, however; with all our ideas of God we may be adoring ourselves. The idolatry of religious concepts is the great danger faced by every religion. We are arrogant when we make for ourselves an image of God or try to capture him in our concepts. Eckhart and Teerstegen rightly say: "A God whom I can comprehend is not God."

Our religious systems are like computer programs. Just as the computer can produce no new knowledge outside of its software, in the same way, theological statements about God remain narrowly limited unless we expand them through mystical experience.

We also must learn that mysticism doesn't necessarily have to express itself in a sweetly pious vocabulary, as if mystic states had something to do with church-mouse religiosity. Rather, mysticism is the experience of the everyday, of the here and now. This experience can be altogether banal. It can be had on a dunghill as well as in a rose garden, in the blowing wind or in a religious ceremony.

We must also be clear about the fact that there are many living creatures whose consciousness has a totally different organization from ours. And there are also beings with a much more comprehensive consciousness than ours.

So it is time to give the certainty of our ego-consciousness a healthy shove and to press forward boldly into other realms of consciousness. Although this sort of thing makes some of us anxious, there is nothing left for us to do except admit our fears and move ahead. Some of us are troubled by doubts because our edifice of faith has been shaken. Of course, a narrow, dogmatically understood profession of faith can be an obstacle to entering this new consciousness. But if we learn to read our sacred books afresh, we will find in them a capacity for transforming our understanding of religion.

Timeless and Incommunicable

The boundaries of "knowledge" are overstepping mystical experience. Human images, symbols, and language are subject to a continuous transformation, while the Divine is beyond space and time. It remains untouched by change, although it is ultimately the essence of everything that changes. Even thinking about the Divine implies a limitation. Here we can understand the "nada, nada" of John of the Cross: "Not this, not this," "*neti, neti.*" We can't say any more than this. The essential core of every religion is the experience of the Ultimate Reality, which transcends all barriers and limitations of space and time.

Barriers and limitations are created solely by the fact that humans want to pin down the ineffable with concepts. Such religious modes of expression are conditioned by time and hence transitory. But experience is timeless and transcends all differences in dogma. It is the common ground on which the individual religions build.

All religions agree that the Ultimate Reality is ineffable, that it can only be experienced. Everything that humans say about it is already a distortion. And so Eckhart argues that "Thou shalt love him [God] as he is, a non-God, a non-spirit, a non-person, a non-image, yet more: as a pure, clear, unalloyed One, free of all twoness."[4]

In his book *Ascent of Mount Carmel,* John of the Cross makes a similar point when he speaks of the damage incurred by the soul when it tries to cling to anything in dogma and images, in memory and fantasy: "For the creatures, whether terrestrial or celestial, and all distinct images and kinds of knowledge, both natural and supernatural, that can be apprehended by the faculties of the soul, however lofty they be in this life, have no comparison or proportion with the Being of God."[5]

John of the Cross calls all images and ideas mere lackeys of the king. The more one looks at the footmen, the less one sees the king: "Wherefore those who not only pay heed to the imaginary apprehensions aforementioned, but suppose God to be like to some of them, and think that by means of them they will be able to attain to union with God, have already gone far astray" (AMC III, Xii, 3).

The Indian mystical poet Kabir (d. 1518) thought along the same lines. He was the son of a Muslim mother but was later raised by a Brahman, and so he found himself caught between the two great religions of Islam and Hinduism. Both attacked him, yet after his death, both fought for his corpse because they wanted to lay claim to him as a great saint. Kabir writes:

> O, thou who serves Me, where dost thou seek Me?
> Behold, I am with you.
> I am neither in the temple nor in the mosque,
> neither in the Kaaba nor on the Kailash.
> I am neither in rites and ceremonies
> nor in yoga and renunciation.
> If you are a true seeker,
> you will see Me at once,
> you will meet Me in the same instant.

Kabir says:

> O Sadhu!
> God is the breath
> of all breath.[6]

Rimi, a Muslim poet, writes:

> What is to be done, O Muslims? I
> no longer recognize myself. I am
> neither Christian nor Jew, neither Persian
> nor Muslim—I am not from the East
> and not from the West, not from the land
> and not from the sea, not
> from the workshop of nature, nor
> from the revolving universe.
> I am not made of earth, water, air
> or fire. I do not come from
> the empyrean, nor from the dust, I am
> neither in the finite, nor in the infinite.
> —I don't come from India,
> China or Bulgaria, nor from the
> Kingdom of Iraq nor from the land of
> Chorasan—I am neither from this
> world nor from that, neither from Paradise
> nor from Hell.
> My place has no place, my tracks leave no trace,
> my body is disembodied, and my soul is soulless,
> for I belong to the beloved.
> All things finite thus become
> infinite. I have overcome all
> separation, I see both worlds
> as universal unity.[7]

Reason can never exhaust the Ultimate Reality. Ramakrishna used to say: "All scriptures and holy books, the Vedas, Puranas, Tantras, and so forth, have in a certain sense been robbed of their purity because their content was expressed by human tongues. What Brahma really is no human tongue could ever describe. For that reason Brahma, now as ever, is untouched and unadulterated."

From the many available Zen texts, I quote just one, by Daio Kokushi:

> There is one reality, which precedes even heaven and earth.
> *It* has no form, much less a name.
> *It* lacks eyes, when they look for *IT*.
> *It* has no voice and so ears cannot discover *IT*.
> O my dear exalted friends, gathered here,
> if you long to hear the thundering voice of Dharma,
> let your talk run dry, empty your thoughts,
> then you will get to the point of recognizing the one Being.

On the level of experience, all religions are one. But individual persons who want to speak about their experience have to be content with the forms of expression available to them from their cultural background. And thus the variety of the esoteric paths reflects the variety of cultures, but in their essence they are all one.

Religion may be compared to the moon; it sheds light on the earth but receives its radiant power from the sun. When the moon comes too close to the earth and thrusts itself between the sun and the earth, there is an eclipse of the sun, and darkness covers the earth.

The sun may be compared to the Divine. It illuminates religion so as to provide light for the men and women on the path to experience. But when religion takes itself too seriously and thrusts itself between God and man, it creates darkness, and God is eclipsed.

Those who have had this experience, that is, "tasted," unencumbered by any word or form, know how relative all words and thoughts are, and how provisional every formulation is. Once they experience reality as it is, they are no longer subject to projections or constricting notions. Anyone who has experienced a tree from within—not as a botanist who sees oaks, beeches, and firs, but as someone who has cast off the garment of speech and experiences "tree"—knows how inadequate speech and verbal expressions are in the religious domain.

An Awakening of God

John of the Cross writes: "Our awakening is an awakening of God, and our uprising is an uprising of God."[8] Thus he clearly and unmistakably calls mystical experience an awakening of God in us. But in the final analysis, this awakening cannot be communicated, and so he says in another passage: "That which the soul knows and feels in this awakening…is wholly indescribable."[9]

All religious books tell the story of this awakening. It is the "love story" between the Divine and the human, with God always taking the initiative. We merely think we are the seekers whereas in reality we are the sought.

The Buddhists have a story like that of the Prodigal Son in the New Testament, which makes the same point. In India there lived an immensely rich man who had only one son. One day the lad was abducted, or else refused to come home. The father did everything he could to find his beloved son, but all in vain.

Years passed, and as the man aged, his longing for his missing son intensified. One day as the rich man looked out of a window on the top floor of his house, he saw a young beggar standing in front of the house. As the beggar was given alms and was on the point of leaving, the rich man saw his face and jumped up in amazement. He recognized his lost son. He called his servants and ordered them to fetch the young beggar back. Some of the servants ran after him and tried to catch hold of him, but the young man refused and said, "I may be a beggar, but I haven't done anything wrong." The servants assured him that they had nothing to reproach him for: "Our master wants to see you," they explained. But they couldn't move him to come back. Rather, the beggar became even more anxious and began to tremble: "I have nothing to do with such a distinguished nobleman." In the end the servants had to return home and tell their lord that they had failed.

Full of love for his son, the rich man ordered one of his young servants to disguise himself as a beggar, like his son, and to make friends with him. When the beggar-servant felt the right moment had arrived, he told the rich man's beggar son, "I have found a good position. The work isn't hard, and the pay is good. We also get a little room. Let's try it." And so the two of them were hired as gardeners by the rich man.

The young man worked for a while as a gardener. When he had gotten used to living there, his father promoted him to house servant. Here, too, he did his work well, and his father appointed him overseer of his whole estate. Finally, he became his father's secretary so that he stayed close to his father and took over his obligations.

Years passed. The rich man became older and realized that he didn't have much longer to live. He gathered his relatives around him and presented the young man to them with the words: "This young man is in reality my son, who disappeared when he was a small child." And he handed over to him all his possessions and his position.[10]

In the Old Testament, God is the jealous lover, and humanity the beloved who keeps running away and being unfaithful. The goal is a loving union and reconciliation. The relationship between God and man is expressed in the word *covenant*, which in archaic society implies absolute solidarity, indeed oneness. The "covenant with God" is something that was and always is there, something that we have to experience personally.

In the New Testament the same message is passed on to us by Jesus Christ. He is "the side of God turned toward us." Through him we can experience the side of God that is turned away, that is, the side that is intellectually and conceptually inaccessible. He is the door through which we can enter into the inner divine domain. And that is the actual goal of humanity, to experience God, the Ultimate Reality. The Buddhists call it Nirvana, the Hindus, moksha. Christians call it heaven, eternal life, or the kingdom of God.

The Hindus speak of Krishna-consciousness, the Buddhists of Buddha-consciousness or Buddha-nature. As Christians, we can call this awakening an awakening to Christ-consciousness. However different religious rites and doctrines may be, in the final analysis, they aim to lead us to this awakening, to the experience of God.

HOMESICKNESS FOR GOD

What ultimately leads the Prodigal Son back home and the beloved to her lover (God) is what C.G. Jung calls the power of individuation. It is that spiritual force that comes from the depth of our essential nature. We can also call it "God's life" or the "Holy Spirit." This power is goal-oriented, even if our ego doesn't always want to follow. Some people feel it very strongly and set off in search of it. People keep saying, "I feel homesick for a place that I don't know—but it's where I belong. There everything is right." Quite simply, they could say, "I feel a longing for God."

When human passions are guided along orderly tracks (and therein lies the meaning of Christian asceticism), this new strength can burst out of serenity. Often it is experienced as a tumultuous power precisely when the individual tastes the meaninglessness of existence because of suffering and strokes of fate.

Because people are not driven at the deepest level by their instincts but by "metavalues," as Abraham Maslow says, the power that comes from them has a teleological function, that is, it is directed. It is the basic

41

force of the whole evolutionary movement in our world. Those of us who take the path of contemplation or Zen are trying to release this force. On these paths nothing can be achieved by our own exertions. There is no "self-redemption." Redemption can only be found. It is always there. The source of power bubbles over in every one of us, and our efforts can only be aimed at clearing away the obstacles that separate us from it. This source pulsates through everything that lives. It flows through all the domains of our existence. It is always there. This power, which drives us forward to fulfillment, to God, accompanies us even after death, if we give it room in this life.

REDEMPTION IS AN EXPERIENCE OF TOTAL REALITY

The difference between the so-called revelatory religions (Judaism, Christianity, and Islam) and the Eastern religions (Hinduism and Buddhism) consists in the fact that for us in the West, God is an ontological Other, that is, something that by its very nature is separate from us and will always remain so. There is a deep cleft between God and man, and the West has not really succeeded in bridging this gap. By contrast, in the main schools of thought of Hinduism and Buddhism, God and man are simultaneously one and different. They are not-two.

In the nonmystic traditions of the Western religions, individuals experience themselves as cut off from God. They have lost their connection with the primal foundation, or at any rate they can no longer recognize it. The unity of God and man is restored through a covenant. God, as it were, joins together what has been broken apart. But for this joining together a high price has to be paid: the death of Jesus Christ.

The East finds it difficult to grasp this notion because it doesn't take *anthropos* (the individual person) but *kosmos* (oneness) as its starting point. This unity can never be dissolved in such a way that individuals or things would be cut off from their Ultimate Source. Separation is merely caused by the egocentricity of everyday consciousness, which deludes us with the idea that we are autonomous and hence separate. The real original sin is the way we constantly fall prey to this delusory tendency of the ego and follow its high-handed, headstrong rule.

Thus in the West, God and man are essentially separate, whereas in the East they are of the same essence. God is both the ideal form and the concrete structure. "He" is nothing that can be seen apart from everything

42

else. The Ultimate Reality is the source of all things, but is never cut off from them and never essentially different from them. Perhaps this is what Jesus meant when he said, "For just as the Father has life in himself, so he has granted the Son also to have life in himself" (John 5:26). And again, "The glory that you have given me I have given them" (John 17:22).

Eckhart writes: "God differentiates himself from man by bearing and being born. But bearing and being born is *one* being, *one* life."[11]

This Ultimate Reality, which we Christians call God, is like the ocean, which is before the wave but not separated from it. It is the vine from which the branch shoots forth, but it is never separated from the branch. Hence this Ultimate Reality is not a Being that exists in separation from everything else. It is the Formless that appears in form. Man, just like all other phenomena of this world, is the form of this Ultimate Reality, form of life, form of God.

If we look at God this way, we will speak about him differently. So long as we see God only from the periphery of consciousness as a Father, analogous to a human father who watches over us, who punishes and rewards us, from whom we can beg for things, and who can deny us something, who gives us eternal life in a place we call heaven, and who can also damn us eternally in a place we call hell, then we will remain mere beggars. But if we see God as an integral whole, then religion has the sense of helping us experience this integral whole. Saving and redeeming then becomes experiencing the whole of reality. It is "looking," it is the beatific vision. We are not a part that is superimposed, but a part in which the whole realizes itself. This is the return to God. In this view, redemption means the integration of our personal ego, which deceives us into thinking we are separated from God, into the whole. This is known as mystical union, enlightenment, liberation, satori, samadhi, and so on, in various religions.

This, too, was Jesus' concern, to help us awaken to God. Redemption is metanoia, the turning to God, to the kingdom of God. "The kingdom of God is among you" (Luke 17:21). "The time is fulfilled, and the kingdom of God has come near; repent, and believe in the good news" (Mark 1:15). Neither in Eastern nor in Western mysticism is redemption something that I myself can accomplish. It is always there, waiting for me, until I can experience it after passing through a process of purification.

EVOLUTION AND ORIGINAL SIN

From the standpoint of both the mystical experience of oneness and the modern scientific study of the evolution of human consciousness, we can take a fresh view of original sin, integrating it more profoundly into the process of human transformation.

The Divine is a mystery. The actual revelation of God lies beyond the level of our daily consciousness, for which it will always be only conditionally graspable. And it will seem utterly new when we press into the depths. The mystics call this deepest level at which revelation occurs the ground, being, mystical union. Here we do not experience something; we just "are."

Revelation occurs in a manner analogous to our knowledge, that is, step by step, because our consciousness, too, unfolds within the framework of evolution.

All religions know about the imperfect condition of humanity. Many speak of a "fall," of "original sin." But original sin is not a fall from a higher state of consciousness into a more imperfect state. Rather, it is the emergence from a "prepersonal heaven," an awakening from the dullness of the preconscious into an ego-experience, a shift out of the state of instinct into the knowledge of good and evil, as the Scripture says. This was a great step forward in evolution, but it also brought with it the whole burden that is bound up with this ego-experience, namely, the experience of sickness, suffering, guilt, loneliness, and death.

Thus the so-called "fall" did not bring mortality, but the knowledge of mortality and the mutability of all things. Previously, humans had been living the life of flowers and animals. Hence the real sin is not eating from the tree of knowledge—that is only an image—but that in the process of becoming an ego the person gets separated from God. "They were naked," Scripture tells us. That has nothing to do with clothes; it implies that they were thrown out into the loneliness of the ego. The expulsion from paradise is stepping out into the personal condition without this experience of oneness with God. Original sin is not guilt in the real sense of the word, as we have long realized. It is a fact resulting from the development of our consciousness.[12]

The path to mystical experience is the path to paradise, but not the one from which the first humans were expelled. That would be regression and would amount to a flight back to the mother's womb. Rather, evolution marches on. One day we shall realize that God always was "walking in the garden" with us, that we never were separated from him. Even if we don't know it now, we will experience it. Paradise lies before us. Hence we Christians call it the "New Jerusalem." It is the experience of oneness with God.

The River of Life

The infinite lights up in the finite. We are bearers of the imperishable in perishable "vessels" and hence more than the form that we run around in. In human beings, life has matured, has ripened to the thickness at which it can become conscious of itself.

As life unfolds into an ego-consciousness, it realizes that in this human form it is finite. All religions tell us that existence between birth and death is only a phase of our entire life. We are caught up in an evolutionary process that is designed to lead to an experience of our definitive, ultimate essence. If we want to mature, we must not cling to anything. Everything we clutch turns into poison. If we cling to the air and refuse to let it go, we suffocate. If we cling to food, it poisons us. Intake and elimination are part of the structural principle of this world. Dying is just as much an active part of growth and maturity as being born.

Our ego resists the process of becoming and passing away. It doesn't want to believe that dying is the gateway to new vistas. But we have to learn that this life of ours is only one act within a play. There are other acts before and afterward. Our ego is inclined to cling to the "theater of the world." This, of course, is a symptom of original sin, thinking we can make our little ego eternal. The passage between birth and death is only an excerpt from our global existence. Our dying is only a transition, a crossing over to something new. But we would prefer to forget that our lives have a prelude and a postlude.

Thus the meaning of our life lies in a permanence that can't be found on the surface, but only in the transpersonal being of our humanity. Stability and continuity are bound up in a dynamic process. The "enlightened" ones are those who experience the stream of life. But they experience it in the here and now.

Thus mystics are people oriented to the world. This is expressed most clearly in the so-called ox-herding pictures of Zen. The last image shows the enlightened person in the marketplace. He buys and sells, laughs and talks, and doesn't in the least resemble a mystic. He has forgotten his enlightenment. He lives on his transformed personality.

Anyone who plunges through the stream of life experiences the eternal Now. Seen from this perspective, life takes on another set of values. Mystics do not think of changing the world; rather, the experience they have transforms their attitude toward the world and all things in it. The projections to which ordinary people constantly fall prey disappear. The world and the things in it are experienced for what they really are. The point then is not the destruction or mortification of evil impulses, but the destruction of the "illusory being" of things, which are falsely valued and treasured by egocentric humans.

When "Conrad and Henry," as Eckhart calls "Tom, Dick, and Harry," are reborn into essential Being, then the things of this world likewise celebrate their resurrection to essential Being. People experience the immanence of God in the world and of the world in God. Their reciprocal interpenetration shines forth. This is how the span between life and death gets its profound meaning. It is given to us for becoming and ripening. Only now are we on the path to full humanity or—if humanity is not our ultimate destination—to the being that we are supposed to become.

In this sort of conscious state, our common life would be transformed. That is, there would no longer be any tensions on our earth. But we shall never create a paradise, of course, and no mystic would be fooled by the idea of such a utopia. Still we could learn to live together without egoism.

Our ego-consciousness is only one organ of our total consciousness. But it behaves as if it were an autocrat; it is in continual conflict with the depths of our being. So long as it has the upper hand, there will be no peace. Only if we press forward into the transpersonal, into that more comprehensive dimension of our consciousness, will we manage to cope with the problems of this world and live in a manner worthy of human beings. It all depends on who gets the upper hand, whether we live increasingly in accord with our inner demands or fail to escape our obsession with feelings, images, and concepts; whether our ego allows itself to be integrated as an organ of our total personality or we allow it to drag us every which way in triumph.

This life is given to us so we can transform ourselves. Those of us who wish to be transformed must learn to let go. Only in that way will we become capable of transformation. Those of us convinced of this will

46

take on a different attitude toward life, society, and the world around us. We will rejoice in feeling ourselves as guests of all things without wanting to possess or dominate them. We will have the courage to live the simple life because life can be tasted far more potently in simple things. We will recognize that it's not a question of quantity but of quality. So once again we are dealing with a change in consciousness, without which there will be no change in people and society.

Those who really break through to the ultimate experience will not remain caught up in any cloud-cuckooland, nor in some sort of ecstasy. They are always there in the particular moment. True experience is experience of fullness in the moment. I would like to clarify this point with a story. A man chopped underbrush at the edge of the forest, sold it, and lived on the modest profits. One day a hermit came out of the forest, and the man asked him advice for his life. The hermit advised him, "Go deeper into the forest!" The man went deeper into the forest and found wonderful trees, which he sold as timber. He became rich, but he suddenly recalled the advice of the hermit: "Go deeper into the forest!" And so he went deeper into the forest and found a silver mine. He worked it and became still more wealthy. One day he again recalled the hermit's words: "Go deeper into the forest!" And so he dared to press farther into the darkness of the mysterious forest. Soon he found wonderful precious stones. He took them in hand and rejoiced at their brilliance, but again the hermit's words occurred to him: "Go deeper into the forest!" Jewels in hand, he walked on and on. Suddenly, at dawn, he found himself again at the edge of the forest. So he took his axe and chopped the underbrush and sold it to his fellows.

From the standpoint of this story, we understand the sixth Zen patriarch who at such a moment said, "How wonderful! I chop wood, I carry water."

Enlightenment leads to the moment. We arrive at the place where we are. What counts is the quality of life not the quantity.

MYSTICAL EXPERIENCE AND SOCIAL RESPONSIBILITY

People who tread an inward path will very quickly face the criticism that they are thinking only of themselves, that they lack social responsibility. That might be so, but then the person in question is surely not on the right path.

Mystical experience breaks through the barriers of the ego and of self-satisfaction. The experience of the common life that pulsates through all things lets us experience the pain and joy of the other as our own pain and joy. The barriers of the ego are shattered. Egoism, the chief vice of humans, is overcome.

Thus Eckhart writes:

> If you love having a hundred marks in your pocket more than in another's, that is unjust…and if you love your father and your mother and yourself more than another person, that is unjust. And if you love blessedness in yourself more than in another, that too is unjust. There are many learned persons who do not grasp this.[13]

> We are one body, and thus every organ serves, in the first instance, the entire body: "The eye sees no more for itself than for the foot, but equally for itself and the individual parts of the body."[14]

The mystical attitude can be seen most clearly in Eckhart's unconventional reading of the Martha and Mary episode. Here the ideal is not Mary who sits transported at Jesus' feet, but Martha who drudges and serves. One of the great misunderstandings by the West about the nature of mysticism is the false notion that ecstasy is the high point of mystical experience. Ecstasy is also a side effect. The goal is the experience of the Divine in every form, in every motion, work, and responsibility. Hence Mary is not yet at the goal. First she has to turn into Martha.

As mysticism sees it, Martha and Mary are not contraries, but two aspects of one reality. Contemplation and action belong together like potency and act. A spiritual path that does not lead to everyday life and one's fellow men and women is a wrong path. The same is true of mysticism in any religion. The most important vow that is daily repeated in every Zen temple is the Bodhisattva vow: "Living creatures are countless. I promise to redeem them all." Compassion for all living creatures is the fundamental virtue of Buddhism. Anyone who has experienced the common life that throbs through all things experiences another's pain and joy as his or her own pain and joy.

A clear example of this is the verse to Koan 46 in the *Mumonkan*: "Don't draw another's bow, don't ride another's horse." That means, when you draw a bow, it's always yours. You are always riding your horse, even if it belongs to another. More specifically it means that if you speak ill of another, you speak ill of yourself. The experience of boundless openness and freedom—the ultimate mystical state—is the foundation of Buddhist compassion. Armapa expresses this in a prayer as follows: "At the moment of enlightenment, as soon as I look upon the original countenance of mind, a boundless compassion wells up in me. The greater the enlightenment, the stronger the compassion."[15]

Buddhism also gets its ethical standards from this attitude, even though such basic truths are sometimes forgotten by Buddhists, as they are by Christians. In mystical experience these truths burst into flame. For this reason the true mystic is not the hermit who looks down at the vile world. Rather, the true mystic wants to grasp God in the things of this world. Eckhart adds: "One can't learn that by fleeing, by taking flight from things and heading externally to solitary places. A person must rather learn an inner solitude wherever and with whomever he may be. He has to learn to penetrate things and grasp his God within them."[16]

TRANSFORMING PERSONALITY, TRANSFORMING THE WORLD

In all religions mysticism is about transforming our personality. We are to experience who we are.

We are more than body and ego-consciousness. The mystical paths aim to lead us into an autoexperience of the whole person, including our transpersonal existence. But here minds have always been at variance. People who reject this other level as irrational, and even as psychopathic, deliberately exclude half of the human personality. In so doing they deny the real forces that produce a change in consciousness that can help us overcome our problems with time. Transformation of consciousness has always stood at the beginning of every new epoch, and that is the goal of the mystical path.

We are in general inclined to solve our problems by following the motto of the German Young Christian Workers: "See, judge, act." That's all well and good—up to a point. We recognize that something's wrong, and so we change it with good intentions and actions. But mysticism has another way. It tries to transform the person from within. The experience of transpersonal levels makes people realize the deeper connections of human life. It transforms the core of the personality. Out of the transformed person come new modes of behavior, values, and intentions. The ethics of this transformed personality proves to be a much more solid basis to build on than even the best of intentions, with which the road to hell is proverbially paved.

But mystics are the last people to be seduced by illusions. They know from their own experience how hard and wearisome the path to personality transformation is. Hence they are open to every form of cooperation to solve the problems of our society. The following old story gives us a glimpse into what could happen if we were ready to accept the help of the transpersonal side of our personality in changing the world. It's the story of the rainmaker.

The village had no rain for a long time. All the prayers and processions had been in vain; the skies remained shut tight. In the hour of its greatest need, the village turned to the Great Rainmaker. He came and asked for a hut on the edge of the village and for a five-day supply of bread and water. Then he sent the people off to their daily work. On the fourth day it rained. The people came in jubilation from their fields and workplaces and gathered in front of the rainmaker's hut to congratulate him and ask about the mystery of rainmaking. He answered them: "I can't make it rain." "But it is raining," the people said. The rainmaker explained: "When I came to your village, I saw the inner and outer disorder. I went into the hut and got myself in order. When I was in order, you, too, got in order; and when you were in order, nature got in order, and when nature got in order, it rained."

In its simplicity this story has a lot more to say than many programs and suggestions for improving the world.

THE TASKS OF RELIGION

On the intellectual level there will be no unity of religions. But these conflicts do no damage to the truth. Truth may be compared to the one light that breaks down into many colors. (See Shelley's, "Life, like a dome of many-coloured glass, / Stains the white radiance of eternity," *Adonais*, 11. 462-3.) Mystical experience is a light that expresses itself in the many facets of various religions.

Religions have the task of reminding men and women of the eternal in the time-bound. Most people are not remotely aware of awakening to God as an ultimate, immediate goal. Too many seek their salvation in the here and now, expecting their happiness from projections onto a provisional scene. They are obsessed by the notion that careers, possessions, vacations, and sex can give life meaning. They identify themselves exclusively with their bodies, their feelings, and intellectual ideas. Yet this brings no interpretive meaning. Anyone who remains stuck in the domain of the ego is stopped halfway down the road. Religion tells us that the eternal, the Divine, is part of the whole person. It is the innermost core of human existence. Religions have always reminded us of this. While their representatives and supporters may be ever so imperfect, our religions continue to be the finger that points to God.

Religions are important for another reason. Those who thrust forward toward the experience of the Ultimate Reality and thereby overstep the bounds of their own denomination still need to celebrate and express this truth. The traditional forms of religion lend themselves to just such a task—unless, of course, an individual should prefer to create his or her own cult and creed. It is best, however, to be at home in a living tradition because people need a framework in which they can understand and express themselves. Those without such a "domicile" run the danger of being more irritated than stabilized by a mystical experience. This is especially true of young people. Hence the mystical paths derived from the great religions deserve full confidence. There people will, as a rule, find the necessary counseling for the road ahead, which is not without its risks. They will be protected from extravagance and exaggeration, and will not fall prey to charlatans.

I believe in the divine core of human beings. The more we can open ourselves to this core, the better and more quickly we shall solve our social and political problems. The men and women of the future will be mystics, or they won't be at all (to paraphrase a line by Karl Rahner). They will grow into this new dimension of consciousness. What is the exception today will one day be the rule. People will transcend and complete their mental consciousness through the transpersonal level. The most important responsibility of religion is to help people in this momentous process.

Chapter 4

Religion or Esotericism?

We refer to God as the power that humans can experience deep within and that leads them from there. When people act against this power they act against themselves. They block their own development. This inner authority drove evolution forward. It is what we indicate by such words as the Being of God or the Life of God, what Eckhart calls Godhead, Zen calls the Void, yoga calls Sunyata, and philosophy calls the Absolute.

But in the following section, I prefer not to use the word *God*. I will speak, instead, of an "inner force," "Immanent Authority," "Ultimate Reality," "totality," "the One," or "the Divine." When I do use the word *God*, it is only in the traditional, I would say archaic, sense of the personal God. By employing the abovementioned terms, I hope to get around the outdated archaic contents of "God."

On the esoteric path we try to open up to this inner power, a power that cannot be communicated through an act of the will or through teaching, but only through direct experience. Theology calls it grace. We cannot dispose of grace, but we can prepare ourselves to receive it. The real meaning of a spiritual guide consists in preparing individuals for the work of grace, to help them move obstacles out of the way, to experience the Divine and make it come out of the depths to unfolding.

This brings us to an important difference between the esoteric school and religion. Esotericism seeks to experience the presence of this inner power in man and in all things. This power is always there in all its fullness, but our egocentricity prevents us from perceiving it. For esotericism, redemption is the experience of this inner reality.[1] And all saints and sages are only companions and helpers that lead others to this experience. Redemption is always there. We can only open ourselves to this redeeming power and let others help us get to that opening.

By contrast, theology tries to reach God by way of the intellect. It works with ideas, images, and symbols. God is thus described as a transcendent God who has an ontologically different being and guides men and women, as it were, from outside. God's mind can be changed by prayer and sacrifice, and God can grant or deny eternal salvation.

How Did the Images of God Come About?

In earlier times people imagined this inner power as a metaphysical being. The Divine appeared to them in visions, as a concrete psychic, indeed a physical force. In "pictorial" visualization of these psychic structures, ancient peoples recognized a personal being who directs the destiny of the world, a perception which gave rise to the creation myths. But this perception also led to the notion of the "near God" whom Moses recognized in the burning bush and whom he proclaimed to the Israelites as the "God who is there." The personal God who accompanies men and women and rewards and punishes them is the "Lord of history" who finds expression in what is called "sacred history." This God, as his followers imagine him, is on the side of humans. He lives among them, as the Bible says, but is uncontaminated by any other living creature.

Even though today's theological language speaks of historical revelation, behind this lies the transcendent, dualistic-mythic idea of God that derives from visions. As we know, visions are an inner perception in which the Divine makes itself known in archetypal images as a force superior to the ego.

These forms that appear in visions have often been taken to be a personification of God. Although all the major religions know that God transcends everything that is comprehensible, and that we should make no image of him, many religious schools of thought cling to these images and concepts and elevate them to the status of unquestionable dogmas. They forget that figures are only a means used by the Divine for

54

sending a message, a message that is to be adapted for real men and women, and thus has to be interpreted anew for every age and human group. The crucial feature is not the personal images but the message. The visions of divine beings are always manifested in accord with the mental patterns and inclinations of the visionaries, and so these can vary greatly depending upon the time, culture, and character of the individual.

ATHEISM AND AGNOSTICISM

Over the course of the last few centuries, science has attempted to dethrone the personal God proclaimed by the theistic religions. Many people believed they could explain the world by means of Darwinism and Neo-Darwinism as a mechanistic development through mutation and natural selection. But typical scientists could not afford the luxury of carrying on research in this positivistic manner, and meanwhile fell back on an archaic notion of God as expounded in Sunday church services. And so they became atheists.

Increasingly, however, this positivistic explanation of the world was felt to be inadequate. Faith in the omnipotence of science and technology was shaken by new findings and research. Today we know more about the cosmos than any other age before us; but we also know that at bottom we know nothing.

Hence people nowadays tend more toward agnosticism. They stand fast by their intellectual incapacity to define reality because they acknowledge that this Ultimate Reality cannot be defined.

REVELATION

But how is the Divine revealed to humans? Revelation. Revelation is understood to mean the manifestation of the divine will. All religious knowledge is based on revelation. It is called supernatural because it did not spring from our senses and our reflection. Rather, it is a direct unveiling of the truth. It is imparted to the seers, prophets, and sages in a manner devoid of images. They frame it in words and pass it on to their fellows. What these seers, prophets, and sages realize in the structureless space of consciousness they then clothe in images, parables, and words they can use to proclaim through speeches, rites, and ceremonies. Experience often flows into a personal "opposite number," which they preach to their fellow men and women as a separate being.

The "seeing" of forms can be bound up with an extraordinary, profound experience. Such "seeing" still occurs to some people in our own time. They see Jesus or Mary and, often enough, a figure from a different cultural milieu, for example, from Greek mythology. Some of them interpret this as an experience of God. They claim that Jesus or Mary has appeared to them. But the Ultimate Reality has merely shown itself in these figures as a means of pointing the way. Hence we have to question the message and not the apparition. In the message is the Word.

The individual is guided by these inner images and, in general, shaped into a more mature personality.

Fundamentally, revelation can be traced back to inner experiences, all of which bear the stamp of the "seer's" cultural affiliation. In some ways religion has still not sufficiently distanced itself from these archaic images of God with which the prophets and visionaries clothed their experience. In fact, some theologians take revelation so completely for granted that they wouldn't dream of analyzing it, while others are more or less aware that their image of God would have to endure a mighty jolt were they to subject revelation to serious questioning.

The esoteric school views revelation as a structureless experience in the depths of consciousness, that is, in transpersonal conscious space which, when it flows into personal space, gets concretized to a certain point in forms, symbols, and shapes. These are images that arise out of the unstructured depths and flow into bits of information and rational knowledge. As esotericism knows, these images are ciphers in which the Divine seeks to make itself conscious.

ESOTERICISM, RELIGION, SCIENCE

The science that dethroned the archaic God has again gotten wind of this inner authority; psychology has gotten started on the track. Primarily, it was C.G. Jung who recognized that in the depths of the psyche there are structures (he called them archetypal images) that embody important messages for the receiver.

Yet, even in the midst of these developments in basic scientific research, there is a rich potential for an up-to-date theology. For example, science has once again discovered "mind," which for the last hundred years was taboo. Of course, this is no longer the mind (or "spirit") that can be equated with the archaic notion of God. It is mind which, together with the solid-material element, forms the other aspect of reality and makes its not-twoness comprehensible. Today, the name of God is more than ever One, Oneness, Simplicity, Wholeness. This One unfolds in evolution like a fan, from "simplicity" into "multiplicity." The Divine reveals itself in a polar fashion. It has two aspects: unity and multiplicity.

Unfortunately, however, theology has for the most part stuck to its archaic ideas. There is very little interdisciplinary research being done in theology, which seems to have fenced itself off even more than other fields. In keeping with the narrow prescriptions of the magisterium, theology has remained bound up in its own system.

And then there is the difficulty of forcing new facts and findings to speak traditional theological language. Unfortunately, religion, as imparted almost everywhere by institutions, seems to thwart many people's access to a deep religious development. For this reason a whole new kind of piety is beginning to develop outside the better known religions.

God is no longer just the One who directs and rules everything. Rather, we use the word *God* to designate the totality of everything that exists. This Ultimate Authority, the Divine, has to be understood holistically. Thus by "totality" and "oneness," scientific research doesn't lead us to the old conceptual notions of God. Otherwise we'd merely have an obsolete idea of God creeping in through the back door. Instead, God reveals himself as mind and matter. Theistic theology falsely calls this pantheism because it can't understand what esotericism is trying to express with not-twoness, namely the experience of conceptual terms as a unit of reality.

Sadly we can't make any statement without forming conceptual pairs. But in mystical experience we learn that such pairs are, in reality, one. Only in experience can we transcend conceptual pairs. And only when we transcend them do we experience what reality is. Zen calls these two aspects of reality form and the void. "Form is really the void, the void is really form." The Divine is a bipolar unity; it doesn't belong on the side of one pole or the other. It is what transcends both poles in oneness.

But this reality must not be described with the usual notions of God. It is, to stress the point once again, not the God that humans have made, but the Ultimate Reality that exists only as mind and matter and can really be grasped only in a transpersonal experience.

A stronger commitment to astrophysics and the theory of relativity would have helped theistic theology keep up with the thinking about God found in the general development of consciousness. After all, many leading scientists, such as Planck, Einstein, Born, Bohr, Jordan, Böhm, and Heisenberg, have pressed forward to the frontier of rational knowledge. They speak openly of this other Authority that can no longer be grasped mentally, that eludes methodical formulas but is part of what we call reality. And they are convinced that this Ultimate Authority has different capacities from those of our ego-consciousness, and that ultimately, these capacities are the force that, with the help of ego-consciousness, drives the whole process of evolution forward.

PANTHEISM AND MONISM

Theologians are still wrestling with these two terms today. The holistic world view is, however, something quite different from the monistic view. In the holistic vision of reality, mind and matter appear as one thing with two aspects. By contrast, monism views mind and matter as substantially one. But that is exactly *not* the case. Holism repeatedly stresses not-twoness.

In Buddhism this is explained with the notion of a "golden lion." Gold can appear only in one form or another (lion). Thus form (lion) and gold are one, but gold is not lion, and lion is not gold. Pantheism would mean that gold and lion have the same substance. That's not what esotericism says. But lion and gold can only occur together; they need each other to appear; they are coexistent.

Another image is light and shadow, which likewise can only occur together. They aren't the same thing, but one can't appear alone. Where there's light, there's shadow; where there's shadow, there's light.

That is why Eckhart says: "At one and the same time when God was, as he begot his eternally equal Son as God fully equal to him, he also created the world."[2] Or, "Similarly it can be conceded that the world has been from all eternity."[3]

As Christians, we can call the two poles or aspects Father and Son, with the Father as the aspect of origin (mind) and the Son as the aspect of form (creation). Both together constitute reality. If you say Father, you imply Son. If you say Son, you imply Father. They are coexistent and one in their form of existence, which is why we speak of the "one

God." But our discursive thought has to break them down into a conceptual pair. The Ultimate Reality is a holistic Authority. The one aspect reveals itself in the other. Thus there is no transcendence that does not reveal itself holistically. This Ultimate Authority is something that manifests itself in material, psychic, and intellectual forms.

BIPOLAR UNITY

Reality has two aspects, just as every staff has two ends. We call the one aspect "form" (in Zen) or "creation" (in Christianity). In the world of forms we see reflected the other aspect of reality, to which we give different names: Godhead, Void, Brahman, the Absolute. The two constitute reality.

In the whole there is no polarity, no time, and no space. But this wholeness or totality is incomprehensible to our human consciousness, and that irritates reason. Mystical experience is the experience of this whole, and so it often comes into conflict with theology, which is anchored in the world of polarity. It's not as if mysticism were against theology; mysticism merely stresses the side of the whole that it experiences but that remains closed to reason.

I would like to cite a remark by Nicholas of Cusa. Since he was a great philosopher, theologian, and mathematician, we need not suspect him of ulterior motives when he writes: "Practically all those who dedicate themselves to the study of theology busy themselves with certain fixed traditions and their forms. And when they can speak this way as do others who present themselves as models, they take themselves to be theologians. They know nothing about the unknowing of that unattainable light, in which there is no darkness. But those who have been led by the knowing unknowing from hearing to seeing mind, rejoice in having obtained the knowledge of unknowing through sure experience."[4]

Every form presents a content that reason and the senses cannot grasp. The world of the forms is the contact point for nonform. The real continues to mirror itself in the world of the forms. The world of the forms is Maya or creation. Behind the world of forms lies the whole, a state that contains all things in an undifferentiated manner.

Still more to the point might be the comparison to a ruler, one side of which measures centimeters and inches while the other has no markings. Both sides constitute the ruler, yet our reason can never see more than one side. Mystical experience, however, grasps both sides as one. Hence mystics speak not just of the whole but of oneness.

The goal of mystical experience, therefore, is not to escape polarity but to experience it as an expression of oneness. Both aspects belong together: unity (wholeness) and polarity (multiplicity) are like two sides of the same coin.

Polarity is a prison cell. As Sakyamuni Buddha says, it brings humans pain, suffering, old age, and death. Within the world of forms, there is no satisfying or fulfilling interpretation of life. But man can escape this prison cell and become one. Esotericism applies a number of different names to the move out of polarity into oneness: enlightenment, the great liberation, satori, mystical union, and others. Since this step leads us out of polarity, it baffles any formulation or representation.

When people succeed in taking this step, they have to clothe their experiences in symbols and images that express the ineffable better than abstract words. But all symbols and images likewise belong to the realm of forms. They are only there to mediate the content. They relate to their content as dream images do to their psychological meaning. If images and symbols are understood literally, if they are absolutized and "worshiped," religion ossifies. The gold is, as it were, confused with the form.

A religion that ossifies into forms sees only these forms and compares them with other religions. Then the arguments and confrontations begin. One's own religion, needless to say, becomes far better or "truer" than the others. One no longer sees that while religions may be very different, formally speaking, they come out of the same absolute truth and aim to lead back to the same truth. The same fluid appears in different containers, but the containers can have quite different sizes and forms. Anyone who sees only the outside will inevitably stress the differences. But whoever tastes the contents, enjoys the same reality. But one must actually drink from it; a description will not suffice. This has nothing to do with syncretism—quite the contrary. Humans need different containers to realize the multiplicity of the Divine.

All founders of religions, all mystics, whether Eastern or Western, have taught one path to the experience of the Divine. Though their words have been utterly different, they have meant the same thing. They showed the path out of polarity into the Whole.

RETURN TO THE WHOLE

People have to find their way back to the Whole. Wholeness embraces everything, there is nothing that could lie outside it. In the Whole there is neither time nor space. Time and space are possible only within polarity. The Whole cannot be described concretely, only in paradoxes, parables, and myths. The only way to illumine the Whole is to frame it in paradoxes.

When the One emerges into creation, it is polar. Creation means that unity crumbles into multiplicity. A popular image attempts to make this clear: light slants through a prism. Light stands for unity, the colors are polarity. The prism breaks down the light into many different colors, but the light always remains what it is: light. Another image is the paper fan; it is a flat sheet of paper; folded it is a fan. In the same way, the One unfolds into the "manifold." It is simple (without-folds) and multiple (many-folds).

Yoga says that when an amethyst is placed in milk, all the milk appears greenish. But the milk and the amethyst remain what they are. This image makes plain that mystical oneness has nothing to do with monism. The not-twoness is still preserved.

In reality the polar world does not exist the way we see it. As the esoteric school keeps telling us, it is a deception, but our ego continually hypnotizes us into believing otherwise. It's hard to realize this so long as we are encapsulated in the deception. But not to see through it means to remain an eternal prisoner of deception. Every esoteric path aims to free people from this illusion. The insight that the world of polarization does not exist is itself liberating.

Dreams can clarify this. When we dream, we take everything to be real. We see forests and people; we fly through the air or dive under water. When we awake, we realize that none of that actually exists. But to reach that realization, we had to wake up. In the same way, the universe, whose meaning we humans strive so mightily to figure out, is only a dream. But we can't experience that until we awaken from sleep. For this reason, enlightenment is also called "awakening." It is being freed from the chains of polarity into oneness.

MYTH: THE LANGUAGE OF RELIGION

Part of the tragedy of theistic religions is that they overstress history. The truth of a religion, however, lies concealed in its symbols, images, and myths.[5] These are like glass windows that are lit up by the "eternal light." Windows give the light structure and color so that we can talk about it. But those who understand these religions only in the historical sense are locking up their true meaning.

In the final analysis the content of myth is always liberation or, as we usually say, redemption. Redemption is carried out in ritual or liturgy as in a drama. In Christianity it unfolds in the course of the Church year. It is the performance of the eternal truth in ritual. But those who see the life of Jesus only as a mystery play are just as far off the mark as those who see only the historical reminiscences. Myth and history belong together. Liturgy becomes a representation of a cosmic mystery play. What is played out is the coming and going of the divine life in the multiplicity of forms. Evolution is the play of the unfolding of the Divine.[6]

We should deal with religious myth as we do with dreams. We need to ask what the images have to say. Those who treat their dream images superficially or even literally are misinterpreting them just as much as those who dismiss them as nonsense. If we want to find out their real message, we have to press deeply into their universal human symbolism. In the same way, images are only metaphors, analogies, and archetypes whose meanings have to be interpreted. We have to do the same with the images and symbols of the sacred Scriptures.

Fortunately, myth contains its own meaning. We simply have to remember that it doesn't recount a historical event. In religion we often remain blocked at the superficial, historical level. If we wish to experience the depths of religion, we have to move beyond an external understanding of faith. We are not limited to seeing Father, Son, and Holy Spirit as persons we can call upon to alter the destinies of our life and this world. We can understand them as metaphors, as well, that convey to us a mysterious underlying truth. Myth does not communicate factual knowledge but a realization of what we really are and what we are meant to experience as truth.

More and more new mysteries will come into being.[7] They are evidently of the greatest importance for leading humanity toward maturity and into the Whole. They help us find the link to our unconscious, where we get the real message for the unfolding of our personality. They bring us objectives designed to make us mature and integrated beings. In the biblical myth of Jesus we are presented with just such a fully developed personality. If we realize this objective ourselves, we, too, will develop into the full "image of God" and become worthy—to stick with the language of the Bible—to be taken into heaven, which ultimately means to become the total, complete person who in the beatific vision comprehends the wholeness of divine revelation.

In Christianity we have the same motif in the Eucharist. The image of the grains of wheat scattered over the field that are made into bread can be traced back to the idea that the One is cut up into pieces and again returns to unity. If the Divine (the Whole) emerges and expands into the many, in other words when creation occurs, oneness dies. It is as if the Divine dies, to arise again as One in the Eucharist under the "species" of bread and wine.

Ego and Self

What is the ego? Our ego is the demarcation that gives us shape and form. It is the "lion" (form) in which the gold is revealed. It is what makes us human beings so that the Divine can resound through us. It is absolutely necessary; it coexists with the other aspects of reality. The only pathological element is the arrogance of the ego, which makes it inaccessible to the Divine.

Thus our ego is something precious. It includes our body, the material level, the psyche, and the intellect. This is the source of the reverence for whatever has form. Here, after all, is where the Ultimate Authority expresses itself.

The ego makes us human. It creates culture and gives rise to progress and development of every sort. At no point need we see it as negative. The only negative feature is that it peremptorily puts itself in the driver's seat and speeds off through life without any clear sense of where it is going. All too often it winds up flipping the car over. It has to learn to get its orientation from the depth of true being. It must find its way back to wholeness.

So often, we carve out for ourselves a piece within this whole and say, "This belongs to me." It's as if we fence off a piece of land and declare, "mine," yet the land has been there since time immemorial and will be there still long after we die. The land is untouched by the fence, as are the sun, rain, wind, insects, and birds that play in, on, and around the land. In reality the fence doesn't exist—unless we believe in it. The idea of "private property" works only if the owners and at least a few other people go along with it. The fence, like the human ego, exists only as an idea. With our ego we fence ourselves off and out. The ego creates polarity. The whole is the inside and the outside.[8]

Every path of salvation necessarily brings about a confrontation with the ego. We have to break the dominating power of the ego and cancel our identification with it. There is no other way of experiencing the whole. This path is called self-knowledge or self-realization. The self is the space where we experience wholeness. It is the *scintilla animae*, the "spark of the soul," of which Eckhart speaks. Teresa of Avila calls it the "interior castle"; Johannes Tauler calls it the "foundation."

Thus the self is a kind of center in which reality may be experienced. It is the place where bipolar reality becomes comprehensible as the One. Thus the self is not the Divine but where the Ultimate Reality is experienced. It is the point of intersection where both aspects, mind and matter, meet and can be experienced as the Whole.

As the story of original sin in Paradise shows, our ego has a drive to keep breaking through these circumscribed limits. In fact, that is what original sin is all about: continually tearing up this oneness with our ego-demarcation. Religion is supposed to help the ego march in step with our innermost essence. Ethical prescriptions offered by religion are designed to animate us to live in harmony with this inner Authority, in other words, to grow up into the definition of a mature personality. The meaning of our earthly existence is to mature and become whole and to return to Oneness.

In long years of practicing contemplation, some people find archetypal images such as light, Jesus, Mary, or Shiva and Kannon (the Buddhist goddess of mercy) to be powerful, heart-wrenching symbolic figures of the Divine. In mysticism these people are taught that such visions are not reality itself, but structures by which the Ultimate Reality communicates itself to ego-consciousness, often with an intensity that transforms lives.

Symbols, myths, and rituals become experiential modes of the Whole, which always has two aspects: the graspable and the ungraspable. Without such forms of experience we could scarcely develop ideas about God.

64

They help us translate the contents of religion into lived life. For this reason all these messages maintain their profound meaning.

For example, "God sent his Son into the world to redeem it by his death, and then the Son rose again to return to heaven" is not only the report of a historical fact but is a symbolical statement for the whole evolutionary process, which is otherwise indescribable. As this myth unfolds in the liturgical year, it has a life-enhancing intensity, and thus makes a crucial contribution to our psychological and overall human maturity.

If we begin to devise formulas, the statements we make will contradict one another. All statements are only like spokes connected to the hub of a wheel. The empty hub is the Void, Godhead, Sunyata, Nirvana. It is not "nothing"; rather, the empty hub is where all spokes come together or go out from. Everything gets its meaning from that empty hub, including the entire wheel itself. If this empty hub did not exist, the wheel would lose its meaning. In the same way, without the ungraspable "emptiness," life has no meaning. Everything that is converges in this void (godhead). The emptiness is not empty. From it proceed all the "spokes of Being."

CHAPTER 5

CHRISTIAN MYSTICISM AND THE EASTERN ESOTERIC PATHS

In recent years astrophysics has made enormous progress and has broken through to discoveries that give us humans and our earth reasons for feeling very modest. We are, beyond a doubt, not the center of the universe, as we have so long believed. Our earth is a speck of dust on the edge of this universe; its home address is on a relatively small Milky Way, of which there are millions, most of them far larger than ours. In all probability the universe began unthinkable billions of years ago with a Big Bang and has been expanding ever since, at nearly the speed of light. We hear of pulsating quasars and black holes, and scientists suspect that after an unimaginably long period of time, this universe will again contract. By then our sun will long since have gone cold, and life on earth will have been extinguished.

We are also in the process of investigating the microcosm. We can split the atom and conjure up frightful consequences, like annihilating life on spaceship earth. Although we have found other subatomic particles such as quarks, we can't specify their exact location or their velocity. In fact, we can't even draw the line between matter and energy since they alternately appear as particles of matter or as waves of energy. True, we continue to experiment and to calculate, but we no longer rightly know what we're experimenting with.

Given all this, we have to steer clear of the notion that the world might be organized according to rational points of view. It is obviously organized in a nonrational manner, and its inner structure has nothing to do with intellectual considerations. In other words, it has dimensions that are not rationally graspable. I recall the theory of superstrings, which defines the world ten-dimensionally, that is, with nine spatial dimensions plus time. Other physicists demand as many as twenty-six dimensions.[1]

So here we are; we live at a tiny point in this cosmos between quarks and black holes. Both the microcosm and macrocosm overwhelm our imaginative capacity. Yet, we insist on assigning great importance to the human race. We claim to know with far too much certainty who God is.

Rational consciousness is only one form of consciousness alongside the others. It views the universe in its own peculiar, limited fashion. Thus we can perceive only four dimensions. Evidently the rest can be grasped only with different forms of consciousness. Reality is something altogether different from what this highly limited rational faculty can disclose to us.

Theology speaks of God only on the level of rationality. Even what we call revelation is verbalized on this four-dimensional level. But science has already moved beyond all traditional mathematical statements about the universe. Doesn't theology, too, have to transcend its rational declarations about God? Why such anxious defensiveness in churches? As always, institutions are afraid of mysticism.

Mystics have always known that there were other dimensions. The ego, they say, has to be transcended to arrive at experience. In the language of mysticism this means that the ego has to die. Mysticism could no more find names for the experience of other dimensions than science could because mystics cannot capture experience in a language based on rational thinking. Nowadays, science recognizes in Eastern esoteric systems a certain relationship to its own "limit experiences."

The Eastern religions have both a theology and a practice that leads to experience. The theology is very complex and subtle; the practice is generally known as "tantra." Tantra comes from Sanskrit and means "weave." One doesn't talk about tantra; one has to do it. In *The Dancing Wu Li Masters*, Zukav explains that "Buddhist philosophy can be intellectualized; tantra cannot. Buddhist philosophy is a function of the rational mind; tantra transcends rationality. The most profound thinkers of Indian civilization realized that words and concepts could take them only so far. Beyond this point lay the actual exercise of a practice, the experience of which was ineffable. This did not prevent them from progressively refining the practice into an extremely effective and sophisticated set of techniques, but it did prevent them from being able to describe the experience which these techniques produce."[2] An important function of Eastern religions consists in giving mind the possibility of escaping the limitations of symbolism. In this view everything is a symbol, not just words and concepts but people and things as well. Beyond the frontiers of symbolism lies pure awareness, the experience of the "thusness" of reality.

Although the Eastern religions have symbols, they use them to escape the limitations of symbols. Religions always have to make use of symbols, that is, words, rites, myths, and sacraments. But they are only the finger that points to the moon. As Christians, we must once again recognize that religion is based on experience as much as on words. The Eastern religions show us this very clearly.

Nowadays one finds more articles on mysticism in journals of science and transpersonal psychology than in journals of Christian spirituality. In the last two hundred years mysticism has emigrated from the Christian churches. This may be one reason why so many people today are dissatisfied with their church. In fact, the new scientific findings are seldom reflected in our ideas and discourse about God. The Christian religion is still too bound up in the Cartesian and Newtonian world picture. Only mysticism, evidently, will bear scrutiny from a contemporary standpoint. Mysticism has always moved beyond the four-dimensional perspective so as to get a more comprehensive view of the Ultimate Reality.

When the Bible was written, humans saw themselves as the center of creation, and the universe revolved around the earth. People believed in a God who had formed and carefully guided all things and who sought out for himself a people for whom he was present in a special way, with whom he made a covenant, to whom he gave laws. From time to time, this God grew angry with this nomadic tribe (for they were no more than that), and then again he was kind to it. Admittedly, even back then this God appeared to be incomprehensible, but he was basically a superbeing, a patriarch who oversaw and directed everything. This notion still plays the decisive role in Christianity, even though in the face of our knowledge of the cosmos it's hard to accept such a patriarchal ruler. In fact, it strikes us almost as an insult to speak of God this way, against the background of the immeasurable expanses of the universe.

In contrast to the Eastern religions, the mystical element is underdeveloped in the West. In fact, it is under suspicion—especially when it borrows from the East—and is often tarred with the same brush as the pseudomystical tendencies of the age. This will surely change some day. Zukav argues that should Böhm's physics or a similar approach become the main thrust of this science, the findings of the East and the West might merge in an extraordinary harmony: "Do not be surprised if physics curricula in the twenty-first century include classes and lectures in meditation."[3]

The authors of the following reports describe the revolution in their piety:

> The deeper conflict in me is the breaking away from a tradition that has left its imprint on all of us, not in the conscious practice of Church tradition, no, on a much deeper, unconscious layer. And strangely enough only now does it come to my mind how greatly this Christianity was alienated in a thousand variations and still resonates as a basic motif in our thought and culture. If the image of the Father God that Jesus Christ gave us is now disintegrating, it's hard to find one's way in a completely new reality. Jesus gave people this image because they already bore it within themselves....But our time can no longer endure the restrictions this imposes.
>
> A few days ago I was reading something by an Eastern Orthodox priest about contemplation: "...when you look at God, you see nothing, and that is precisely the point: When you're looking at nothing, then there is no knowledge or experience. In fact there you have what God is, God is nothingness." And immediately thereafter I saw Nothingness. It was the unfenced reality, the reality with no wheels, confined to no track; and all my attachment had disappeared in this seeing....The more ego-consciousness falls away, the more one finds oneself in this inner reality, in this Nothingness. It was as if the past and the future had ceased to exist. I couldn't even manage to remember myself. There was only the freedom of seeing, of hearing, and of doing.
>
> *A priest*

For some time now I have been in inner conflict with my Church; overnight the nest has become too cramped. So, although nobody around me noticed, I secretly "emigrated." I left behind the external fabric of forms and structures, but still I would like to lead people to a place where in a homey religious environment they can discover and experience the foundation of their life as a precious treasure.

Religion is something other than what the Church "stages." When I question what brought about my retreat from the usual structures—especially from the whole area of the liturgy—I can't explain my behavior rationally or psychologically....A powerful longing to spiritualize my religious experience no doubt shapes my attitude of flight as far as the liturgy goes: flight from ceremonies, rites, gestures, words, images, decorations, signs, in which the religious person expresses himself or herself....

God, who burst into my life as such a powerful reality, would like to fill up the depths of my soul. This is like a core transformation in which becoming one takes place, and I can only observe this process of becoming one, of fusion in the present, and let it happen without translating it symbolically. I myself don't understand the way I have changed; perhaps it's only a transitional phase. And it hurts me that I can't celebrate with you (her fellow Catholics) as I used to. The form for doing that has yet to be born.

A woman

There are far more mystics in our time than people generally suppose.

Mystical experience has always and everywhere transcended narrow dogmatic thinking, even though it was often forced into the confines of traditional concepts and symbols. Ever since gnosticism was banished from Christianity, mysticism has surfaced in peripheral movements such as alchemy and astrology, but also in theosophy, the *philosophia perennis*, and in parts of psychology (above all Jungian and transpersonal psychology).

People who have been exposed to deeply moving religious experiences often look for help from professional therapists, not least of all because they have gotten so little understanding from the Church's representatives. There is an international organization called the Spiritual Emergency Network which links a variety of people, most notably psychologists, therapists, and social workers. This organization supplies the addresses of persons to whom you can turn if you're having problems dealing with a transpersonal experience. The crisis such individuals go through is expressed in the following account by a young woman:

> At my first Communion I had a profound experience. On that day I experienced with my whole being what I had hitherto believed, namely that God *is*. And God wasn't just in me. He was in all the men and women around me, and he was everywhere. He was the center of all things. This experience was so powerful that I had to share it, but when I turned to my spiritual adviser, he told me "You've imagined something; you've been fantasizing." This answer shocked me, because the depth of the experience made it impossible for me to label it imagination or fantasy.
>
> I carried it around inside me until about the age of eighteen, and then I began to look for explanations. Since I had searched in vain in the Christian Church, I went to the theosophists. Among them I discovered that this experience, which still shapes my life, was an authentic mystical event. In theosophy I also learned about paths that can lead to such an experience. I am still thankful today that I found trusting people who understand me.

Integrating our religious experiences into the fabric of our lives is crucial to self-understanding. If we fail to do that, we can easily slip into neurosis because our experiences give us an entirely new and persuasive understanding of reality, an understanding of reality that contradicts the convictions of the world around us and hence is extremely difficult for our ego to maintain amid everyday life.

Religious experience lets people enjoy more and more independence. This is especially striking with women. As far as I can see, women come to religious consciousness much earlier and more frequently than men. I would say that the feminine qualities of the person—letting oneself go, giving oneself, opening and accepting oneself—play an especially important role here. Easterners find this easier to do than Westerners, and thus mystical experience has always been acknowledged in the East as a central concern. Today many women are discovering this feminine legacy which opens the way to mysticism. This makes men feel anxious. Thus a number of women have pointed out to me that the lack of understanding on the part of a male-run Church caused them to leave that institution. The development of femininity, which is basic to any continuation of the mystical tradition in the West and in Western Christianity, would be the best response to the religious longing of our Western contemporaries. In this era, with our tremendous possibilities for communications, we have the opportunity to learn from the East and thereby reanimate our mystical tradition. The very survival of the Church and society may perhaps be at stake.

ESOTERICISM AND EXOTERICISM IN THE WORLD RELIGIONS

I no longer believe that the crucial difference between religions is the boundary separating individual faiths, such as Buddhism, Christianity, Islam, and Hinduism (to mention only those with the largest following). Rather it is the difference between esoteric and exoteric spirituality. So as to avoid misunderstanding, I must briefly explain what these terms mean.

Esotericism comes from the Greek *esoteros* which means "inside, within." Exoteric comes from *exoteros* which means "popular, comprehensible to the lay person." However, I am not using the word esotericism here in the sense of something accessible only to initiates, that is, people belonging to an esoteric group. Nor do I use the word exoteric to refer to noninitiates or outsiders. By esotericism I mean rather a spirituality that is oriented toward experience and that sees in this goal the meaning of religion. By exotericism I mean a spirituality that is based exclusively on scriptures, dogmas, ritual, or symbolism. Thus an esotericist is not a person with some sort of elitist consciousness but someone who has started off on the path to experience the Divine in himself or herself and in all things.

Thus the fundamental difference between religions consists not in their doctrines and rituals but between their esoteric or exoteric spirituality. The dividing line runs horizontally, not vertically. I would like to illustrate this with a diagram:

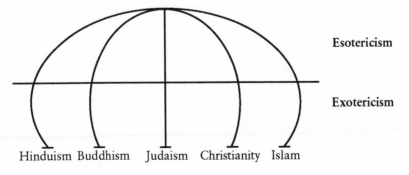

Esotericism

Exotericism

Hinduism Buddhism   Judaism   Christianity   Islam

73

The Ultimate Reality, variously named by religions as the Absolute, Godhead, the Tao, Sunyata, Nirvana, defies every kind of naming or visualization through reason and the senses. The attempt to give it a name that everyone can accept is what divides the religions, and, as history shows, what has led to wars of religion, persecution, defamation, disparagement, and so forth. Today we have at least arrived—well, not completely—at the stage of dialogue. Religions are paths on which individuals should be led back to their origins, or what we call our deepest essence or the Divine within us and within everything that exists.

Experience is so deeply concealed in human existence that it resists every attempt at communicating it. This is why mystics are often criticized for being antirational and arrogantly "enlightened." Even if this experience is spelled out somehow or other, exotericists have difficulty accepting it because it's not intellectually graspable. Esotericists, by contrast, have no problems with religious formulas because the formulas aren't posited as absolute. Thus over the course of history mysticism has had a two-sidedness: it can effectively support dogmas or it can undermine them. Eckhart's writings make it clear that mysticism doesn't have to be the enemy of subtle theological reflections. Nevertheless the esotericists in most religions have suffered harsh penalties from the dominant institutions of their day. Many were not just excommunicated but were thrown into prison and burned at the stake.

Exotericists are afraid of betraying the truth of their religious beliefs. Since their faith is lodged in an altogether special creedal statement, they find it difficult to accept that truth is to be found in other religions as well. That, of course, would relativize their own faith and lead them into great insecurity because their religious certainty is grounded precisely in the differences between their own and other religions. Tolerant individuals may well concede that truth may be found in other religions, but there can't possibly be as much of it as in their own.

The truth common to all lies in the heart of every religion. But since this truth transcends any and all forms in which it appears, only a few people are fortunate enough to press forward to it. That is why religion is important. A religion can no more exist without forms of expression than a person can live without a body. Holy Scriptures, theology, and ritual are like the map that believers require to find their way to God. They need direction, encouragement, and companionship so as not to lose their way. Humans live in a world of symbols, images, and forms;

and these modes of expression are needed to communicate their religion to others. The foregoing remarks are not meant to impugn religion as such, but to invalidate a narrow, exclusively exoteric understanding of faith.

Religion may be compared to a glass window. It remains dark unless it's lit from behind. The light itself is not visible, but in the window of religion it takes on a structure and becomes comprehensible to everyone. Although religion often tends to bind its followers to the structures of the window, the ultimate thing is not the window but the light that shines behind it. Only those who see the light of God behind all the structures can realize the meaning and goal of religion. The danger is that symbols and images of God will obscure rather than illuminate the reality they are supposed to shed light on.

THE MEANING OF EASTERN ESOTERICISM FOR WESTERN MYSTICISM

Zen helped me to understand an important part of our Christian spirituality that has been lost in the traditional teaching about prayer—namely the mystical element. Christianity usually teaches oral and meditative prayer, a certain moral behavior, and social commitment. But this isn't much more than the grammar school of a religion, and so many Christians remain stuck in an infantile state. When they grow up, they drop the childish forms without having learned a grown-up form of prayer. That is how things are in almost all religions. In Buddhism and Hinduism, too, most believers never get past a very simple form. Thus, as I see it, all religions are only on the way toward outgrowing a childish notion of the self and growing into an adult understanding.

I make a distinction between spirituality and religion. Spirituality teaches a path into experience and deals with what is experienced. Religion, by contrast, is instruction that has evolved into dogmatic theology. These dogmas do, in fact, derive from experience, but they have been absolutized, and only a few believers understand them in an experiential fashion. In esotericism there is instruction but no dogma. "Dogma" here relates to traveling a path to come to one's own experience.

These thoughts might give rise to the misunderstanding that esotericism could subsist all by itself. Not so. Religion needs the two pillars of esotericism and exotericism, otherwise it can easily fail to reach its goal. Esotericists, too, have found the way to mystical experience by means of religion. They will never reject religion, but they clearly recognize the one-sidedness that every formulation brings with it. Humans are creatures of mind-and-body, and so they need religion as a profession of faith and they need language as a means of expressing themselves. But true religion attempts to lead its adherents beyond itself to the experience of the Divine.

The Christian religion is my home, even though I cannot identify myself with everything tradition has made of it. We have received a great legacy, and few of us would have made it to the path of contemplation if Christianity had not put us on the right track. I myself feel responsible for this legacy and would like to bring back into the light some of its features that I think have been submerged.

ESOTERICISM AND EVERYDAY LIFE

Esotericism is not primarily concerned with elevating the mind to a level of experience on which it forgets all its earthly ties. Rather it aims to bring about a sharp-eyed vision that lays aside all egocentricity and allows us to grasp the world in its "thusness." That alone will lead to the comprehensive love that makes human life possible to begin with.

There is an old mandala, known in both the East and the West, that clearly and pointedly expresses the standpoint of the mystic: two overlapping circles. Christians call this a mandorla. In Romanesque art, Jesus Christ is represented by these two circles, just as Sakyamuni Buddha is in Buddhist art. The mandorla is no doubt older than both religions. It designates the supernatural and the natural, the Divine and the human, mind and matter. In the area where the two circles overlap sits the "Godman." Here is where both aspects of reality coincide and become one.

The mandorla designates the union of apparent opposites, the *coniunctio oppositorum*, or, as Nicholas of Cusa would say, the *coincidentia oppositorum*. This is the bipolar unity of which the mystics speak. Our ego-consciousness divides reality into subject and object, whereas our true self experiences unity and harmony. In the mandorla both aspects coincide. Nicholas of Cusa writes: "I have found the place where one can find Thee undisguised. It is surrounded by the coincidence of opposites. This is the wall of Paradise in which Thou dwellest. Its gate is guarded by the highest spirit of reason (*spiritus altissimus rationis*). Unless one overcomes it, the entrance will not open.

On the other side of the walls of the coincidence of opposites one can see Thee, on this side never."[4]

Thus esotericism does not mean exiting from the world. On the contrary, it sees the world and reality as they are, not as our reason and senses deceptively present them. The process of human maturation consists in making these two circles more and more congruent. Esotericism and exotericism belong together. Even in the Gospel according to John there are passages that say as much, for example when Jesus tells his disciples, "Whoever has seen me has seen the Father" (14:9). Some apocryphal texts speak even more clearly about this unity: "When you make the two one, and when you make the inside like the outside and the outside like the inside, and the above like the below, and when you make the male and the female one and the same, so that the male may not be male nor the female,...then you will enter the Kingdom"[5] (*Gospel of Thomas*, v. 22).

Ultimately esotericism is concerned with a new experiencing and grasping of reality. The true esoteric paths don't lead out of this world, but into the heart of the moment, into life. The point is to feel not contempt for the world, but an entirely new form of love for it. And with that we come to the essence of mysticism in both the East and the West: religion is life, and life is religion. When I experience the fact that my rising in the morning and putting on my slippers is a profoundly religious act, then I have recognized what religion is. But this is simply not possible without deep experience. In the Eucharist we solemnly proclaim that this is not just bread (in other words, not just form) but the essence of divinity appearing in this form. In the Eucharist we solemnly proclaim that nothing exists that is not God, which means that we actually ought to experience even our breakfast as one more way the Divine expresses itself. It is a sacred action to live one's life here and now. In the final analysis, the sacrament of the moment is nothing else but "living in the will of God." That is the way to happiness.

BREAKING DOWN PREJUDICES

Esotericism aims to provide a clear-sightedness that sets aside all egocentricity and enables us to grasp the world in its "thusness," but also to relativize it. The East often calls "emptiness" or "the void" what European languages would most readily translate as "the Numinous" or "the

Absolute." Eckhart would use the word *godhead*. Ultimately, things have no independent or lasting substance. They are pure phenomenal forms that cannot appear outside of the Divine, that is, outside of the void. When the East says, "All things are empty," it doesn't mean that things don't exist, but that they are nothing but phenomenal forms. Things have no existence on their own. Thus the void makes form possible to begin with and simultaneously links all forms together.

Everything that has been said thus far could be easily confused with monism, pantheism, quietism, animism, gnosticism or—to mention more recent intellectual trends—anthroposophy, theosophy, and Christian Science. But that would be true only if I were trying to interpret mystical experience from a rational standpoint—a level on which it is simply incomprehensible. Mystical spirituality is mature piety that can emerge from any religion. Everything is ontologically one with God. There is no domain of life or experience that could be excepted from this rule. Every school of mysticism tells us this, insofar as it is allowed uncensored freedom of speech.

We also have to emancipate mysticism from all superpious religiosity, indeed from what we Christians call the gift of prophecy or visions. That doesn't mean that something like this couldn't happen to mystics and might not be important for the individual and even for the group. But a mystical experience can also be something quite banal—and nonetheless completely fulfill a person. It doesn't absolutely have to be expressed in religious language. Its primordial language in the West is the love song. Followers of Zen know that a mystical experience can occur in the bath or on the toilet, while having sex or chopping wood. The Divine reveals itself in everything and whenever we receive the gift of being able to let go.

A further objection is that in esotericism the understanding of God remains at the mercy of individual subjectivity. There are criteria for genuine experience, however, though naturally these, too, are grounded in personal experience and thus can't be nailed down rationally. This renders esotericists powerless to come up with "proof." And that is why mysticism will always come off the worse until a larger portion of humanity is blessed with such experiences. The number of people who have had a transpersonal experience is on the rise. Unfortunately, many of them have to set up their tents outside the organized Church because they are rejected inside it.

Another prejudice involves the idea that contemplation is self-redemption. The fact is, neither Zen nor the higher forms of yoga nor the Christian practice of contemplation have anything to do with self-redemption. Redemption is always there, but it is not something people achieve. Humans can only prepare themselves to experience it. They can only try to clear away the layers that separate them from it. As for the relation between divine grace and human effort, Eckhart says: "It is one moment: the being ready and the pouring out. When nature (that is, humans and their efforts) has done its utmost, then God gives grace. At the same point in time that the (human) spirit is ready, God enters it without delay or hesitation."[6]

I think it's important to take a new look at ideas that over the course of history we have branded as heretical. In the future, real religious dialogue will be conducted on the level of experience, not on the level of theology. One can only hope that Christian churches will recognize the signs of the times and not oppose the new religious awakening. Perhaps they can rediscover in their own tradition the very things that people today are yearning for so passionately.

C.G. Jung reduced the whole problem to a very simple common denominator. For him mysticism was not a matter of faith but of experience. He writes: "Religious experience is absolute, it can't be discussed. One can only say that one has never had such an experience. Then one's opponent will say, 'Sorry, but I *have*,' thereby ending the discussion. It doesn't matter what the world thinks about religious experience: the person who has it possesses the great treasure of a thing that has become for him a source of life, meaning, and beauty and that has given the world and the human race a new brightness."[7]

CHAPTER 6

CONTEMPLATIVE PRAYER: AN OLD CHRISTIAN TRADITION

Contemplation is the word that was used throughout the Middle Ages for prayer with no concrete object. It was the highest form and the goal of all instruction in prayer.

Three forms of prayer were distinguished: *oratio* (oral prayer), *meditatio*, and *contemplatio*. Teresa of Avila handed down to us a still more precise classification: oral prayer, mental prayer, meditation (possibly with reading), and the prayer of recollection (active and passive). After these forms, Teresa tells us, begins actual contemplative prayer: the prayer of quiet and contemplation (also called mystical union, immersion, or the art of loving).

Teresa's four forms address the intellectual and sensory endowment of human beings. That is, they involve the senses, feelings, and reason. These forms of prayer are concerned with the contents of consciousness, that is, with images, words, metaphors, or nature, through which the powers of the soul are stimulated.[1] Mystics call this meditation.

Contemplation, on the other hand, is possible only when reason, memory, and will have come to rest. All psychic forces behave passively in contemplation. Something happens to the person at prayer. No cognitive contents are accepted; religious images, visions, inner speeches, and pious thoughts are left behind. Contemplation is pure gazing. Something happens to the pray-er. It is an awakening to one's true divine essence.

Kataphatic and Apophatic Spirituality

There is no religion that doesn't point out a twofold path to God. To express this, scholars have coined the terms "kataphatic" and "apophatic," from *kata* which means "according to," and *apo* which means "away from," and *phatis* which means "discourse, word." Thus the first is "positive," the second "negative." The first makes use of language; the second does not.

Kataphatic spirituality works with the contents of consciousness, that is, with images, symbols, ideas, and concepts. It is content-oriented and starts out from the assumption that people need images and concepts to come to God, that such things are of the greatest importance for the unfolding of the religious life.

Apophatic spirituality is oriented to pure, empty consciousness. It sees contents as an obstacle. As long as consciousness clings to images or concepts, the actual experience of God does not take place. Rather than shed light on the Divine, these images and concepts obscure it.

Most men and women doubtless take a kataphatic path, that is, the path of images, ideas, and words about God. They have been taught that way in their childhood, and they find support in it. For this reason kataphatic spirituality plays the larger role. But the more forcefully religion gets into the mystical realm, the more it becomes apophatic; it abandons images, ideas, and concepts because after a certain point they make God even harder to see.

Thus on the one hand, religion needs words and images because faith cannot be communicated without them. On the other hand, however, the danger of reifying and ultimately even worshiping words and images is very great. Images and symbols are authentic paths leading to the Ultimate Reality, but they can also become obstacles.

From time immemorial apophatic spirituality has been rather suspect to the revelatory religions, especially to Christianity. Granted, it always represented a more or less broad current that sometimes flowed more beneath the surface, but it often shot heavenward in a great surge. Still, the institutional Church always nurtured a certain mistrust of it. At times this feeling was justified, especially when the mystical path took a strong anti-theological or anti-intellectual turn and descended into uncritical fantasies or even into the excesses of parapsychology. Mysticism and theology are the two pillars of religion. Only when both are allowed to maintain a strong, well-balanced existence does religious life flourish.

RELIGION AND THE STRUCTURE OF PERSONALITY

The religious path people choose greatly depends on their personality structure. People who are strongly subject-object oriented generally feel anxiety over losing control of their ego or, as mysticism says, letting it die. Such persons need an "opposite number" to whom their ego can cling. In most cases that purpose is served by religious images and theological concepts. Images can bring the mystery of God closer to an individual, of course, but they can also distort it. Ego-consciousness is only too happy to shield itself against its own disintegration. Thus critics of the imageless contemplative way are often motivated by fear, believing that if the image of God is let go, the ego will disappear as well. For this reason images are often confused with what they merely represent. They turn into idols. Clinging to images and concepts seems to be one of the refined tricks of ego-consciousness to prevent a deeper union with God.

Ego-consciousness and the experience of oneness are mortal enemies; they cannot subsist together. For the duration of mystical experience, a person loses his or her ego-consciousness. This *mysterium* has something threatening about it. The individual stands for some time in its presence, full of reverence but also full of fear. A deeper readiness to open oneself to the mystery is slow to develop because this always means letting go of the ego and its ideas.

Our ego is something that is continually constituted by memory but has no existence in itself. In the course of the contemplative path, we learn that our real self lies far deeper than this superficial ego, which is formed by intellect, senses, and will. This false self-image is what we must relinquish if we want to experience the greater Reality: God.

No doubt every person relies on a blend of both ways in prayer. Mystics take part in church services and also generally proclaim their faith. Their spiritual experience, however, transcends all of that.

TRAINING IN CONTEMPLATION

The question keeps arising whether the *path* to contemplation should already be called contemplation. Most of the medieval masters speak of *training in* contemplation. Thus John of the Cross says that one "must set forth on the contemplative path."[2] He even speaks of a "ladder" leading to contemplation.[3] Madame de Guyon (1648-1717) speaks of the short and easy way to inner prayer that everyone can take without difficulty and on which they will make good progress in a short time.[4]

Thus contemplation is something one can be trained to do. It's comparable to mountain climbing (see John of the Cross, *Ascent of Mount Carmel*). John of the Cross writes about a "state of progressives."[5] Osuna even says that one must build the house of contemplation.[6]

Training forms a state of soul through which it can be shifted to "gazing."[7] The state of contemplation, or loving knowledge, is acquired only gradually because at first the soul cannot yet perceive what it is seeking, although it is there.[8]

Before Osuna, John of the Cross, and Teresa, Hugh of Saint Victor (d. 1141) pointed out a clear path to contemplation. Hugh speaks of the threefold eye of man: "the eye of the flesh, the eye of reason, the eye of contemplation." The eye of the flesh grasps outer things, while the eye of reason grasps intellectual things, and the eye of contemplation grasps divine things.[9] These same three steps, more or less, are noted by Richard of Saint Victor (d. 1173), Bonaventure, and others. In each case the highest stage is called contemplation. So it would make sense for us Christians, in keeping with tradition, to hold onto this word to designate our object-free way of prayer. Contemplation is a path that runs parallel to the paths of Zen, Vipassana, and yoga—all of them headed to the same goal.

In his *Itinerarium*, Bonaventure describes this path. As he sees it, contemplation is the real purpose of Christian life, and to it everything, including philosophy and theology, must render service.[10] We also see a clear path presented by that fourteenth-century English mystic known only by his writings, *The Cloud of Unknowing* and *The Cloud of Silence*.[11] For these authors, mysticism was not something they primarily wanted to describe, but something that could be reached, that had to be striven and struggled for. The ultimate experience is grace—nobody questions that. But all writers on this subject know that human effort and the help of others on the path are extremely useful.

Who Should Take the Path of Contemplation?

"Everyone is suited for inner prayer. It is a great misfortune that almost everyone takes it into his head that he is not called to inner prayer. We are all called to inner prayer, just as we are all called to salvation," writes Madame Guyon.[12]

In *The Ascent to Mount Carmel,* John of the Cross writes: "[This book] treats of how the soul may prepare itself in order to attain in a short time to Divine union. [It] gives very profitable counsels and instruction, both to beginners and to proficients."[13]

For Louis Blosius, a fourteenth-century French mystic, the status of contemplation was absolutely to be taken for granted, at least for monks: "If you say that this perfection is too high for me…then I answer you: You are no monk." There is a quotation from Zen quite similar to this: "A monk without kensho (contemplation of essence) is not worth a cent."

People keep signing up for courses in contemplation after they have already had a profound mystical experience. Among them are Christians and also men and women who have never practiced their Christianity and are strangers to any connection with the Church. Others taking these courses very quickly break through to a genuine mystical experience. It's altogether possible that the experience of Christians may express itself in nonreligious images, while agnostics may suddenly come up with Christian images. Both groups may be horrified at this situation.

As Christians, we run the danger of not letting anything count as authentic mystical experience unless it fits into the framework of dogmatic declarations. But experience is not tied down to any definite faith or denomination. God has always revealed himself to—among others—people without any particular religion. In other words, experience always flows into a person's channels of consciousness, which for their part depend upon his or her upbringing and personality structure. From this fact and from practical experience, even people who are alienated from their religion can take this path and come to authentic mystical experience. Some return to some sort of connection with a church, others see no need to do so.

BASIC FORMS OF TRAINING

It seems that the mystical paths of the East and the West can be reduced to two basic forms of exercise: recollecting consciousness and
emptying consciousness. The first could be called the concentrative way
and the second the receptive way.

The path of gathering consciousness consists in the bundling or con-
centrating of psychic powers on an object of meditation, for example, a
word or koan. When we continue the exercise of dwelling on this object
for a longish period of time, we are led to the loss of the ego level of
consciousness. The stream of thoughts revolving around the ego and
the ego itself are, as it were, sucked up by the object. In the end the
experience of the absolute One emerges, for where only One fills the
whole consciousness, everything else disappears, including the ego. In
its place comes the experience of oneness.

The way of consciousness-emptying has its basic structure in the
nonreaction of consciousness. It is wide-awake, but doesn't bind itself
to any thoughts, doesn't let itself be captured by any ideas or carried
away by any emotion. Whatever appears in the field of consciousness is
perceived and then let go. Thus the core of consciousness resembles a
mirror. Whatever steps in front of it is reflected. The meditating person
senses that the observing ground differs from the observed contents of
consciousness but resists the tendency to identify itself with these contents.

Naranjo describes meditative training as follows: "It is an ongoing
effort to track down all conditions, all compulsive processes in the mind
and body, and all emotional reactions conditioned by habit that poison
the totally simple situation. It is an effort that the exercitant needs to
make to free himself from all those things."[14]

Thus pressing forward on the mystical path leads to the
deautomatization of consciousness. Reaction or behavior patterns, both
in grasping the complete reality around us and in coming to grips with
situations, are dissolved, taken apart, and finally put aside through meditation. The person meditating once again becomes capable of seeing
everything that appears in the field of consciousness as it is and not as
his or her projections and anxieties have hitherto made it look.

Recent years have brought us an enormous amount of research in
psychology. Anyone who deals with mysticism today can no longer ig-

nore what transpersonal psychologists have published on the subject. Psychology can, up to a certain point, shed light on what happens in mystical experience and "demystify" many aspects of it, though it cannot describe or define the final condition.

Not only the Christian, but, as Karl Rahner said, any man or woman of the future will be a mystic. Humanity has once again arrived at the end of one of its evolutionary epochs, in this case the mental phase.[15] It seems that our survival is bound up with our success or failure to take the leap to the level of consciousness (which Jean Gebser calls the perspectivist level). Young people already show themselves much more open and gifted for the mystical path than the older generation. The mystical current is unfolding more outside the organized Church than inside it. For these days the humanities and the various branches of psychology and psychiatry are showing more interest in the depth-dimensions of the human soul than are the religious institutions.

Breathing practices: The Christian monastic tradition has always known about entering into a state of immersion with the help of breathing exercises. Here are some examples from the *Philokalia*:

> You know, brother, how we breathe: we breathe the air in and out. On this is based the life of the body and on this depends its warmth. So, sitting in your cell, collect your mind, lead it into the path of the breath along which the air enters in, constrain it to enter the heart together with the inhaled air, and keep it there. Keep it there, but do not leave it silent and idle; instead give it the following prayer: "Lord Jesus Christ, Son of God, have mercy on me." Let this be its constant occupation, never to be abandoned.
>
> A man who wishes to learn this doing should know that, when we have accustomed our mind to enter within while inhaling, we shall have learnt in practice that at the moment when the mind is about to descend within, it forthwith rejects every thought and becomes single and naked, freed from all memory but that of calling on our Lord Jesus Christ.
>
> St. John of the Ladder says: "May the memory of Jesus combine with your breathing; then you will understand the use of silence."…Hesychius says: "To keep silence as you should and to be sober in your heart without effort, let the Jesus prayer cleave to your breath."[16]

The practice of sitting: From time immemorial, long, quiet sitting has been considered important. One can plump into a church pew or a chair at home or a bench anywhere. Some people prefer to squat on their heels. If you place a cushion between your buttocks and heels, you can maintain your position for a longer time and with greater ease. From the earliest days, Christian monks were aware of the value of long sitting and persistent practice. This training, however, had to be continued on a daily basis.

Cassian, a monk, reports to us about the prayer life of eremites and cenobites in the desert. He describes the practice of mystical prayer and recommends a short ejaculation:

> "Come to my help, O God; Lord, hurry to my rescue." Our prayer for rescue in bad times and for protection against pride in good times should be founded on this verse. The thought of this verse should be turning unceasingly in your heart. Never cease to recite it in whatever task or service or journey you find yourself. Think upon it as you sleep, as you eat, as you submit to the most basic demands of nature. This heartfelt thought will prove to be a formula of salvation for you. Not only will it protect you against all devilish attacks but it will purify you from the stain of all earthly sin and will lead you on to the contemplation of the unseen and the heavenly and to that fiery urgency of prayer which is indescribable and which is experienced by very few. Sleep should come upon you as you meditate on this verse until as a result of your habit of resorting to its words you get in the habit of repeating them even in your slumbers.
>
> This verse should be the first thing to occur to you when you wake up. It should precede all your thoughts as you keep vigil. It should take you over as you rise from your bed and go to kneel. After this it should accompany you in all your works and deeds. It should be at your side at all times. Following the precept of Moses, you will think upon it "as you sit at home or walk along your way" (Deuteronomy 6:7), as you sleep or when you get up. You will write it upon the threshold and gateway of your mouth, you will place it on the walls of your house and in the inner sanctum of your heart. It will be a continuous prayer, an endless refrain when you bow down in prostration and when you rise to do all the necessary things in life.[17]

The monks of the Thebaid and of Skytis likewise knew about the custom of sitting for long periods. "The monk squatted in his cell on a mat or on a low bundle of papyrus—it may have been for ten hours a day or more."[18]

The *Philokalia* observes: "After sunset, having asked the help of the all-merciful and all-powerful Lord Jesus Christ, sit you down on a low stool in your quiet and dimly lit cell, collect your mind from its customary circling and wandering outside, and quietly lead it into the heart by way of breathing, keeping this prayer: 'Lord Jesus Christ, Son of God, have mercy upon me,' connected with the breath."[19]

Practice with the Word: The author of *The Cloud of Unknowing,* a mystical text from the fourteenth century, advises making use of a word—and a short one at that—to collect our consciousness. Experience in fact teaches that a short word is better than a long one. It also shows that a dark vowel flows more easily and brings better vibrations with it than a light one. In Christian contemplation, for example, "Jesus," "Christ," and "shalom" have proven appropriate formulas. As we pronounce (inwardly) these words and then breathe out, we quite naturally lengthen the final vowel. If the word has two or three syllables, for example, "Jesus" or "Lord Jesus," the word can be divided as follows: "L-o-r-d," upon breathing in, "J-e-s-u-s," upon breathing out, or the first syllable, "J-e," upon breathing in, and the second syllable, "s-u-s," upon breathing out.

When you have advanced sufficiently in your exercises, you no longer direct your attention to breathing but to the sound. The vowel is, as it were, sung internally; it guides the breathing. The goal is to become one with the word, or rather with the process of internal pronunciation or singing. The point is to become this sound itself. This brings your inner self to rest. You gather your consciousness, so to speak, at this word or vowel, thereby letting go of the many other things. Only one thing is left in consciousness: this process of pronouncing the long, drawn-out vowel, bound up with the breath. Thus contemplation does not thrust aside the contents of consciousness in the sense of repressing them. It merely concentrates on this one word and thereby lets go of the many other things. While contemplative prayer lasts, thoughts, feelings, and moods withdraw. The word or vowel rivets all your attention.

Letting go of thoughts: Mere reflection on a word is meditation about something—and a basic directive of all mysticism states that one must *stop* reflecting. Even the most pious thoughts get us no further on the path. Pious feelings must remain behind.

The author of *The Cloud of Unknowing* gives instructions (in Chapters 7 and 36) on the use of words in contemplation:

> Take just a little word, of one syllable rather than two; for the shorter it is the better it is in agreement with the exercise of the spirit. Such a one is the word *God* or the word *love*. Choose which one you prefer, or any other according to your liking—the word of one syllable that you like best. Fasten this word to your heart, so that whatever happens it will never go away. This word is to be your shield and your spear, whether you are riding in peace or in war. With this word you are to beat upon this cloud and this darkness above you. With this word you are to strike down every kind of thought under the cloud of forgetting; so that if any thought should press upon you and ask you what you would have, answer it with no other word but with this one. If the thought should offer you, out of its great learning, to analyze that word for you and to tell you its meanings, say to the thought that you want to keep it whole. If you will hold fast to this purpose, you may be sure that the thought will not stay for very long.
>
> For here it is not a question of analyzing or elucidating these words rationally or listing their various meanings in the hope that such consideration would increase your devotion. I do not believe this to be so, or that it could ever happen in this exercise. These words must be held in the wholeness.
>
> No man can think of God himself. Therefore, it is my wish to leave everything that I can think of and choose for my love the thing that I cannot think. Because he can certainly be loved but not thought. He can be taken and held by love but not by thought. Therefore, though it is good at times to think of the kindness and worthiness of God in particular, and though this is a light and a part of contemplation, nevertheless, in this exercise, it must be cast down and covered over with a cloud of forgetting.[20]

> If any thought should rise and continue to press above you and between you and that darkness, and should ask you and say: "What do you seek and what would you have?" you must say that it is God whom you would have....Say to the thought: "Go down again." Tread it down quickly with an impulse of love, even though it seems to you to be very holy; even though it seems that it could help you to seek him.[21]

The practice of self-surrender and love: The author of *The Cloud of Unknowing* advises his readers to charge their words with devotion, love, and trust. Although this seems to contradict the command not to cling to feelings, it doesn't, for love, devotion, and longing are fundamental movements of the soul that can accompany the word every step of the way. They orient us and help us "collect" ourselves. When we are thirsty we don't have to think of water; the longing for water is riveted in our body. It's the same way with love. When we really love, really yearn, really surrender, we are not distracted and we are likely to succeed in the practice of contemplation. But we should not be surprised if such feelings are often lacking. The path leads over long dry stretches, it leads through the wilderness and night, as the mystics say. When that happens it is extremely important to keep practicing even—in fact, especially—if there are no feelings at all.

Awareness of one's own being: Along with the path of recollection of consciousness, the author of *The Cloud of Unknowing* is also familiar with the receptive path to mystical experience, namely the emptying of consciousness. He often speaks of the awareness of one's own being. In the course of training, one notices that in the depths of thoughts, feelings, and intentions, something else exists independently of the movements that ripple across the psyche. Thoughts and feelings arise from it, but they are not the same as this ground. *The Cloud of Unknowing* calls it "Being." Perhaps one enters a state where one experiences the fact that one is—without knowing where or who one is—naked Being. In this condition there are always two elements, an ego that experiences and the object of that experience. Moving beyond this point is very hard. Yet the goal is to leave even this ego behind and to experience only the Being of God. But this can't be achieved by an act of the will. There is nothing to do but go on exercising faithfully. Continue with the practice of prayer. Flow into it completely. Then the experience can be granted to you.

Mantric prayer: Through the power of our senses, that is, through our seeing, speaking, touching, hearing, and so on, we enter into contact with the outside world. But we can also direct our senses' capacity inward. There they can become our guide to a deeper reality.

Sound has its own dynamism that goes far beyond its vibrations and can lead into the depths of our consciousness. The rosary and litanies, of course, belong to the mantric forms of prayer. For simplicity's sake, I'll use the word *mantra* to refer to any such prayer.

All religions are familiar with holy words and signs that are constantly repeated, such as the mantra. Islam, for example, has the ninety-nine names of Allah that are repeated on a string of beads. It is said that only the camel knows the one-hundredth name of Allah because the name of Allah can only be experienced. The Sufis have wazifas, the Hindus have their mantras, the Buddhists repeat the nembutsu or sutras. We Christians, too, have words and prayers (mantras) that are constantly repeated, such as the Jesus prayer ("Lord Jesus, Son of God, have mercy on me"). *Kyrie*, too, is such a word, as well as *allelujah, Maranatha,* and *shalom.*

Mantras capture the infinite in the finite. Because the infinite is experienced in the sound, the mantra is not a magical incantation; it has nothing hypnotic about it, no power of its own. Rather it strengthens the forces that are already present within us. It connects us with something that is there to begin with. It links our everyday consciousness with the depths of our being.

These depths are more comprehensive than language and concepts. Hence the mantra is prelinguistic and very well adapted to leading us away from everyday consciousness into a comprehensive experience. The content of the word itself is not important because its effect works on the psychospiritual level that is not subject to our discursive thinking. The mantra connects us with forces and currents that are always flowing through our body but that get strengthened by this constantly repeated practice of prayer. The mantra starts something vibrating in us, sets us on an inward path, and leads us to the actual sources of our being.

The ancient scriptures of Tantric Buddhism say about the *OM*: "This mantra is the mightiest of all; its power can impart enlightenment all by itself." And the Upanishads say: "Whoever says this mantra, the mantra of the Holy Word, thirty-five million times, will be set free from his karma and from all his sins. He is redeemed from all bonds and reaches absolute liberation."[22]

In the *Sincere Tales of a Russian Pilgrim*, we read of the starets' directive to repeat the Jesus prayer twelve thousand times a day.[23] Anyone who practiced that for ten years would reach a number similar to the one in the Upanishads, namely 43,800,000,000. In mantric prayer, repetition plays a crucial role. After a certain amount of time the prayer develops its own dynamic: it prays in us.

There are certain details about the mantra that we now consider.

VIBRATIONS AND HARMONY IN THE MANTRA

Today we know that every particle in the universe has its own frequency. The identity of a thing seems to lie in its frequency. Many centuries ago the philosopher Pythagoras said that a cliff was music turned to stone. Science has realized that every particle in the physical universe has its own pattern of frequencies and vibrations. The world is really sound even though we can't hear all the resonances.

We humans are far more dependent on vibrations than we think. A lie-detector expert named Cleve Backster once made an unusual discovery with plants. He wanted to study how they reacted when their leaves were burnt with a candle. Curiously, the measuring device registered the highest levels the moment Backster merely had the idea of singeing a plant. Plants, in other words, understand our thoughts.[24] We know that plants do better with some people rather than others, that they evidently react very strongly to vibrations. Might we humans be much more strongly influenced by them than we think?

Thus frequencies have a major effect on our lives. If only we were more aware of this, we would better understand, for example, how malicious and envious thoughts can wreak far more havoc than we think on our family, our society, our partners, or our colleagues at work. Naturally all benevolent thoughts that we have for one another have a positive effect. A harmonious life together has its starting point in the nonverbal messages we send.

Such a harmonization can actually be measured. When two people carry on a good conversation, the waves of their gray cerebral cortex coincide. The same thing happens when there is a good connection between a preacher and the congregation. And, of course, we see this with married couples. We can even observe it in animals, for example, when a school of fish or flock of birds changes direction as if on command. One researcher writes: "The flock is more like an individual being, an organism."[25] The orders are issued by the collective. Physics call this "harmonization and resonance." Scientists also now assume that sicknesses are above all rhythmic disturbances. Pains and illnesses seem to arise not least of all from the fact that our bodies can't resonate harmoniously in all places.

Sounding: Mantras consist of vibrations. When we set off resonances, we vibrate. It is important that we don't "make" the sound but that we become a body of sound, an orchestra. The sound should vibrate through our entire body. We can even address the individual parts of our body separately, such as our legs, pelvis, chest, neck, arms, and head. Mantric recitation and sound can even ease cramps. We can also charge the sound with feeling, for example, with devotion, love, trust, or good will. Sounding is also appropriate for releasing aggression so long as we don't aim it at anyone.

But those are only intermediary goals. Actually we should try to become one with the sound so that sound is all there is. Everything else disappears alongside of it, goes under it, so to speak. To experience sound in us and in everything is the goal of "sounding." To become one with the sound brings about an opening of consciousness. Everything vibrates in the same rhythm. The ego-boundaries fall, and we experience ourselves as one with the Divine in us and in all things.

The rosary: The rosary is doubtless the mantric prayer best known among Christians, above all among Catholics. It exhibits its greatest power when it is prayed in common, indeed when recited in a rhythmic drone.

My first experiences with prayer are tightly associated with the rosary. When I was about six years old I took part in praying the rosary in church. It was led by a couple of women in the usual monotonous drone, with the congregation murmuring the responses. This rhythm led me into a state of consciousness that was unlike my everyday awareness. I knew that behind all the words there was a reality beyond everyday consciousness. I had a similar experience with litanies; their repeated sing-song rhythm carried me to a deeper experience of prayer.

The rhythmic droning is an important component of mantric prayer. Yet so many Christians dismiss that aspect with contempt, and that's unfortunate, for the rhythm and repetition bring the real pray-ers onto a track headed inward toward more intimate contact with God. Something similar happens, as previously mentioned, in the Jesus prayer. It has the same effect as the rosary. Instead of despising this form of prayer, we should try it sometime.

Repeating a word: The repetition of a word in contemplation qualifies as mantric prayer. This word accompanies us through our entire life, indeed beyond death. It is a form of letting go of all images and ideas, so as to give ourselves over entirely to God's will. It releases us from our cramped condition in the world of forms so that we no longer beg to go to heaven, but that God's will may be done in us. "Father, into thy hands I commend my spirit."

For all this, to be sure, we must practice with perseverance. The only people the "word" of prayer will help are those for whom it has become continual prayer in their lifetime.

In the West we have almost forgotten the mantric forms of prayer. In the Eastern religions, however, they are highly prized. In his book *The Power of the Holy Sound*, John Blofeld tells of an old monk who was asked the origin of the cheerful serenity that he radiated. He answered that it was the sound of the mantra that enabled his mind to experience in a mysterious way his hidden harmony with the Tao, the primal way, and the primal meaning of Being. Blofeld writes: "I myself finally managed to experience the superiority of the mantric form as compared with prayer. Prayers have a conceptual meaning, but that conjures up thoughts, which disturb the silence of the mind. Hence the mind can't reach a quiet and serene condition, in which its silence is reflected. It remains hung up on dualisms—such as 'I, the pray-er,' or 'He, the prayed-to.' At best prayer is a proto-form of mystical union. And as for prayers that contain a request, hardly anything could be more unspiritual than to pray for victory or for a certain kind of weather or for happiness, which in the final analysis can only be attained at the cost of others."[26]

Angelus Silesius expresses the same idea in a poem: "Whoever pleads with God for gifts / Has badly gone astray. / He worships not his Master / But the creature of a day."

CHAPTER 7

GREAT MYSTICS' PATHS OF PRAYER

THE FATHERS OF THE DESERT
(Third and fourth century)
Puritas Cordis (Purity of the Heart)

The Desert Father John Cassian was born in Constanza (in modern-day Romania) around the year 360, into a family of Roman colonists. With his friend Germanus, young adult Cassian headed to Bethlehem. He didn't find what he was seeking there, so he moved on to the monks in the wilderness, about whose prayer life he gives us an extended account. Later he wandered further, founded two monasteries in Marseille around 415, and died around 435. In his *Conferences*, Cassian has left us the teachings of the Abbot Isaac on prayer. The following material adheres to that tradition.

For Cassian, the chief capacity of knowing or experiencing is *cor* (heart). Heart is that spark of the soul with which we not only experience our true divine life but which *is* this divine life. This experience is not achieved through reflection or through words that remain fixed in the memory.

> For the manner of these things can by no means be understood or
> taught or kept in the memory through leisurely reflection or a mere
> word because almost everything here is based on experience alone.
> And just as these things can be learned only from someone who
> has experienced them, so they can be grasped and understood only
> by the person who strives to learn them with the same zeal and
> industry.[1]

Rather, the path to experience goes by way of knowledge about the
path, through *praktiké*, which is divided into three sections:

- work on the inner person (struggle against sin)
- service to the brothers
- modeling oneself on Christ

Purity of the Heart

Seeing is the actual goal of monasticism, but it is a gift and is not subject
to our will. Hence the immediate objective is purity of heart (*puritas
cordis*). "The aim of our profession is the kingdom of God, or the kingdom of heaven. But our point of reference, our objective, is a pure heart"[2]

We misunderstand, however, if we interpret this as sinlessness in the
moral sense. Rather, it is a psychic disposition that is pure, that is to say
free from obsessions, confusion, and excitement. It is tranquillity that
has let go of everything so as to be free and open for God. "And so anything which can trouble the purity and peace of our heart must be
avoided as something very dangerous."[3]

The process of breaking free, which John of the Cross later named
active and passive purification, is a psychospiritual process aimed first
at clearing away psychic defects such as anxiety-ridden childhood experiences, traumas, and similar disturbances in the personal unconscious.
Further purification also means emancipation from all instinctual domi-
nation.

Our passions, given us by our Creator, are good. Only their perverted
use is evil. For example,

> The drive to nourish ourselves is not bad, but gluttony is, because
> it paralyzes us. Cassian sensibly advises his readers not to eat be-
> tween meals and not to be picky eaters. Actually he is more con-

cerned with inner fasting: not abandoning ourselves to everything that reason supplies us with.

Fornication is a special form of being occupied. Work helps to counteract it.

Greed is the sin of the lukewarm who make themselves an idol.

Sadness is compared to the image of the moth, the wood worm, and rust; it dislodges the mind from the state of purity.

Weariness leads to laziness and lethargy. It fogs the mind.

Thirst for glory and pride are the vices of the perfect who have already made some progress on the spiritual path.

A certain quality of heaviness, of imperviousness and dullness, clings to all these vices. They cause unrest and disturbance and thus prove to be obstacles on the path to purity of heart.

Praxis

The monks squatted in their cells on a mat, a bundle of papyrus, or a footstool for as many as ten hours a day. Even after the midnight psalmody they didn't lie down. Cassian reports how Abbot Theodore once cautioned him not to squander this precious time. Abbot Theodore "…came unexpectedly to my cell around midnight, secretly inquired with fatherly concern about what I, a still inexperienced hermit, was doing. When he found that immediately after the solemn night prayers I had given my weary body to rest and lay there on the coverlet, he released a sigh from the depth of his heart and spoke, calling me by name: 'O, John, how many people are speaking with God in this hour, embracing him and holding him in their heart, and you let yourself be deprived of this great light, dissolved in lazy sleep.'"[4]

Even during manual labor, contemplation went on. "Thus while they earn their livelihood with apostolic work (that is, with manual labor as the Apostles did), some, like excellent fishermen, may catch in the depths of their tranquil heart the schools of swarming thoughts with attentiveness and calm. Meantime, as it were from a towering rock, they look intensely into the depths and with salutary discretion, decide which one they will reel in on their pole, but also in clever (discretion) which ones they will dismiss and reject as bad and harmful fish."[5]

Desert, cell, work, fasting, and reciting the Scripture form the core of *praktiké*. Individuals could gauge their progress from their dreams. "When the spirit of a man begins to see his own light, when he can't be unsettled by dream stories, and when even in the face of the events of life he can remain serene, then such a person has reached apatheia."[6]

The path of praxis is a transformation and ripening into a purely receptive state of consciousness. For the monks, Jesus is the perfect mystical prayer. His prayer on the mountain was *apatheia*, the vision of God. Just as Jesus stood on the mountain praying and having a profound experience of what he called his Father, so should every monk persist in this prayer.

> Our Lord, too, represented this condition in the prayer that he made silent and withdrawn—as it is written—when he, himself an inimitable model of self-sacrifice, poured out drops of blood in the agony of his prayer.[7]

Cassian encourages the monks to attempt to transcend all words and images. He speaks of monks who can't pray because they can't imagine any picture.

> These (uncultured monks) think they have nothing left at all unless they picture some image to themselves, which they constantly address in their prayers, carry around with them in their minds, and always keep right in front of their eyes.[8]

> According to the measure of his purity...every spirit in his prayer will be set up and given his general formation, namely by distancing himself so far from the contemplation of earthly and material things as the state of his purity leads him, and insofar as Christ— either still humble and in the flesh or glorified and coming in the glory of his majesty—lets him look with the inner gazes of the soul. For those will not see Jesus come as king who—still entrapped in a sort of Jewish weakness [*sic*]—cannot say with the Apostle: "Even though we once knew Christ from a human point of view, we know him no longer in that way" (2 Corinthians 5:16). But the only ones who see his godhead are those who rise above the lowly, earthly world and thoughts and withdraw with him to the high mountain of loneliness, which—free from the noise of all earthly thoughts and confusion...reveals the splendor of the divine face and the image of his transfiguration to those who are worthy to look upon him with pure gazes of the soul.[9]

Exercising With the Formula

Cassian reports of a powerful saving formula that serves to recollect the mind. He has Abbot Isaac say, "The formula of the spiritual vision must be handed over to you. You must always freely fasten your glance on it, through which you will learn to move it in a salutary constancy, and through its use and your meditation, climb to a higher vision."[10]

Mantric prayer—the constant repetition of the same prayer word—awakens powers in us that have always been there. It links our everyday consciousness to the depths of our consciousness. Our sounding, too, awakens forces in us. It synchronizes body and psyche in the same vibration and opens up the deeper layers within us.

One such mantra used by the Desert Fathers was evidently the verse: "O God, come to my aid. O Lord, make haste to help me." Cassian shows us how we have to use this mantra.

> The thought of this verse should be turning unceasingly (*volvatur*) in your heart. Never cease to recite it in whatever task or service or journey you find yourself. Think upon it as you sleep, as you eat, as you submit to the most basic demands of nature. The heartfelt thought will prove to be a formula of salvation for you. Not only will it protect you against all devilish attacks but it will purify you from the stain of all earthly sin and will lead you on to the contemplation (*theoria*) of the unseen and the heavenly and to that fiery urgency of prayer which is indescribable and is experienced by very few. Sleep should come upon you as you meditate on this verse until, as a result of your habit of resorting to its words, you get in the habit of repeating them even in your slumbers (*decantare*)....You will write it on the threshold and gateway of your mouth, you will place it on the walls of your house and in the inner sanctum of your heart. It will be a continuous prayer, an endless refrain.[11]

MEISTER ECKHART
(1260-1328)
The Birth of God in the Soul

Hitherto scholars have found Eckhart interesting as a theologian and independent thinker, consigned primarily to philosophers and theologians. Few asked about Eckhart the mystic, the man who taught a path to experiencing God. In fact, Eckhart left us no systematic exercises, but his writings say enough about inner communion that we can easily make out a "path" in them.

Eckhart lived in a time of religious searching that has scarcely been matched by any other epoch in human history. Dominic, Francis of Assisi, the Beguines, and the renewal of the old orders caused a great number of religious communities to come into being. The English chronicler Matthew Paris has supplied us with a few statistics. According to him, there were seven Dominican monasteries and eighty-five Beguine houses in Strassburg during Eckhart's time. In Cologne, where Eckhart worked, there were one hundred sixty-nine Beguine houses. Matthew Paris assumes that in Eckhart's Germany, which had between eight and fourteen million inhabitants, there were one million Beguines, a hugely disproportionate number of people living in monastic communities. In those days, extreme ascetical practices and mortifications of all sort were the order of the day in most monasteries.

Eckhart wanted to guard people from such exaggerated and self-destructive external asceticism and to win them over to a spiritual way of life and an inner imitation of Christ. He was interested in the training that inwardly transforms a person—we would call this a person's consciousness. He makes a distinction between the "natural man" and the "God-born man," who knows himself to be one with the Divine. The question for Eckhart is: "How can an individual find oneness with God and live, thus becoming a true person and fully alive?"

Eckhart's path is the path of the birth of God in the soul. He continually stresses that the experience of God is not something we can produce on our own, and that it cannot be forced by training or violent asceticism. It was—and is—grace. One cannot earn the Divine: "Because they are gifts of grace, we can't acquire them with our own strength."[12]

To Eckhart, seeking for God is pointless. The wish to experience the birth of God actually prevents us from getting closer to God: "The more one seeks God, the less one finds him. You should seek him in a way that you find him nowhere. If you are not seeking him, you will find him."[13] On this point Eckhart is no different from other mystics. Thus the author of *The Cloud of Unknowing* argues that one should conceal from God one's longing for God. The following Zen text has a similar message:

Joshu asked "Should I turn to the way or not?" Nansen said, "If you turn to it, then you're going against it." Joshu asked, "If I don't turn to the way, how can I know that it *is* the way?" Nansen said, "The way does not belong to knowing or not-knowing."[14]

Eckhart himself asks whether, in that case, a person is at the mercy of God's whim. No. For Eckhart, as for all Zen masters, there is the path: "If you don't seek it, then you'll find it." Seeking lies too much on the level of ego. We still want something; our ego is still too involved. Only when we have fully let go are we ready for grace. All training is practice in letting go. If we really have let go and have let ourselves become empty, God must pour himself in. "It is one moment: the readiness and the inpouring. When nature reaches its summit, then God gives the grace. At the same point in time that the mind is ready, God enters it, without delay or hesitation."[15] Being ready and inpouring occur in the same moment: "For this reason God must necessarily give himself to a secluded heart."[16]

When we leave behind our ego, the Divine appears in the depths of our soul. But the letting go has nothing to do with an act of the will. We can't voluntarily let go. We must, as it were, enter into ourselves until our will, too, goes under in seclusion. Our will has to put us on the path, has to motivate us, but then it must go under in the exercise of prayer.

Two Kinds of Prayer

Eckhart distinguishes between two kinds of knowing: the knowing that transcends all sensory and intellectual cognition, and the knowing that limits itself to the finite. The former is knowing in a "divine" fashion, the latter in an "earthly" fashion. To press forward to "divine" knowledge, we have to let go completely. In Sermon 32, Eckhart cites a multitude of exercises that prepare the readers for the grace of the divine birth: "ruling over passion," "the reception of faith," "love of God and neighbor," "a conduct pleasing to God," "constant multiplication of good works," "zealous absorption in divine things," "a constant perseverance in obedience."

Although Eckhart does not take a negative stance on the sacraments, he sharply distinguishes between external action and the right inner attitude, which must not be understood in a magical or mechanical fashion.

Eckhart, concerned with a spiritual way of life, opposed the extreme forms of penitential life common in his day, such as "fasting, vigils, praying, kneeling, mortifying oneself, wearing hairshirts, and sleeping on hard surfaces."[17] He also prescribes no definite number of exercises. All he cares about is inner transformation. There, too, he resembles the Eastern master who one day was polishing a brick. When his disciples asked him what he was doing, he replied, "I am polishing the brick until it turns into a precious stone." When his disciples replied that that was impossible, he answered, "No more can you become the Buddha through sitting." All exercises have only one function: to teach us to let go. Eckhart calls these preparatory moves "inner exercises." They help, "if one trains oneself from within, with understanding and circumspection."[18]

At first, the exercises are practiced in the monastic cell and the church. The important thing is, however, to live the state of inwardness out in the world as well. Once more we may recall Zen, where the climb up the mountain of ecstatic enlightenment is only the beginning of the path. It is crucial to descend from the mountain into the everyday world. The Eastern saint ends in the marketplace of life. Only there does he show whether he is truly enlightened.

Directives for Training

What then are the exercises that Eckhart recommends? What can we contribute to the birth of God? The key principle of his directives can be found in the discourses of instruction: "In addition he (the person) should attain to imagelessness and remain fully free vis-à-vis things. In the beginning this will necessarily call for reflection and an attentive recollection, as the disciple must have in his art."[19]

A certain intellectual realization or intuition is presupposed for the path. It is the sure intuition that God can only be found beyond intellectual realization. But such knowledge puts us on the path: "Knowledge has the key and opens up and presses and breaks through and finds God undisguised."[20]

This statement has misled many scholars into thinking that Eckhart's "birth of God" is an intellectual achievement. But Eckhart gives the following explanation: "Thus, too, in truth, neither the knowledge of all creatures nor your own wisdom nor everything you know can bring you to the point where you are able to know God in a divine fashion. If you want to know God in a divine fashion, your knowledge must become a pure unknowing and a forgetting of yourself and of all creatures."[21] For Eckhart knowledge is a "virtue of the heart" and not "headwork." It is rather what mystics call experience, a "divine knowing."

Inner Exercise

For Eckhart, the prerequisites for "inner exercise" are fivefold: quiet, recollection, calm, poverty, seclusion. Here, too, there is no systematic presentation, but Eckhart's work as a whole provides that. His readers at the time, of course, could simply take many such things for granted.

Quiet: Only in pure quiet can a person see God.[22] Only in quiet does God give birth to his Son in the soul. For Eckhart, this exercise comes before any other. "God does not esteem and require vigils, fasting, prayer, and all sorts of mortification. He does demand tranquillity."[23] Eckhart mentions two steps: "Withdraw from the unrest of outer works! Flee further and hide from the storm of inner thoughts."[24] It's not enough to seclude ourselves externally; we can't learn that by flight. Our heart must be set at ease. "All voices and sounds must be gone, and there must be a pure silence, a complete silence."[25]

Eckhart knows very well that this inner quiet is much harder to come by than the external sort.

Recollection: "Whoever is to receive God's teaching has to recollect himself and shut himself off from all care and affliction and the bustle of lower things."[26] What at first glance looks like a narrowing of consciousness leads, in fact, to a broadening of consciousness.[27] Thus conscious recollection is the preliminary stage for expanding consciousness. Recollection is a letting go of all other possibilities of consciousness.

Composure *(Gelassenheit):* To Eckhart, composure means something different from the usual sense of the term. This becomes clear from a scriptural quotation: "No one can hear my word or my teaching unless he has abandoned (*gelassen*) himself."[28] Thus *gelassenheit* has to do with abandoning and with letting go. Only those who abandon their ego can comply with their Master's bidding. Here, too, Eckhart shows the consistency of a Zen master. We must abandon ourselves in such a way that we never for one moment look back at what we have abandoned.[29] "No one who puts a hand to the plow," says Jesus, "and looks back is fit for the kingdom of God" (Luke 9:62). But neither may we look forward to what we would like to get. "If you have looked ahead to what will fall to your share, and if you peer at it out of the corner of your eye, it will not be yours."[30]

Poverty: This is another of Eckhart's words for letting go. It doesn't mean physical poverty, but as Sermon 32 (*Beati pauperes spiritu…*) clearly shows, Eckhart uses the term to designate a letting go of intellectual activity. In it we find sentences like "Hence we beg God that we may be free of God. Therefore I beg God that he may get rid of God for me, for my essential being is above God." And then he says with matchless radicality that we must even abandon the will to carry out the will of God. We must be so poor that we don't even recognize and perceive that God is living in us and that God also wants to be the scene in us where he operates. The works that we do are then no longer our own, but God's works.

Kabir suggests the same thing when he writes:

> The moon shines in me,
> but my blind eyes can't see it.
> The moon is in me, and the sun too.
> The unbeaten drum of eternity
> can be heard in me;
> but my deaf ears can't hear it.
> As long as a man still shouts
> for "me" and "mine"
> his works are nothing.
> When all love for "me" and "mine" is dead,
> then is God's work done.[31]

Every human activity must shrink and retire on this path of contemplation. Only then can the Divine shine out in us.

Seclusion: Eckhart understands seclusion not so much as a retreat into solitude but as an inner seclusion from ideas and concepts. "When I preach, I am accustomed to speak of seclusion, and how the individual is to become free of himself and of all things...."[32] Seclusion surpasses all virtues. Seclusion compels God's self-communication. We are to maintain this seclusion even in our external acts. Here Eckhart cites the parable of the door hinge which remains immobile even when the door swings. Likewise, we maintain an inner coming-to-rest of the soul, memory, and will in all things so that divine knowing and mystical experience can shine forth. The heart "must stand on a pure nothing."

This taking back of the activity of ego-consciousness is mentioned in all esoteric paths as an indispensable prerequisite. It is the alpha and omega of every training path and leads men and women to uniformity with God. Eckhart interprets the saying of Jesus, "It is good for you that I go away," as: "Therefore slough off the pictorial appearance, unite yourself with the formless Being." Even the image of Jesus and all images of God have to be abandoned if we are to really experience God. If we are to realize the nobility and usefulness of perfect seclusion, we must observe the words Christ spoke about when he said to his disciples, "It is to your advantage that I go away, for if I do not go away, the Advocate will not come to you" (John 16:7). As if he were saying, "You have taken too much pleasure in my present appearance, hence the perfect joy of the Holy Spirit can not be imparted to you. So slough off the pictorial appearances and unite yourself with formless Being, for God's spiritual comfort is very fine in nature."[33]

Seclusion is like the door hinge that provides quiet even in the stormiest times. "A door swings open and shut on its hinge. Now I compare the outer panel to the outer person, but I equate the hinge to the inner man. When the door opens and shuts, the outer panel moves backwards and forwards, and yet the hinge remains immovable in its place and so is never changed. That's just how it is here, if you rightly understand it."[34] "When seclusion reaches to the Most High, it is knowledgeless from knowledge and loveless from love and dark from light."[35]

Contemplation and Action

Quiet, recollection, and composure are mere prerequisite for right action. We come out of solitude to experience all three in everyday life. "Pay heed to this, how you are turned toward your God, when you are in church or in your cell. Maintain this same state of mind and bear it among the crowd and into unrest and dissimilarity."[36] The works that we do are no longer our own works, but God's. Here, too, Eckhart's statements are reminiscent of Zen, where for example Koan 46 in the *Mumonkan* seeks to explain: "You must step out from the top of a one-hundred-foot-high mast and manifest throughout the entire world to the world and in the ten directions."

Contemplation and action belong together. One should be "without ties in the midst of his works."[37] Like John of the Cross, Eckhart points to the actual mode of being of things, which is divine. "Nevertheless the external phenomenal forms are to the practiced interior person an inner divine mode of being."[38] John of the Cross calls this "recognizing things in God." When the birth of God has occurred in us, we must no longer withdraw into solitude. Rather, we experience the "ultimate reality" in the course of events.

JOHN OF THE CROSS
(1542-1591)
Loving Attentiveness—The Dark Night

John of the Cross wants to teach a path to mystical experience. Nowhere can this be seen more clearly than in the introduction to his book *Ascent of Mount Carmel,* whose opening lines are "(the *Ascent*) treats of how the soul may prepare itself in order to attain in a short time to Divine union."

The description of the path may be readily abbreviated, as we see in his book *Living Flame of Love*: "And the soul has then to walk without loving awareness of God, without performing specific acts, but conducting itself, as we have said, passively, and having no diligence of its own, but possessing this simple, pure, and loving awareness and determination, as one that opens his eyes with the determination of love."[39]

The path to contemplation described by John of the Cross is loving attentiveness or, as he calls it in another passage, "passive and loving awareness."[40] Like other mystics, John teaches that even pious thoughts and feelings have to be left aside during the practice of contemplation:

> For the spirit needs to be so free and so completely annihilated
> that any kind of thought or meditation or pleasure to which the
> soul in this state may conceive an attachment would impede and
> disturb it and would introduce noise into the deep silence which it

is meet that the soul should observe…so that it may hear the deep and delicate voice in which God speaks to the heart in this secret place.[41]

This loving awareness is an inward listening; God is in us. "The center of the soul is God."[42] Normally we can't perceive or experience that because our reason, our senses, and our will are so loud. It's not easy to maintain our footing on this high ridge of inward listening. We must neither drift off into discursive thought nor into daydreaming nor even into sleep. Ultimately it is just this loving attentiveness that—without ideas of God or specific expectations—listens and looks, since "God is the center of the soul."

Reason, memory, and will have to remain completely turned off. The tender relationship of this loving awareness to the center of our own being is destroyed by the slightest stirring of those psychic forces. Thus John of the Cross warns in the commentary on the third strophe.

> These blessings, with the greatest facility, by no more than the slightest act which the soul may desire to make on its own account, with its memory, understanding, or will, or by the application of its sense or desire or knowledge or sweetness or pleasure, are disturbed or hindered in the soul, which is a grave evil and a great shame and pity.[43]

He goes on to write of lulling the senses to sleep,[44] and of the darkening of relations with God.

> I say, then, that the soul, in order to be effectively guided to this state by faith, must not only be in darkness with respect to that part that concerns the creatures and temporal things, which is the sensual and lower part (whereof we have already treated), but that likewise it must be blinded and darkened according to the part which has respect to God and spiritual things, which is the rational and higher part, whereof we are now treating. For, in order that one may attain supernatural transformation, it is clear that he must be set in darkness and carried far away from all that is contained in his nature, which is sensual and rational. For the word supernatural means that which soars above the natural; so that the natural self remains beneath. For, although this transformation and union is something that cannot be comprehended by human ability and

sense, it must completely and voluntarily void itself of all that can enter into it, whether from above or from below—I mean according to the affection and will—so far as this rests with itself. For who shall prevent God from doing that which He will in the soul that is resigned, annihilated, and detached? But the soul must be voided of all such things that can enter its capacity, so that, however many supernatural things it may have, it will ever remain as it were detached from them and in darkness. It must be like to a blind man, leaning upon dark faith, taking it for guide and light, and leaning upon none of the things that he understands, experiences, feels, and imagines. For all these things are darkness, which will cause him to stray; and faith is above all that he understands and experiences and feels and imagines. And if he be not blinded as to this, and remain not in total darkness, he attains not to that which is greater—namely that which is taught by faith.[45]

At first, this loving recognition of the inner light is almost imperceptible, says John of the Cross, because "When the soul has been accustomed to that other exercise of meditation, which is wholly perceptible, it cannot realize, or is hardly conscious of, this other new and imperceptible condition."[46] He compares this process to the perception of external light, whose visibility is best where it is reflected. The sunbeam shining through the window can be made out better by the eye when flittering specks of dust reflect its light. Thus the soul initially clings to the dust particles that flitter about in its inner space because it can't yet grasp the darkness of uncreated light. "Light is no proper object of vision," says John of the Cross, "but the means whereby that which is visible is seen."[47] Thus looking inward goes through a long process of development.

The Practice of Loving Attentiveness

John of the Cross presupposes that beginners in contemplation have intensively cultivated image-oriented meditations.[48] But when the joy of that fades, the soul should begin to busy itself with loving awareness, even if this seems to be doing nothing.[49] God's light will never fail the soul. Yet because of the images and veils that cover the foundation, it can't be perceived. Hence we must learn to dwell before God in loving attentiveness.[50]

This dwelling must take place frequently and regularly, so that as he says, it leads to a condition, or act: "And, just as many acts, of whatever kind, end by forming a habit in the soul, just so, many of these acts of loving knowledge which the soul has been making from time to time come through repetition to be so continuous in it that they become habitual."[51]

Thus constant training is of utmost importance. Peaceful sitting and evenly paced breathing make exercise easier, as we can learn from the writings of the monastic fathers. But loving awareness is not something we should have only while sitting or kneeling; it should accompany us all through the day and always be there when our mind is not busy with intellectual work. The hours of sleepless nights should become precious hours of exercise. The orientation inward, where "God is the center of man," and the firm decision to continue exercising is, all the spiritual guides tell us, one of the most crucial preconditions for progress on the contemplative path. It is well known that in Zen and yoga during periods of special exercise, individuals can spend up to ten hours a day in deep recollection. Both the monastic fathers and the masters of Eastern meditation teach us that the path essentially consists of an ongoing commitment to the relationship with our own center. In the beginning we must be active, do things, take pains, in order to remain in the state of alert, loving attentiveness, until through perseverance we arrive at the maturity of contemplative prayer. As soon as reason, fantasy, memory, and will fall silent, the path of contemplation begins. The soul should give itself to this practice, says John of the Cross, so that it may become accustomed to developing a condition in itself that then shifts it into contemplation.[52]

That doesn't mean that mystical experience can be "done" or "forced." It will always be a pure gift. The point is to prepare ourselves through practice in letting go and becoming empty. John of the Cross reports that he gave himself to this prayer for hours, even nights at a time, and that like Jesus his master, he preferred doing it out-of-doors or at an open window.[53]

The Purification Process—The Dark Night

None of the ego-directed psychic forces, such as reason, memory, or will, are allowed to be active in the state of contemplation. This exercise is not easy because reason may not hold onto anything. Emotions, too, should pass over. It is a loving awareness that knows nothing and wants nothing. When we set out on this path, we quickly notice how crowded we are by thoughts of everyday life.

But such thoughts are not the only thing that make exercise difficult. Everything that has been repressed into our unconscious in the course of the years, "swept under the carpet," begins to claim its place on the inner stage. For this reason, beginners usually struggle with anxiety-ridden childhood experiences, traumas, and neurotic blockages. For some of us, the inner difficulties become so strong that we can no longer continue in contemplative exercise. This is the point when the support and direction of a spiritual guide is crucial.

The disturbing cores in the unconscious often appear as anxiety. We don't know what we're afraid of, but it prevents us from proceeding on the contemplative path. We might be able to succeed in accepting our anxiety, ignoring it, and boldly continuing to direct loving attentiveness to God. We might find ourselves having to stop contemplation and undergo therapy first. For most of us, it's enough to accept the states of anxiety, to ignore them, and to move on. With time, in fact, such anxiety attacks generally diminish and disappear altogether.

During this active purification phase, we can make yet another contribution to our internal transformation. But with the beginning of "passive purification," which appears primarily to cleanse the collective unconscious, all activity falls away. These layers of consciousness are closed off to active access. The final purification must be endured.

The whole process can be incredibly painful. Only those who have been through it or have worked a long time with others affected by it can know how terribly hard it is. Chapter VI of Book II of *Dark Night of the Soul* by John of the Cross gives us a glimpse of all this.

> The third kind of suffering and pain that the soul endures in this state results from the fact that two other extremes meet here in one, namely, the Divine and the human. The Divine is this purgative contemplation, and the human is the subject—that is, the soul. The Divine assails the soul in order to renew it and thus to make it Divine; and, stripping it of the habitual affections and attachments of the old man, to which it is very closely united, knit together and conformed, destroys and consumes its spiritual substance, and absorbs it in deep and profound darkness. As a result of this, the soul feels itself to be perishing and melting away, in the presence and sight of its miseries, by a cruel spiritual death, even as if it had been swallowed by a beast and felt itself being devoured in the darkness of its belly, suffering such anguish as was endured by Jonah in

the belly of that beast of the sea. For in this sepulchre of dark death it must needs abide until the spiritual resurrection which it hopes for.[54]

These words of John of the Cross give some sense of how frightful this purifying process can be.

The lamentations of death—the pains of hell—flung into darkness—they have set me in the deepest and lowest lake—in dark places and in the shadow of death—the lamentations of death and the pains of hell—a most afflictive suffering (as if a man were suspended or held in the air so that he could not breathe). Heap together the bones and I will burn them in the fire; the flesh shall be consumed and the whole composition shall be burned and the bones shall be destroyed (Ezekiel 24:10).

This phase of contemplation can be terrible and can last a long time. In general its symptoms resemble those of deep depression. It's important here that this not be looked upon simply as a suffering that has to be endured, but as a process of spiritual purification. Only then can we manage to summon up the energy to bear with this process till the end. Our attitude toward the inner experience makes all the difference. This can be seen from the following example. Think of two tourists who have been left behind in the wilderness, with nothing but water for the next four weeks. The first tourist constantly looks for food, imagines nothing but things to eat, dreams of eating, gets hungry, and finally, at the end of four weeks, starves to death.

The second tourist prepares himself for a four-week fast, a time of psychic and physical cleansing. Because he knows how to fast, he emerges strengthened and purified from this deficit phase, while the first man remains stuck in need, fear, and hopelessness.

Passive purification can be a time of helplessness, pain, constriction, despair, panic, and horror. Not without reason did the mystics label this state *horror vacui*, horror of the void. Only a few persons will be able to go through these trials without a guide.

The dark night will sound frightening and negative to some readers. For John of the Cross, however, this cleansing is an emancipation from obstacles that separate a person from the experience of God. The "loving soul" doesn't make a list of things that she has had to forgo for the sake of her beloved. She doesn't count the costs. In fact, it doesn't even hurt. Thus the entire path of purification can be accompanied by a great tenderness that one day definitively leads to joy.

Guidance on the Path of Contemplative Prayer

John of the Cross places great importance on spiritual guidance. Anyone without guidance, he says, is a garden without a fence.[55] In many chapters of his works he speaks of spiritual guidance, of spiritual fathers and confessors—whom, to be sure, he also sharply takes to task. In the view of Fernando Urbina, one of the leading experts on John of the Cross, John wrote his books only because fear of the Inquisition kept the confessors of his time from advising gifted men and women about the contemplative path. John of the Cross pointedly criticizes these counselors for their lack of understanding because they try to take people who are on the point of entering the darkness and emptiness of contemplation and drag them back into meditation and pious exercises.

> These souls turn back at such a time if there is no one who understands them; they abandon the road or lose courage; or, at the least, they are hindered from going farther by the great trouble which they take in advancing along the road of meditation and reasoning. Thus they are weary and overwork their nature, imagining that they are failing through negligence or sin. But this trouble that they are taking is quite useless, for God is now leading them by another road, which is that of contemplation, and is very different from the first; for the one is of meditation and reasoning, and the other belongs neither to imagination nor yet to reasoning.[56]

> The way in which they are to conduct themselves in this night of sense is to devote themselves not at all to reasoning and meditation...although it may seem clear to them that they are doing nothing and are wasting their time and...that is because of their weakness that they have no desire in that state to think of anything.[57]

> At times...they (the souls) have no desire to enter it (the dark night) or to allow themselves to be led into it; at other times,...they understand not themselves and lack competent and alert directors who will guide them to the summit. It is sad to see many souls to whom God gives both aptitude and favor with which to make

progress remaining in an elementary stage of communion with God, for want of will, or knowledge, or because there is none who will lead them in the right path or teach them how to get away from these beginnings. And at length, although Our Lord grants them such favor as to make them go onward without this hindrance or that, they arrive at their goal very much later, and with greater labour, yet with less merit."[58]

This is a crucial point on the inner path. Instead of calling their advisers back, spiritual guides should encourage them to move ahead, bravely and loyally, with the practice of loving attentiveness, despite all the dryness, loneliness, and emptiness. In *Living Flame*, John of the Cross deals with this at length:[59] For example, he threatens:

Great is the indignation of God with such directors, whom he promises punishment when he speaks through Ezekiel and says: "Ye drank of the milk of my flock and clothed yourselves with their wool and ye fed not My flock. I will require My flock at your hand."[60]

In the Prologue to *Ascent of Mount Carmel*, John of the Cross calls the disqualified spiritual advisors "builders of Babel." In *Living Flame* they are described as having "no knowledge save of hammering souls and pounding them with the faculties like a blacksmith,"[61] "little foxes which tear down the flowering vine of the soul,"[62] "blind guides" who disturb the workings of the Holy Spirit and "barriers and obstacles at the gate of Heaven."[63] Hence he advises people to be careful on the spiritual path and not to put their trust in everyone. "It is of great importance for the soul that desires to make progress in recollection and perfection to consider in whose hands it is placing itself; for, as is the master, so will be the disciple, and, as is the father, so will be the son."[64]

All mystics point out that the time comes when we have to leave behind reflecting about God—and along with that quite a few pious practices—if we are to make progress on the path of contemplation. Nonetheless even today many confessors and pastoral counselors advise people against moving forward when they get to this point. Anyone who has no personal experience in this area naturally has a hard time releasing others into object-free prayer.

Let me quote Johannes Tauler (d. 1361), who evidently had to deal with the same problem in spiritual guidance. In his twenty-ninth Sermon we read:

> If you have not arrived at this foundation, then you will not get there with external effort. Do not strain yourself pointlessly! If you have overcome your external man, turn to your inner self, go within yourself and seek this foundation: You will not find it in external things, in directives and intentions....
>
> Anyone who takes over such people (those seeking their foundation) and drags them down into his coarse method of external exercise, so that they lose such grace as they had, is preparing for himself a terrible judgment. Some people, truly, with their particular exercises of piety, to which they want to win over those men and women, are putting more obstacles to their progress in their path than the pagans or Jews ever did. You, therefore, who judge with your vehement words and wrathful language, beware when you speak about the inner man.[65]

Tauler is deeply disturbed that "pagans" know the path to the foundation of their souls better than the Christians do. For he goes on to say in the same sermon:

> On this point a pagan teacher, Proclus, says: "So long as a person is busy and has dealings with the images that are among us, he will, I believe, never arrive at this foundation. We consider it a superstition that this foundation is in us. We cannot believe that something like this could be and could be within us. Hence," he continues, "since you wish to experience the fact that he *does* exist, then abandon all the manifold varieties of things, and observe only this one object with the eye of your understanding. But if you wish to rise higher, then let go of rational looking and gazing, for reason lies beneath you, and become one with the One." And he calls the One a divine darkness, quiet, silent, sleeping, supersensory. Ah, my dear ones, that a pagan could understand it and have discovered it, while we stood so far apart from it and so little up to his standard, that means for us an insult and a shame.[66]

John of the Cross doesn't demand unquestionable holiness from a guide to contemplation—just experience. In addition there are some necessary psychological prerequisites for counselors.

> And let it be noted there is hardly anyone who in all respects will guide the soul perfectly along the highest stretch of the road, or even along the intermediate stretches, for it is needful that such a guide should be experienced as well as wise and discreet...if a guide

have no experience of the nature of pure and true spirituality, he will be unable to direct the soul therein, when God permits it to attain so far, nor will he even understand it.[67]

Perhaps the following section best expresses what John of the Cross demands from a spiritual guide:

> Let such guides of the soul as these take heed and remember that the principal agent and guide and mover of souls in this matter is not the director, but the Holy Spirit, Who never loses His care for them; and that they themselves are only instruments to lead souls in the way of perfection by the faith and the law of God, according to the spirituality that God is giving to each one. Let them not, therefore, merely aim at guiding these souls according to their own way and the matter suitable to themselves, but let them see if they know the way by which God is leading the soul, and, if they know it not, let them leave the soul in peace and not disturb it.[68]

John the Cross also refers to reason and common sense. No one should blindly follow his own experience, but check with his or her director.

> And thus, men were not authorized or empowered at that time to give entire credence to what was said by God, unless it were approved by the mouths of priests and prophets. For God is so desirous that the government and direction of every man should be undertaken by another man like himself, and that every man should be ruled and governed by natural reason, that He earnestly desires us not to give entire credence to the things that He communicates to us supernaturally, nor to consider them as being securely and completely confirmed until they pass through this human aqueduct of the mouth of man. And thus when, whenever he says or reveals something to a soul, He gives this same soul to whom He says it a kind of inclination to tell it to the person to whom it is fitting that it should be told. Until this has been done, it gives not entire satisfaction, because the man has not taken it from another man like himself.[69]

This is a counsel that has been given to spiritual advisors again and again. Thus Augustine writes that humans are saved by a human being and hence they, too, should let themselves be guided by a human. On this matter he refers to John Chrysostom, who in his first homily makes a similar point, and to Paul, who had a mystical experience on the road to Damascus, but then was sent to Ananias for further instruction.

Above all, the "dark night" phase requires the accompaniment of a guide. This night is a last touch of God's hand on a person, and it is often marked by feelings of meaninglessness and abandonment by God.

MADAME GUYON
(1648-1717)
The Way of Night

Egner-Walter's *Das innere Gebet der Madame Guyon* (Münsterschwarzach, 1989) contains a brief description of Madame Guyon's life. Born Jeanne Marie Bouvier de la Matte, she became a leading author of the Quietist school. In 1688, she was locked up in a convent by the government because of her supposedly heretical opinions, and from 1695 to 1702 she was imprisoned in the Bastille.

According to Madame Guyon, everyone is called to inner prayer for two reasons. First, we all have a natural inclination toward God; we need only be shaken up. Second, we are all called to salvation.

Madame Guyon argues that we can approach God in three different ways, which derive from the path of purification. She calls these three "the active path of light," "the passive path of light," and "the path of night." This classification was drawn up by Peter Poiret, who has edited the writings of Madame Guyon.

Our sole responsibility is to return home to God during this life by finding our path to essential oneness with him. This is also described as union with our own center.[70]

After testing all three paths, Madame Guyon is convinced that only the path of night leads to union. She uses the image of the three rivers that flow back at different rates of speed to our true origin.

The Active Path of Light

This is the path of people who meditate, for example, on a text from Scripture or an image. They try to understand the truth intellectually. They try to purify themselves by means of "good intentions." They love communities that are active in charitable work.

118

They undertake a thousand enterprises and a thousand practices to come closer to God, to maintain themselves in God's presence. Yet all this is done on the strength of their efforts, supported and fostered by the grace of God. For these people, their own doings seem to outweigh God's doing, which relates to their own only as a source of help and confirmation.[71]

In Madame Guyon's view, such people are strongly shaped by their unstable feelings. They don't find their path to inner peace, which is the precondition for a deep encounter with God. "They never have that halycon cheer, that deep peace, that quiet of God's people (Hebrews 4:9-10) that others enjoy even in the midst of distractions."[72] To use the river image, this stream doesn't have enough water because the source flows feebly and often dries up. Those who take this route reach salvation, but in their lifetime they will surely never get back to the sea.

The Passive Path of Light

Madame Guyon's second way is one of belief in the light and of revelation. This way may lead to insights, even to visions and transports. Such people find themselves surrounded by others because they demonstrate parapsychic abilities. In the East, the saying goes, when a mountebank and a sage enter a city, the people run after the mountebank. "Many saints who shine in the Church's heaven like stars of the first magnitude never got beyond this stage."[73]

Madame Guyon has great respect for these people. They are seized by a powerful love that helps them endure temptations. They also have experiences of the presence of God. Indeed God gives them powers with which they can work miracles. Their language is the language of mysticism. They talk about mortifying, abandoning, and losing: "As for their own activity they have also actually died to him (God). But they are not dead as regards their deepest foundation."[74]

But capabilities and gifts are rather obstacles on the path. We can become proud of them and deceive ourselves. At such a crossroad of spiritual life, it's good to have an advisor to press us on. The gifts are still provisional. They are supposed to lead to their giver. Unfortunately, it's often the other way around: they become hindrances.[75] Thus Madame

Guyon doesn't bother asking whether the gifts are from God or from somewhere else. Since they are not the goal, the question is irrelevant, even if this is a matter of ecstasies, visions, prophecies, or similar phenomena.

> It is unnecessary to try to distinguish whether these things are from God or man because, in any case, one is supposed to transcend them. If they are from God, they will come to fulfillment through his Providence, to which we have committed ourselves. If they are not from him, but from ourselves, then at least we will not be deceived since we did not dwell on them.[76]

In the image of the three rivers, these people resemble broad, slow, majestically flowing streams that either come to the sea late or not at all.[77]

The Path of Night

As a general description, this path consists of simple looking within, which Madame Guyon calls "simple contemplation."

> The very best method of all is to withdraw the reason into the interior, by means of the will that loves God, which seems to gather all the powers of the soul to itself and to unite itself with them. This is a loving contemplation, which looks to nothing distinct in God, but loves him all the more, the more reason submits to dark faith, not by compulsion, nor by rational effort, but out of love. One does no violence to one's reason by removing it, but as the soul sinks deeper and deeper into love, it accustoms reason to let all thoughts fall away; not, as already mentioned, with work and rational reflection, but by no longer holding on to them, they fall away of themselves. Then the soul takes the right path, the path of inner recollection, in which it finds the presence of God and a wonderful inflow of his goodness. This means that all multiplicity, all effectiveness, all talking has to fall away unobtrusively, bringing the soul to a sweet silence.[78]

> Such practice leads to uniformity with God and frees us from distracted thinking. This last way is, in the language of the three rivers, extremely swift. Its course no longer meets any obstacles.
> What can we say of the men and women of the third path? They are like the rivers that plunge down from the mountain crest. They

burst out from God himself and never rest for a moment until they have lost themselves in him once more. Nothing holds them back. They bear no burdens. They are quite naked and bare and storm forth with a rapidity that puts fear into the heart of even the most plucky…Without binding itself to its own riverbed as others do, its current still follows certain rules. One sees those on this path ceaselessly forcing their own way. They smash against the rocks and plunge with a roar down the precipice…till finally after long going astray, whipped and dashed this way and that, losing their way and then finding it again, they reach the sea and lose themselves in it, never to be found again.[79]

The path of night is the only one that leads to union with God, even in this life, because on this path alone does the purification process really take place.

The purification process: The great obstacle on this way is egocentricity, which Madame Guyon calls arbitrariness (high-handedness): "Nothing is more opposed to God than arbitrariness, and all human wickedness has its source in it."[80] She also emphasizes the obstacle of ego-activity: "It is still necessary to understand that by the term arbitrariness must be understood, both spiritually and temporally, all particular actions, self-seeking, everything that has to do with us, as well as all intervals between God and the soul, all resistance, indeed all aversion, everything that has to do with oneself: self-love is in all that, and so is idiosyncracy."[81]

Like all mystical paths, the way recommended by Madame Guyon works by means of withdrawing the ego. According to the view of scholasticism, the ego's activities are reason, memory, and will. Perhaps Madame Guyon read John of the Cross, who writes extensively about these powers. The point is to take back ego-activity so that more comprehensive capacities for experience can awaken in us. This is a purification process, which is the precondition for all experience of God.

This process runs through four stages:

1. Being touched, which invites the individual to move inward while the outer senses dry up.
2. A passive purification process, in which God takes control, while the "inner senses" (reason, memory, and will) die.

3. The letting-go of religious support. God can no longer be experienced. The person feels abandoned. This is the level of mystical death.
4. Here the return to life occurs, the resurrection and integration of experience into everyday existence.

The path to Everything goes by way of Nothingness. "There are only these two truths, Everything and Nothing. Everything else is a lie. We can honor the divine All only by coming to nothing. And hardly have we come to nothing when God, who never allows a vacuum without filling it, will fill us with himself."[82]

First Stage of the Purification Process

Madame Guyon teaches two different forms of inner prayer: meditative reading and meditation. In meditative reading (*lectio divina*) we stop at a truth that appeals to us for the purposes of relishing it. Only when we cease to taste any pleasure in it do we read on. But very little should be read at one time—half a page at most.

Meditation, on the other hand, aims at perceiving the presence of God in our own interior. We collect our senses, read a sentence from a spiritual book, and take it into ourselves and taste it—rather than reflecting on it. We let our soul rest in silence and peace. If we notice our senses drifting, we return to the exercise. This constitutes the first stage.

The experience of the presence of God leads to the second stage, the prayer of simplicity. This prayer is also called the prayer of quiet, or contemplation. We relish the presence of God. When this happens, we remain in this form of prayer, bothering with nothing else. Words are no longer necessary. A glance within is perfectly sufficient. At this point, we should be prepared to face dryness, a dryness that has a purifying effect. In any event it would be false to fetch back the presence of God by dint of reason and the senses. We should seek God for God's own sake, not for pleasant sensations. A central concept for Madame Guyon is abandonment—and on the way to God, this is the most important exercise.

Madame Guyon demands that we change our religious behavior when we feel compelled to do so. We should lay aside practices if they become hindrances.

Just let him [God] act and for your part do not be attached to anything. Even if it seems good to you, it is not, if it turns you away from what God wants of you. The will of God is to be preferred to everything else.[83]

If someone has to say prescribed prayers, he should do that. But he will soon notice that he is drawn to his own prayer exercise. And the time will come when it is no longer possible to recite prayers. Should he force himself to do so, he would lose inner peace.[84]

But then Madame Guyon says that up to this point everything has been child's play: "Up to here, however, everything has been just a game that a person could easily get used to, if the divine friend did not change his conduct. You people who love God, who complain at how fleeting his presence is, you do not know that hitherto everything has been only like a game, a teasing, trials and tests. Soon the hours of his absence will turn into days, into weeks, months, and years...."[85]

Second Stage of the Purification Process

The following text is clothed in a language that is no longer to our taste. But it clearly shows the ups and downs of the contemplative path at this stage.

Suffering, without the divine beloved's knowing it, suffering while he seems to disdain us and to turn away from what we endure in order to please him, suffering, while he shows only revulsion at what we once used to delight him with, seeing him regard all this with coldness and alienation, whatever we may try to do to give him joy, and still not stop doing the same thing; seeing that the more zealously we pursue him the more fleetly he slips away from us, letting everything be taken away from us without complaint, everything that he earlier gave us as a proof of his love, and what one thinks to have paid for with love, loyalty, and suffering, not only seeing this robbery without complaint, but also seeing how others are enriched with what has been stolen from us; and then despite all, not giving up, continuing to do everything that could delight the divine friend, not stopping to pursue him, and when one has stood still for a moment in self-forgetfulness and has lost time, replacing that through doubled haste, pressing straight ahead in one's course, without avoiding the abysses into which one might plunge, paying no heed to the dust and mud that one could besmear and besmirch oneself with, paying no attention to whether one falls again and again, and falling a thousand times, struggling to one's feet again countless times, until one finally lies utterly exhausted and powerless, languishing away, while the "all too harsh" One does not turn around once and thrill us with a look of love: All that does not belong to this level, but to the one that follows.[86]

Now God himself intervenes to bring the individual ahead. On this level the point is not to annihilate intellect, memory, and will. There is nothing one can contribute to this purification. Love can no longer be sensed; joy and peace are lost. We can no longer work on ourselves. We can only endure. "The mightier God becomes in us, the weaker we become."

Third Stage of the Purification Process

At this stage there is nothing to hold on to. After periods of quiet, a new abyss opens up—and mystics can never go around abysses; they must go through them. "He goes on his way softly and imperturbably when all of a sudden a new abyss opens up before him, steeper and more threatening than the one before. He steps back, in vain. He has to fall into it. And fall ever more deeply. From cliff to cliff, from chasm to abyss!"[87]

The false handles to hold on to, the supposed props to provide safety are continually snatched away from those who are truly on the path. The end is mystical death. There is nothing left that the individual might take pleasure in; even interest in religion disappears. "This suffering person then realizes that the way leads to dying. He finds life nowhere. Everything becomes the cross to him. Only death: prayer, reading, conversation, everything is dead. There is no longer anything for him to take a liking to."

Fourth Stage of the Purification Process

At this stage, the disposition to receptiveness, as Eckhart calls mystical capacity, broadens. In the image of the river, this is seen as follows: the stream has flowed back into the sea and shares in its immensity. At first it differs from the sea by the color of its water. But with time, and by way of a very slow process, it takes on the color of the sea. "Just as the person is only stripped bare slowly and by degrees, so is he also enriched and animated again only by degrees."[88]

The person is at peace, though of course that doesn't mean there is no experience of suffering. The mind and senses are still perfectly capable of that.

> It is true that they [these people] suffer the greatest pain. At the same time it is true that they do not suffer everywhere, but are left in perfect quiet and undisturbed satisfaction. Even if they should be taken to hell, they would to be sure suffer the torments of hell, but that contentment would remain within them.[89]

> There is nothing about these people that gives them away. At most, one notices the freedom with which they go through life. Some are offended by this. Their emotions and passions remain. However it is no longer possible to sin.[90]

Such statements naturally irritated the theologians and led to Madame Guyon's being persecuted. But she meant nothing more than what Augustine did with his famous "Love and do what you want."

The person remains human with human character traits.

> He will speak, write, act, attend to business, more perfectly and successfully than ever he did when he was still doing things his way and not God's way.[91]

> For him there are no longer any special times and places where he would pray or would have to seek God. God is in all things. The person could spend eternity in hell or heaven, for he sees God both in the archangel and the devil.[92]

> Here everything is God. God is everywhere and in all things. So, too, the divinized person is everywhere and in everything. His hope is God. His joy is God. His prayer is God. Always the same, always and uninterruptedly. His prayer is free of content, uninterrupted, formless. This is the condition of the person. He prays at all times, at all times. It is a matter of complete indifference to him whether he is in the wilderness or among people, whether he is free of the bond of the body or still has to bear the body around with him.[93]

Persecution and Downfall of Mysticism
The prayer of contemplation until the sixteenth century

Until the high Middle Ages the meaning of Christian teaching on prayer lay in the experience of the Divine. The goal of all instruction in prayer was object-free praying, called contemplation. Today this approach has been lost to a large degree; instead, we are rediscovering *meditation.* In Buddhism and Hinduism, the form that corresponds to Christian contemplation aims at encountering the Ultimate Reality. That is not the least of the reasons why today many Christians are turning to Zen and yoga. They find there what they evidently miss in contemporary Christianity.

And yet only two centuries ago, contemplation was something taken for granted in the teaching of prayer.

In her directives for contemplative prayer, Madame Guyon stressed: "Inner prayer is suitable for everyone. It is a great misfortune that almost everyone gets the notion into his head that he is not called to inner prayer. We are all called to inner prayer, just as we are all called to salvation."[94] She emphasizes that this prayer is very easy, and regrets that it is not taught by the priests.

John of the Cross gives instructions for all his readers in the opening words of *Ascent of Mount Carmel:* "[This book] treats of how the soul may prepare itself in order to attain in a short time to Divine union. [It] gives... counsels and instructions, both to beginners and to proficients...."

In *The Cloud of Unknowing,* by the anonymous fourteenth-century mystic, we learn that contemplation is a path for every serious Christian. In Chapter 74 the author points out that the call to contemplative prayer goes out to all religious and lay people.

Downfall of Contemplative Prayer

Prior to the Enlightenment, it was taken for granted that contemplation was the goal of Christian prayer life. It was the esoteric path of Christians, as Zen and Vipassana are the path of Buddhists, yoga the path of Hindus, and the Sufi forms the path of Islam. In his overview of the history of contemplation, Abbot Thomas Keating, an American Cistercian, argues that various events are responsible for the disappearance of this mode of prayer.

- the unfortunate tendency to abbreviate the spiritual exercises (of Ignatius) into a method of discursive meditation[95]
- the confrontation of the institutional Church with Quietism, and the Church's harsh condemnation of this movement. Quietism teaches a passive attitude of letting things happen and self-surrender to the guidance of grace. This provoked the institution's latent fear of any kind of mysticism, and so mysticism fell into discredit.
- Jansenism and its aftereffects. Jansenism is very close to determinism. The individual is predestined and cannot change very much about that. God chooses the person and lends to that person the grace to behave well and thus work out his or her own salvation.
- the overstressing of appearances and private revelations and the resultant devaluation of the liturgy
- the confusion of the true nature of contemplation with phenomena such as levitation, glossolalia, stigmata, and visions
- the confusion of mysticism with sanctimonious religiosity
- the distortion of the image of mystics and the equating of mysticism with otherworldly asceticism
- the increasing legalism of the Roman Church

Abbot Cuthbert Butler summarized the spirituality of the nineteenth and twentieth centuries with the following words:

> Apart from a few unusual vocations, normal prayer for everyone, including contemplative monks and nuns, bishops, priests, and lay people, was systematic meditation according to a precisely stipulated method. There were four choices available: either meditation in accordance with the three powers, as laid down in the Spiritual Exercises, or following the method of St. Alphonsus Liguori (a slight reworking of Ignatius' Exercises), or the method described by Saint Francis de Sales in his *Introduction to the Devout Life*, and lastly the method of Saint Sulpice.[96]

> The final nail driven into the coffin of traditional teaching (about contemplation) was the claim that it was presumptuous to strive for contemplative prayer. Thus novices and seminarians were given a mutilated picture of the spiritual life that did not coincide with Scripture, with tradition, and the normal experience of growth in

prayer. For if one tries to persevere in discursive meditation after the Holy Spirit has called one beyond it, as often happens, one ends up in a state of extreme frustration....As pious men and women had involuntarily pressed forward to such a development in their prayer, they suffered from the negative attitude toward contemplation....Finally they gave up mental [contemplative] prayer altogether as something for which they were evidently altogether unsuitable. Or, thanks to God's mercy, they found a way in which, despite the almost unsurmountable obstacles [to contemplation], they could make progress.[97]

Persecution of the Mystics

Very few mystics failed to be persecuted for their teachings. Between 1531 to 1533 Juan de Avila (1499-1569) was thrown into prison for several months while his teaching was scrutinized.[98]

Ramon Llull (1232-1316) was not declared a saint because his opponents falsely imputed to him alchemical-magical writings, which brought his canonization trial crashing to the ground.[99]

Luís de Granada (b. 1504) had to leave Spain for Portugal. "It is assumed that the passionate preacher, with his mystical inclinations, had aroused the suspicion of the Inquisition."[100] Teresa recommended his writings to her Carmelite Sisters.

Francisco de Osuna (1492-ca.1542), from whose books Teresa of Avila drew, as she herself tells us, was not actually bothered during his lifetime. Afterward, however, his books were placed on the *Index*. Although he was Teresa's real guide, she was not allowed to read him.

Teresa of Avila (1515-1582) was often at loggerheads with Church authority in her own country as well as in Rome. She was suspected of heresy and repeatedly had to assure the Inquisition that her writings were orthodox. When she was fifty-one, she wrote a prayer that soon fell into the hands of ecclesiastical censors: "My creator...when you were on earth, far from despising women, you met them with great benevolence. You found greater love and more faith in them than in men; for among them was your most holy mother....When I look upon our world of today, I find it unjust that persons with a virtuous and strong disposition are despised, purely and simply because they are women."[101] With that, the papal nuncio began to watch Teresa with a suspicious eye. In 1578, he gave her a certificate of bad conduct, and in a letter to Rome called her "a restless female, always gadding about, disobedient, and impenitent. Under the semblance of piety she thinks up false doctrines. She lectures like a professor of theology, although Saint Paul says that women are not allowed to speak." Pope Gregory XIII lent a favorable ear to such calumny, and in a letter he called Teresa "a filthy and immoral nun who is indecent in the highest degree and simply uses her busy efforts at founding convents that observe the original rule as an excuse for indulging in her dissipated lusts."[102]

John of the Cross (1542-1591) was imprisoned by his Carmelite Brothers for nine months and was repeatedly charged before the Inquisition. During this time he was given no change of clothes. When the General Chapter of the Order met in Madrid under Doria in 1591, John was deprived of all his offices. Father Doria assigned Father Diego to gather material against Gracián and John of the Cross. His method was simple: he went into the Carmelite convents and questioned the intimidated nuns until they repeated the answers he put in their mouths, for example, that John had kissed a nun through the grille. A dossier was drawn up against John that would be burned after his death as nonsensical garbage. Under pressure, John declared himself ready to go with a missionary group to Mexico, the contemporary equivalent of Siberia for the Spaniards, but he died before he could be exiled there.

Luis de León (1527-1591) spent five bitter years in prison.

Margareta Porete was burned at the stake on June 1, 1310. She voiced her mystical views in the *Mirror of Simple Souls*.

Madame Guyon was locked up in the Bastille for seven years.

Miguel de Molinos, a Spanish priest, was arrested in 1685 and brought before the Inquisition, which condemned him to lifetime incarceration. He died in prison in 1696.

Because of his supposed connections with Molinos, Père La Combe was imprisoned. He died in prison in 1715, totally deranged.

As soon as he went public with his experiences, Jacob Böhme (1575-1624) was fought by the theologians, above all by Pastor Gregor Richter von Görlitz. Using the slogan, "Shoemaker, stick to your last, not to the pen," an attempt was made to heap ridicule on Böhme. He suffered incredible acts of spitefulness. But then, against the will of the clerical magisterium, the magistrate of Görlitz insisted on giving Böhme a decent burial. The chief Protestant pastor who had to deliver the eulogy, however, couldn't help saying that he would rather have gone twenty miles away than comply with the will of his honorable city council.

Angelus Silesius (alias Johann Scheffler) lived from 1624 until 1677, hence during the Thirty Years War. In 1653, the personal physician (he held doctorates in both medicine and philosophy) of Duke Sylvius Nimrod converted to catholicism. Upon being confirmed, he took the name Angelus Silesius and left the service of his Protestant employer. Freedom of religion was badly off in the country. Under the principle, "*Cuius regio, eius religio*," the lord of the region functioned as its "*summus episcopus*," or highest bishop, and determined the faith of his subjects. Angelus Silesius went back to Breslau and died in 1677 near the city.

Skepticism toward contemplative forms of prayer has remained with the Church to this day. Journals on spirituality spend more time criticizing and warning about mysticism than presenting, advising, and recommending it. One can find more detailed treatments of mysticism in psychological publications than in Christian ones. Even scientists are more interested in the topic than the clergy are, so much so that Gary Zukav could write: "Do not be surprised if the physics curricula in the twenty-first century include classes in meditation."[103]

Personally, I doubt that theology will have made that much progress by then. It is no wonder, therefore, that people who are looking for a path to transpersonal experience pitch their tents outside the Church—resulting in mysticism emigrating from Christianity.

It is no mystery that one of the main reasons people are distancing themselves from the Church is that they can no longer accept absolute theological pronouncements. There is no satisfying theoretical answer to the question of the meaning of life, not even in religion. Only in the depths of our being, when a foreshadowing of the Divine flares up in us, does our life acquire meaning. Like all mystics, Eckhart knows that when he writes, "Man should not be satisfied with a thought-of God. For when the thought fades away, so does the God."

A human being is a "*Homo religiosus*." The Divine is the human's deepest essence. But the expression of that religion need not be of the traditional churchly sort, as the experiential accounts at the end of this book will indicate.

CHAPTER 8

JESUS CHRIST
IN CONTEMPLATION

Contemplation deepens and transforms our faith in Jesus Christ. It leads us from Jesus to the Christ.

At the farewell discourse in the Gospel of John, Jesus says, "It is to your advantage that I go away, for if I do not go away, the Advocate will not come to you" (John 16:7). The mystics, above all John of the Cross, interpret this passage to mean that the figure of Jesus must withdraw so that the real Jesus Christ may be experienced. We must let go of all ideas about Jesus if the true Jesus is to appear.[1]

John of the Cross says that in contemplation a person should flee from everything that comes by way of the physical senses. He believes that this was the reason Jesus said to Mary Magdalene and Thomas, "Do not touch me." John of the Cross insists that "they [the things experienced by the senses] are a hindrance to the spirit, if they be not denied, for the soul rests in them and its spirit soars not to the invisible. This was one of the reasons why the Lord said to His disciples that it was needful for Him to go away that the Holy Spirit might come (John 16:7); so, too, He forbade Mary Magdalene to touch his feet, after his resurrection (John 20:17)."[2]

In *Ascent of Mount Carmel*, Chapter XII, John of the Cross says the same thing about imagination and fantasy, and in Chapters XIII and

XIV he states why and when a person is to enter into contemplative prayer. From this point on the pray-er must leave behind all images and ideas of Jesus during the time of contemplative prayer.

TRANSFORMATION, NOT IMITATION

Contemplation is about a process of transformation, rather than of imitation. The same thing should take place in us that took place in Jesus Christ. Jesus Christ, who is wholly God and wholly human, is like all of us. We are all confronted with the same task that Jesus faced: We all have to let the Divine in us be expressed without hindrance. In the act of living our own lives, we become just like Jesus. "There is an endless preachment in Christendom about what happened after the death of Jesus, how he conquered, and how his teaching triumphantly swept over the entire world. In a word, one hears all sorts of sermons that would end more appropriately with hurrahs than with amens. No, Christ's life here on earth is the model; I must try to shape my life to copy his."[3]

We have turned Jesus Christ into a cult object. We have declared him the object of faith and, by means of dogmatic theology, we have ascribed to him various precise functions. He has become an "object of imitation," an example that we are supposed to emulate. Jesus Christ has become too much a religious subject and hardly the actual subject of an internal process, a becoming filled with the divine fullness (Ephesians 3:19). Many people no longer have access to this figure of Christ, as one-sidedly presented by institutional religion. And so in their quest for authentic experience of God, they often pass our churches by.

And where lies the failure in our preaching of Christ?

> As way, door, and light, Christ opens up for us an inner access to the divine ground with which we are supposed to become one, as he has become one with us. As bread, water, and sap of the vine, he is to enter us, so that we can sense the divine life that has been made available to us in him. The Johannine symbols of Christ are not intended for objectification but for spiritualization. They open the divine center of our life and make it clear that Jesus Christ incorporates the form of our true redeemed being. What we experience in him is what we would actually like to be. He doesn't meet us from outside; he awakes in us from within.[4]

The key to all this is not so much *imitatio* as *conformatio*. The divine in us has to be laid bare just as it was manifest in Jesus Christ. The redemptive process in us aims at a process of becoming Christ, which in the final analysis is the process of becoming fully human, indeed of "becoming God."

WAY OF PURIFICATION

This process leads us through passive purification. According to John of the Cross, Jesus has redeemed the world in the *kenosis*, the ultimate emptying on the cross.

> At the moment of His death, He was likewise annihilated in His soul, and was left deprived of any relief and consolation, since His Father had left him in the most intense aridity, according to the lowest part of His nature. Wherefore He had perforce to cry out, saying: "My God! My God! Why hast Thou forsaken Me?" This was the greatest desolation, with respect to sense, that He had suffered in His life. And thus He wrought herein the greatest work that He had ever wrought…that the truly spiritual man may understand the mystery of the gate and of the way of Christ, in order to be united with God.[5]

To become Jesus Christ in this annihilation is the highest state the soul can reach. This supreme state consists in the experience of death on the cross, sensorily and spiritually, inwardly and outwardly. For John of the Cross the "conformation" with Jesus Christ in his deepest state of abandonment is the precondition for a mystical experience. But abandonment and emptiness are not the goal, only the transition and prerequisite for the resurrection.

LETTING GO OF ALL RELIGIOUS IDEAS

Words such as *peeling away, mortification*, and *dying* awaken negative associations in us. We think immediately of ascetical exercises in the form of fasting, self-castigation, denying the world, and similar things. For John of the Cross, however, the main point is the letting-go of ideas and images of God. He teaches us not to cling to such things even if they appear in the most pious clothing:

> Wherefore those that imagine God beneath any of these figures, or as a great fire or brightness, or in any other such form, and think that anything like this will be like to Him, are very far from approaching Him…these considerations and forms and manners of meditation are necessary to beginners, in order that they may gradually feed and enkindle their souls with love by means of sense.[6]

For John of the Cross real knowledge of Jesus Christ consists in "conforming" with Jesus Christ, and he deeply regrets that this is not preached by those who speak a great deal about Jesus Christ and are very learned….

> I see that Christ is known very little by those who consider themselves His friends…men of great learning and influence, and all others who live yonder, with the world…may be said not to know Christ,…for to them it was fitting to speak first this word of God, as to those whom God set up as guides, by reason of their learning and their high position.[7]

JESUS CHRIST, THE ARCHETYPE OF UNITY

Jesus Christ is, as it were, the archetype of the unity of God and humanity that we bear within us. This is certainly one of the reasons so many people have felt drawn to him over the centuries. He clearly manifests the fact that the whole person is "divine and human." The Church's official prayers close with "through Jesus Christ, our Lord," thus reaffirming this oneness. Moved by such an experience of unity Angelus Silesius wrote:

> The noblest prayer is
> when he who prays
> is inwardly transformed
> into what he kneels before.

and:

> Would you know the new man
> and his new name,
> then first ask God
> what name *he's* used to taking.

The Divine sleeps in every one of us like a seed of grain. Just as it unfolded in Jesus Christ, it is to awaken and unfold in us. Jesus Christ was completely transparent; God shone through him. God shone forth in him. The same thing has to happen with us. God would like to unfold in us, show himself, make himself felt, present himself, as Paul said: "I have been crucified with Christ; and it is no longer I who live, but it is Christ who lives in me" (Galatians 2:19-20).

Jesus came to cure us of the misconception that we live separated from God. His death on the cross dealt a fatal blow to this false notion. If it is given to us to die with him, we shall also live with him (Romans 6:4). The path of contemplation is the path through suffering and dying into the experience of oneness with God. Thus the point is to allow the Divine into us, to give it room. Ethical striving serves the unfolding of what lives in us, so that the doings of humans become the "doings of God." All the negative expressions (peeling loose, mortification, and so on) are not meant to designate anything except the freedom at which we should arrive. Dying in the sense of contemplation is really gaining—the gain of full and total life. Of course that is possible only when we withdraw our ego-activity so far that our real self, the life of God, can shine through.

JESUS CHRIST, LEADING US TO THE DIVINE

While the New Testament offers us a broad selection of texts in our understanding of Christ, not all the theologies developed by all the various Christian communities are contained in it. In fact, until the fourth century a whole series of different gospels was in circulation. Each had an understanding of Jesus that could complete the one we get from the New Testament. This is especially true of the apocryphal gospels collected in the Nag Hammadi library, which was discovered in Upper Egypt in 1945. The most important of these are the *Gospel of Thomas, Gospel According to Philip, Protoevangelium of James, Apocalypse of Paul, Letters of Peter to Philip,* and *Apocalypse of Peter.*[8]

Although written in Coptic, these writings go back to earlier texts, some of which are as old as our four Christian gospels, perhaps older. These writings present Jesus as a leader who has an esoteric message to impart.

I don't believe that Jesus wanted an institutionalized religion. He called himself the son of man. He understood himself as an embodiment of the new person of God's creation, as the person who will "inherit the kingdom." He spoke of a new age of God's kingdom, a kingdom that can be entered only by those who have gone through a *metanoia*. We must be reborn into a higher state of consciousness. We must be born into the kingdom of the Father, that is, into that new foundation of being that Jesus called eternal life or becoming a child of God. We are challenged to become another Christ, that is, to press forward to that transpersonal structure of being in which our divine essence dominates. Jesus did not lay claim to this structure of being for himself alone:

> Though he was in the form of God,
>   [Christ Jesus] did not regard equality with God
>   as something to be exploited,
> but emptied himself,
>   taking the form of a slave,
>   being born in human likeness.
> And being found in human form,
>   he humbled himself
>   and became obedient to the point of death—
>   even death on a cross.
>
> Therefore God also highly exalted him
>   and gave him the name
>   that is above every name,
> so that at the name of Jesus
>   every knee should bend,
>   in heaven and on earth and under the earth,
> and every tongue should confess
>   that Jesus Christ is Lord,
>   to the glory of God the Father.
>   *Philippians 2:6-11*

Jesus was a historical person. But Christ is a symbol for the eternal transpersonal mode of being that is built into all humans and designed to unfold in them. We have to live this form of being as he did. We must, in a certain sense, become Christ, that is, Christs. Jesus has not called on us to revere him; there is more at stake than that. We are to follow him, to become like him. His form of being is our form of being. He is the firstborn of this creation. We are his brothers and sisters.

136

Jesus wanted to be our leader into God's kingdom. By contrast, we have overstressed his divinity. And as long as we set up an unbridgeable gap between Jesus and ourselves, Christianity will not fulfill its true mission. As long as we merely adore Jesus, we will not follow him as our leader. He is the one who told us who we really are: children of God. This mode of being—as children—has to be experienced. What's more, the Divine would like to break through in us.

Unfortunately, however, we have forgotten our origins. This seems to me to be the sin against the Holy Spirit. It cannot be forgiven, because it is a false orientation, that is, we go in the wrong direction so that we miss the goal and meaning of life. This has nothing to do with a sin that is followed by punishment. Instead we punish ourselves because we distance ourselves from life. The denial of the Divine in us is the real sin. Redemption is liberation from this ignorance to knowledge of our true divine being.

Thus Jesus wanted to lead us into the experience of God, into the fullness of life. He called this fullness of life "the kingdom of God" or "everlasting life." He wanted to prompt our conversion to this life. To experience that conversion, we must "be born again," as Jesus says to Nicodemus. We must experience our real life. Physical birth alone did not bring us this experience. We have to enter into continual communication with God, that is with our deepest being, which is divine.

Life is not just religious; it is religion. We don't really enter onto a religious path unless we recognize that the path of life is a religious path. Religious life means constant communication with God in everyday life, not only in prayer, ritual, and sacrament but in the performing of everyday actions. The point of contact with God is here and now because there is nothing that might not be divine. Here and now is also hell. Heaven and hell are separated only by our ego. If we can abandon the ego, we enter the kingdom of God. There are no magical rituals that take us there, only the dying of our false ego. Only love gives us the power to abandon everything so as to enter into this new order of being.

CHAPTER 9

PSYCHOLOGICAL ASPECTS
OF THE INNER PATH

One day a man from the people said to the Zen master Ikkyu, "Master, would you write down for me some basic rules of the highest wisdom?" Ikkyu immediately reached for the paintbrush and wrote "Attentiveness."

"Is that all?" asked the man. "Wouldn't you like to add something more?" Whereupon Ikkyu wrote twice in succession: "Attentiveness. Attentiveness."

"Now look," said the man, rather irritated, "I really don't see anything very deep or brilliant in what you've just written. Then Ikkyu wrote the same word three times in a row: "Attentiveness. Attentiveness. Attentiveness."

In a huff the man demanded, "What does this word *attentiveness* mean, anyway?"

And Ikkyu answered gently, "Attentiveness means attentiveness."[1]

> A rabbi was asked how, in spite of his many activities, he could always be so composed. He said, "When I stand, I stand; when I go, I go; when I sit, I sit; when I eat, I eat; when I speak, I speak."
>
> His questioners cut him short: "We all do that, but what do you do besides?"

The rabbi said once again, "When I stand, I stand; when I go, I go; when I sit, I sit; when I eat, I eat; when I speak, I speak."

Once again the people said, "We all do that too."

But the rabbi said to them, "No, when you sit, you're already standing; when you stand, you're already running; when you run, you're already at the finish line."

Attentiveness is probably the hardest but most important ascetical practice. It is a constant interruption of ego-satisfaction, for as attentive people, we no longer flow with the current of custom or allow our consciousness the arbitrary course that would prevent an advance into the depths. With the practice of attentiveness, we are led into our deep, true self—and thus away from our ego. Hence we are no longer so dominated by our egoistic way of thinking. Other ascetical practices and privations may occasionally be necessary, such as cutting down on sleep, comfort, and sexual gratification. But to come into contact with true life, the practice of attentiveness seems more important than all others.

"Our ego-consciousness is like an ape," says a Zen sutra. An ape swings from branch to branch, from tree to tree, all through the forest. Sometimes we should look at it and realize that it's only an ape, not our consciousness. But we shouldn't chase it away. It's better simply to return to our exercise.

Forms of Attentiveness

Attentiveness in the body: This means paying attention to our breathing, to our sense perceptions, to the different movements of our limbs, to everything that plays out on the physical level in the body.

The different forms of feeling: We experience everything with an affective quality. When the feeling is strong, it becomes the object in our exercise. Because of our feelings, we wish for things or reject them. We should look at these feelings, but not identify with them.

Moods in our consciousness: When we are angry, we should know and admit that we are angry. When we are afraid, we should concede the fact to ourselves. When we rejoice, we should rejoice without judging. These psychic events are just as real as material things. But just as we don't identify ourselves with matter, we shouldn't identify with these emotional sequences. For we are not anger; we are not joy. These are mere moods in our psyche. Our consciousness is continually colored by moods. When we clearly realize that emotional conditions prevail only in the "outer part" of us, we won't be driven about by our feelings. Instead, we can watch as if a performance is in progress on the stage of our ego. But if we identify with the performance, we suffer. When we manage to maintain our distance, the mood or feeling may not necessarily go away, but we are no longer swept overboard by it. Then anxiety doesn't turn into panic, and joy doesn't become euphoria. We become spectators, watching the events in our own psyche emerge and recede.

Intellectual events: Like emotions, thoughts come and go. We have to learn to look at them without identifying with them. When we can notice how pauses occur between thoughts coming and going, when we can look attentively into our interior life, we will note that events slow down and we become peaceful and serene. This is the first experience of quiet.

The Ego: The Point of Intersection
of Our Thoughts, Feelings, Desires, and Emotions

What we call our ego is nothing more than the point of intersection of our thoughts, feelings, desires, and emotions. The path of contemplation teaches us to refrain from identifying with these expressions of our psyche. Then, for example, when we've been insulted, the insult remains, the aggression still vexes us, but we maintain our distance from these emotional stirrings. The path of exercise helps us arrive on a level where the fixation on thoughts or feelings is canceled. Thus on the ego-level, anxiety can certainly continue to exist, rage can torment us, but we discover that our real being lies far more deeply beneath the surface. We learn to have feelings and to admit we have them without being taken over or blocked by them. Finally, we simply *let be* these movements of our psyche, rather than try to repress them. Still, letting them be doesn't mean we want to get rid of them.

Which brings us to the actual problem. If we want to get rid of certain emotions, we tend to think that repressing them will help. But when we repress emotions like sadness, hopelessness, rage, and anger, however, we only succeed in getting caught up in them further. At best these emotions will bury themselves deep in the unconsciousness where it's hard to get at them, and where, eventually, they will exert their disruptive influence. We are utterly at their mercy.

We should repress nothing. What is there is there. Look at it, accept it, let it come! Make friends with your fear and your rage. They belong to you. After all, you don't cut off your toe if it hurts. Try this some time with sadness: accept it, but don't wallow in it. Don't make a big deal about it. Look at it; and then go back to your exercise. Sadness can be a good point of departure for the exercise.

Let's consider the same with anxiety. So many of us are plagued by anxiety, but we don't know why. We don't know where it comes from or where it hides itself. We can say "yes" to anxiety. We can say, "Yes, I am afraid." We can take it into our exercise. When we repress anxiety or sadness, these emotions will disguise themselves and hide in some corner of our psyche. Then, when they pop up, they appear with a totally different face, perhaps as aggression, pride, or even virtue, which can deceive us even further.

If we don't want to fall victim to this subtle trick, we have to realize that sadness, jealousy, aggression, and so on, belong to the psychic energy of our personality structure and hence to our life, and that ultimately they are as much expressions of the Divine as joy, peace, and harmony. Everything we can *let be* has the tendency to change into something pleasant. But the things we fight grab on to us.

We practice pure observation, pure attentiveness, without any evaluation or preoccupation. Emotions must be lived—even welcomed—steadfastly and imperturbably. No commentary, no getting swept away, no distorting. Feeling is like a cloud that moves across the blue sky; it may darken the sky, but it never stays.

Ken Wilber summarizes this:

> Here we're interested only in observing our specific troubles, simply and harmlessly becoming aware of them, without condemning them, avoiding them, dramatizing, processing them or justifying them. If a feeling or a tendency arises, we take note of it. If hatred of this feeling emerges, we're aware of it. If hatred arises against the hatred, we observe that. There's nothing to do, but if an action arises, we take cognizance of it and remain a "non-preferential consciousness" amid all the troubles. This is possible only if we understand that none of these represent our real self. So long as we are

bound up with them, there will be an effort, however subtle, to manipulate the troubles. If we understand that they are not the center of the self, we won't curse our troubles; we won't scream at them, won't let them disgust us, won't try to reject them or surrender to them. Every measure that we take to get rid of a trouble simply strengthens the illusion that we are the plague in question. So in the end, the attempt to avoid the trouble merely guarantees that it will endure. What is so upsetting is not the trouble itself but our connection to it. We identify with it, and that alone is the real difficulty. Instead of attacking a trouble, we adopt the guilelessness of a distanced nonpartisanship toward it. The mystics and sages like to compare this condition of registering to a witness with a mirror. We simply mirror all sensations or thoughts that arise without clinging to them or throwing them away, just as a mirror reflects with perfect impartiality whatever goes on in front of it.[2]

Disidentification

Psychotherapy tries to get people to identify with their feelings and moods. By contrast, contemplation and all other esoteric paths teach disidentification. Disidentification helps neutralize the movements of our psyche: desires, expectations, fears, aggressions. As a result, we don't project so much onto our problems. We don't blow them out of proportion. We realize that it doesn't pay to waste our energy on getting rid of these bubblings in our psyche. What does it bother the mountain when a few clouds gather around it? Our deepest being remains untouched.

When we are in the center, we know perfectly well when we may act and when not. There can be something that hammers against our center, that would like to make itself independent, tear itself away, take action. But the center is stronger. We don't repress the aggressions that well up inside us, but we know perfectly well that they are only an event in our psyche, something that, so to speak, flits over us like a cloud across the blue sky. As wishes and projections pop up, we can run after them, but we already know that they won't satisfy us. Then there is our laziness. Right now we would rather sleep, we'd prefer not to strain ourselves, but we can also continue to be attentive. We can be attentive to the fact that we are sleepy.

All these are psychic conditions, not our deepest essence. They are processes that disappear when their energy fizzles. These psychic powers belong to us, and they're very important for our humanness, but we have to learn to have them and to direct them and not let them have us and direct us. When we don't identify with them, and don't let ourselves be carried away, their intensity slackens. But if we do identify with them, they become the cause of much suffering.

Disidentification opens up to us the possibility of pressing forward into transpersonal space and of realizing our true essence, a place where there is rest. The danger is, however, that we'll go right back and identify ourselves with a psychic state, rest, for example. But after all, rest is not the ultimate thing to experience. And so the basic directive remains in place: let go!

Then one day we can say, "I have a body, but I'm not my body. I can see and feel my body, and what can be seen and felt is not the true seer. My body may be tired or excited, sick or healthy, heavy or light, but that has nothing to so with my inner self. I have a body, but I'm not my body.

"I have desires, but I am not my desires. I can know my desires, and what can be known is not the true knower. Desires come and go, they flow through my consciousness, but they don't touch my inner self. I have feelings, but I am not the feelings.

"I have thoughts, but I am not my thoughts. I can know my thoughts and intuitively grasp them, but what can be known is not the true knower. Thoughts come to me and then leave me, but they don't touch my inner self. I have thoughts, but I am not my thoughts."[3]

Events, thoughts, images, feelings, moods, are nothing but a storm on the ocean. What does the ocean care if there is a storm in the Bay of Biscay? The storm is something we suffer until it blows over. The less we identify with it, the less force it develops. That doesn't mean we no longer feel, get angry, experience depression. Rather, it means that, despite these emotions, there is a core that remains untouched. We are no longer handcuffed or swept away by feelings.

In the course of time the hunger for new impressions subsides, and the addictive need to busy ourselves internally lessens. When desiring stops, contemplative seeing becomes possible. Once we have reached this stage, we also realize that nothing lasts. There's nothing we can cling to. The only constant is the flow. Permanence lies in flux, not in any status quo. Attentiveness awakens in us the capacity to experience this flow and yet to know tranquillity amid all the hustle and bustle.

THE SACRAMENT OF THE MOMENT
LONGING FOR GOD

Homo sapiens is also *homo religiosus*. The Divine is our deepest essence, and we tend back toward it, whether we know this or not. John of the Cross says, "Our awakening is an awakening of God, and our uprising is an uprising of God."[4] The awakening of a human person is an awakening of God. The awakening of society is an awakening of God in society. The awakening of the cosmos is an awakening of God in the evolution of the cosmos. Human beings of the future (not just Christians of the future) will be enlightened people. They will be mystics. That is our sole chance of survival.

Deep down in human beings lies a yearning that is the Divine itself. God presses toward unfolding in us. Deep within us, the awakening of the Divine appears as deep longing: the longing to go home and to find the place where everything is good, where we are loved and accepted. But we learn very early in life that no human being, not even the most beloved, can give another person this ultimate certainty. Until we find our true self or rather until our true self breaks through all the incrustations and faulty developments, there remains an unbridgeable gap of separation. Thus we head off on the path to God because we bear this deep longing within, a longing that is ultimately the longing of God himself.

There is an old story that expresses this very clearly. It is told in the East and the West: the story of the Lost Son. Here is a central Asian version:

> In India there once lived a fabulously rich nobleman, who had only one son. One day this son was kidnapped or no longer wished to return home. The father did everything he could to find him, but in vain. Years passed without his learning anything. Then one day as the rich man looked out of the window, he saw a young beggar standing in front of his house. He asked for, and was given, an alms and wanted to go away immediately. The rich man saw the beggar's face and jumped up in great surprise, for he had recognized his lost son. He called his servants and ordered them to fetch back the young man. Several of them ran after the beggar and tried to hold him back, but the young man refused and said, "I may be a beggar, but I haven't done anything wrong." The servants assured him that they had nothing to reproach him for. "Our master wants to see you." But they couldn't convince him to return. On the con-

trary, he became increasingly anxious and began to tremble. "I have nothing to do with such a distinguished nobleman." Finally, the servants had to go back home and tell their lord that they hadn't been able to accomplish anything.

Full of love for his son the rich man ordered one of his young servants to disguise himself as a beggar, just like his son, and to make friends with him. When the servant-beggar felt the time was right, he said to the rich man's son, "I have found a good position. The work isn't too hard, and the pay is good. We also get a little room. Let's try it." So they were both hired as gardeners on the rich man's estate. When the young men had settled in, the rich man promoted his son to house servant. Here, too, he performed his work well, and so the father put him in charge of all his property. Finally he became his secretary, so he remained close to his father and took over his business.

Years went by. The rich man got older and realized that he didn't have much time to live. He gathered his relatives around him and introduced the young man: "This young man is in reality my son who disappeared when he was a little child." He then handed over to him his entire estate and his position.[5]

Thus the path of human life is a going home to God, and described as such in all religions. We seek the roots of our existence because we have forgotten who we really are. That is why we go out and search until we learn that we have already been found. We aren't seekers at all; we're the sought.

Granted, this human longing can have narcissistic features; it can be a flight from reality; it can attempt to compensate for deficits in our childhood. But it arises primarily out of the realization that our being contains realms of consciousness that can give life more meaning and help, and enable us to have a more comprehensive experience of God.

Dying So That We Might Be Reborn

Psychology stresses that to live we must have a proper sense of self-worth and a corresponding ego stability. But the esoteric paths demand the death of the ego. Actually, all contemplative practice ultimately aims at the withdrawal of ego-activity. Jesus says, "He who would save his life must lose it." Thomas à Kempis writes in his *Imitation of Christ*: "Be assured that you must have a dying life." John of the Cross argues that,

146

"He who knows how to die in all things will have life in all things." Several thousand years ago the *Tao te Ching* already knew that "to die without going under means eternal presence." All these approaches say one thing: the path to the experience of unity and love is a path of self-surrender, a dying so as really to live.

The Dying of the Ego

The dying of the ego is more than the above-mentioned withdrawal of ego-activity. It is a stepping out of the structures and patterns that we have grown fond of and that give us security. It is an event that touches the whole person, shaking us to our very roots. The dying of the ego is accomplished in what mysticism calls the dark night of the senses, the soul, and the mind. It is the way of purification that constitutes the actual task in all esoteric paths. It is the letting go of all safeguards.

The dying that mysticism speaks of is far more difficult than physical dying. It can't just remain a wish to fall into God's protecting hand. It must be an absolute letting go: "Father, into thy hands I commend my spirit." Some things about such a situation may appear pathological and even rightfully classified by psychologists as such. But it is a dying in order to live. The goal is the return to live, so long as this body is granted us. We have to experience and manifest the Divine here and now. What's more, individual mystical experience is not the last word. Rather, the integration of an experience into everyday life is the main task to be performed on the mystical path.

The Transforming Power of the Moment

Mysticism speaks of the healing and transforming power of the moment or, as Jean P. Caussade calls it, the "sacrament of the moment," a phrase I found for the first time in his book *Surrender to God's Providence*. Caussade writes:

> God truly dwells in this place, and I did not know it, as Jacob once said. Thus you seek God, too, and meanwhile he is everywhere. Everything proclaims him to you. Everything gives him to you. He went alongside you, he surrounded you, he pervaded you and dwelt in you...and you seek him. You fret and fuss over an idea of God

and meanwhile in essence you already possessed him. You chase after perfection, while it lies in everything that meets you unsought for. In the shape of your sufferings, your activity, of the impulses you receive, God himself comes forward to meet you. All the while you strive in vain for exalted notions that he refuses to clothe himself in.

Yet don't reason and faith reveal to us the real presence of divine love in all creatures and in all the happenings of this life just as surely as the word of Christ and the Church guarantee for us the presence of the sacred body under the eucharistic forms of bread and wine? Don't we know that divine love wants to unite with us through all creatures and events? That only for this reason does it cause, arrange, or allow all the events that surround us and happen to us, so that we come to this union, which is their only purpose?[6]

But if that is how things are, what prevents every moment of our life from being a kind of communion with divine love and this communion from bringing forth at every moment in our soul just as much as the communion that entrusts us with the body and blood of the Son of God?—To be sure the latter enjoys a sacramental effect that the former lacks. Yet how much more frequently can the first kind of communion be repeated and how meritorious can it become if it is received in a perfect state of soul.[7]

Caussade comes to the subject of the Eucharist to express this idea: "How mistaken we are not to see you [God] in everything that is good and in all creatures. Why deliberately seek you in things other than those through which you wish to communicate? Do people seek you in the Eucharist under other forms than those you have chosen for your sacramental presence?"[8]

In the Eucharist we see a solemn proclamation of what actually was always and everywhere the case. Thus, for example, the presence of the Divine would have to be just as conscious in eating breakfast as in taking communion.

God is the symphony that resounds in everything. It's not true that once upon a time he composed it and now he's performing it. The symphony's name *is* God, and nothing is excluded from it—not suffering, not our psychic handicaps. To experience that is *satori*. What's more, some people learn that suffering and pain are as much an expression of the Divine as joy is. Unfortunately we easily forget this.

For Caussade, the source of "living water" gushes forth in the present moment. We need look no further. The wellspring flows continuously. Why go looking for streamlets? "God has ceased to be an object and an idea, now he is only the origin and source."[9]

"Grace-giving present moment! You communicate God in such inconspicuous forms as manger, hay, and straw."[10]

Ultimately, the "sacrament of the moment" is simply the acceptance of God's will. "Still easier is the passive part of holiness. For it is exhausted by simply accepting what mostly cannot be avoided anyway, and that one lovingly puts up with—that is, with loving confidence and composure—what we otherwise all too often unwillingly endure."[11]

There is no transcendence removed from what is here and now. As Angelus Silesius wrote, "God does all things in the saint that the saint may ever do / He walks, stops, lies down, sleeps, / wakes, eats, drinks, and has good cheer too."

The Moment Brings Us to the Experience of Life

Life is in the moment. God can be experienced only in this moment. Again, referring to Angelus Silesius' writings, we read, "You think that you'll see God and his light, you say. / O fool, you never see him, and you won't see God today."

But how does this path look, practically speaking? It has nothing to do with affected elitist behavior. Andreas Gryphius writes:

> Mine are not the days that time has already taken.
> Mine are not the days that have yet to come my way.
> The moment is mine, and I pay heed to that,
> Thus is he mine, who made time and eternity.

> Look well to this day,
> For it is life,
> The life of all life!
> Yesterday is nothing but a dream
> And tomorrow only a vision,
> Today, however, rightly lived,
> Makes every yesterday a dream
> Full of happiness
> And every morning a vision
> Full of hope.
> So pay careful heed to this day.[12]

Meister Eckhart and the Moment

Eckhart keeps telling us that we have to experience God in things. I cite a few passages:

> Thus we too should in all things be consciously on the lookout for our Lord. That necessarily requires diligence, and one must be willing to spare no expense, doing whatever one can with one's sense and powers. Then it will be well with people, and they will grasp God equally in all things, and they will find just as much of God in all things.[13]

> If all is well with a man, then truly, wherever he may be, whomever he may be with, it is well with him. But if things are not right with him, then everywhere and with everybody it is all wrong with him. If it is well with him, truly he has God with him. But whoever really and truly has God, he has him everywhere, in the street and in company with everyone, just as much as in church or in solitary places or in his cell. But if a man really has God, then no one can hinder him.
> Why?
> Because he has only God, and his intention is directed toward God alone, and all things become for him nothing but God. That man carries God in his every work and in every place, and it is God alone who performs all the man's works.[14]

> Let a man go across a field and say his prayers and recognize God, or let him be in church and recognize God; if he recognizes God more because he is dwelling in a quiet place, then that comes from his own deficiency, not because of God; for God is equally in all things and all places and is ready to give himself in the same way, insofar as it is up to him; and the only one who recognizes God rightly is the one who recognizes him as the same.[15]

> The man who has God essentially present to him grasps God divinely; and to him God shines in all things; for everything tastes to him of God, and God forms himself for the man out of all things. God always shines out in him, in him there is a detachment and a turning away, and a forming of his God whom he loves and who is present to him. It is like a man consumed with a real and burning thirst, who may well not drink and may turn his mind to other things. But whatever he may do, in whatever company he may be, whatever he may be intending or thinking of or working at, still

the idea of drinking does not leave him, so long as he is thirsty. The more his thirst grows, the more the idea of drinking grows and intrudes and possesses him and will not leave him. Or if a man loves something ardently and with all his heart, so that nothing else has savor for him or touches his heart but that, and that and nothing but that is his whole object. Truly, wherever he is, whomever he is with, whatever he may undertake, whatever he does, what he so loves never passes from his mind, and he finds the image of what he loves in everything, and it is the more present to him the more his love grows and grows. He does not seek rest, because no unrest hinders him.[16]

A man cannot learn this by running away, by shunning things and shutting himself up in an external solitude; but he must practice a solitude of the spirit, wherever or with whomever he is. He must learn to break through things and to grasp his God in them and to form him in himself powerfully in an essential manner.[17]

It is ultimately the healing power of God or the healing power of life that is at work in the moment.

God in the Everyday Moment

Many know the healing power of knitting and crocheting. Others have a similar experience in a long nature walk. Our spiritual path takes in such simple basic activities. We don't do anything special; we try to enter the moment and become one with whatever it is we are doing just then. That's where God is closest to us. The slightest action that we perform—going up the stairs, opening the door, washing our hands, waiting at a red light—should be accompanied by inner alertness that gives us a special gait, for we are no longer by ourselves. We are no longer in the moment. We are no longer in life. Thus life is only in the moment.

There are so many opportunities to practice real life, that is, to be entirely "at home," entirely involved with what we are doing. It may then seem difficult, for example, to read and listen to music at the same time. They don't go together. Or, to make my point in a much more banal fashion, you shouldn't take the newspaper with you to the bathroom. We have to learn all over again how to eat, rinse lettuce, go to work, and call it a day. A good number of people who take to the path of Zen or contemplation have absurd expectations. *Satori* is in the moment. It's not a state of being exalted above the world, but the experience of the world in this moment.

DEEP STRUCTURES AND STAGES ON THE INNER PATH

Every spiritual path should be backed up by the results of scholarly research, otherwise it might easily lose all sense of direction. Genuine esotericism doesn't reject scientific findings, it treasures them. Thus the question of universal deep structures in the human personality is a question for psychology, but at the same time, it is a critical issue for esotericism, providing much food for thought.

Can we recognize different stages of an esoteric path? Can they be classified systematically and hierarchically? Or are they only snapshots of a development, incapable of representation in the form of a model? Is there any continuous development at all? What side effects show up? Don't pathological structures sometimes reveal themselves too? What does the fully developed person actually look like? Isn't what psychology understands as normality (a fully differentiated and integrated ego structure) really a momentary developmental stage? Doesn't a person have to reach out to the transpersonal realm? Isn't this level part of being human too?

Stages of Development

Most esoteric approaches have developed a "path" or "way," on which its disciples are led through various stages. However, these stages don't necessarily follow one another in perfect sequential order; rather, there are many overlapping phases. Not everyone goes through all the phases, and the sequence of phases can be different.

First stage: Orientation: This is often introduced by the question of meaning. We look for a path because we have doubts about the meaning of existence. We suffer from what Viktor Frankl calls a noögenic neurosis, that is, a neurosis whose causes are not psychic but existential. The question often runs: "Why am I alive anyway? Why this misfortune? Why me?" Such reflections lead to a reorientation, and we begin to be on the lookout.

We take a renewed interest in the spiritual life and begin to notice certain pieces of spiritual literature. This reorientation alone has a significant influence on our life and leads us to an attitude of expectation that strengthens our belief in a metastructure of this world. The stream of consciousness begins to run in a different direction. It has discovered the "meta," what lies behind things, or the vertical dimension, which is necessarily part of the horizontal dimension. The realization that the horizontal isn't all there is to life increases. This is of inestimable value, because our life remains a prison cell as long as we don't look beyond the surface.

At this stage we can become very thin-skinned. Things that formerly left us cold can move us and cut us to the quick. This shows how awake ego-consciousness has become. The readiness for accepting situations and for letting things pass grows, but so does the sensitivity to pain, both our own and others'. Shifts and changes in life take place. We read different books, eat more carefully, perhaps get a different wardrobe. We recognize what is detrimental to the new way of life and change our behavior. Some things happen through conscious changes in life, others through a shift of values. External distractions are limited.

Second stage: More awareness: The second stage is characterized by more awareness. First comes training in physical awareness. Events occurring in body and psyche are experienced wide-awake. Unconscious random living gives way to a certain presence.

We begin to place a greater value on external bearings. That doesn't mean affectation or attention-seeking, but a posture in keeping with the inner process. Christian tradition has little to say about this, but the Eastern paths make specific recommendations. Legs, spine, chest, neck, hands, tongue, and eyes are supposed to be kept in a state of attentiveness. Any unreflecting, restless activity of the body is recognized, and the stray movement is again recalled to the attitude of attentiveness.

Calming of the breathing process leads to calming of thought. The never-ending chatter of everyday consciousness quiets down; so-called daydreams diminish. We entrust ourself to the steady rhythm of breathing in and breathing out. Consciousness becomes quieter, and associative trains of thought decrease. The contents of thoughts become more conscious, and the whole stream of consciousness moves in the direction of greater order.

Third stage: Standardization of consciousness: We begin with a specific practical exercise, our goal being to reduce the stream of consciousness. This includes seeking out a quiet place, fixing consciousness for longish periods of time on a (possibly external) "object," and controlling of the eyes. Our glance is no longer questioning and analytic but measured and sober.

This leads to a connection of the mind with an object, but also to a change in the experience of the object. The object loses the character of abstraction and is no longer experienced as a concept, but the way it really is. A book is no longer a book, but an oblong object with color and form. Normally we see things other than as they are. We filter the objects and force them into categories. Through nonjudgmental looking, the object again becomes what it is.

Something more important than this, however, is concentration on an inner event. The wandering consciousness has to be trained to stick to an inner object. The Tibetans use visualizations for this; yoga prefers physical energy currents, or *OM*; Zen has *MU*; Christian contemplation gazes on naked Being. This exercise leads to standardization of consciousness.

The problem of inadequate stimuli can arise, for example, noises, smells, touches, flashes of light, that are experienced only internally. Our perceptual capacity gradually exceeds mere sense perception so impressions that don't exist during normal use of the senses come into being. This perception is constantly changing: vibrations, oscillations, colors, light patterns, shapes appear. Zen calls this *makyo*.

Every serious kind of esotericism warns against ascribing any particular importance to these impressions—and under no circumstances should we cling to them. The best way to get over them is to relax our exercises a bit. We simply let the dance swirl past until it ebbs away.

Although our mind quickly begins to reflect on these phenomena and to analyze them, we should resist this. Our reason is constantly searching for objects because it can't yet manage contemplation without an object. John of the Cross says that the mind clings to the dust particles floating in the air because it cannot yet see pure light. But eventually, the coarse contents of consciousness scarcely continue to appear. The coarse-grained world disappears, and peace and quiet enter.

Fourth stage: Emptying of consciousness: The next step is recollection of consciousness without any prop for the ego. The *koan*, the word or external object of the exercise, becomes increasingly more subtle. They now readily vanish from consciousness, not because they have been forgotten, but because they have become so fine. We may perceive flashes of light, but this light has nothing to do with external light. It may flow and effect a certain *samadhi*. In between, however, coarser perceptions keep intruding because our intellect is incredibly persistent in producing forms. But the effort of exercising makes these constructs withdraw in favor of a continuously flowing light energy. We hold fast to the river of light. The river can flow faster. The intensity of the light can increase.

The process is further disturbed by ego fragments that are used to keep ourself on this level. Here, too, there is still attentiveness, striving, and letting go of ideas. But now everything structural has a disturbing effect. It's not easy to maintain tranquillity.

The amount of effort expended to exercise correctly must once again be diminished. Letting go becomes crucial. Our ego has to accompany us to the threshold of experience, without getting in the way. The effort must be increasingly well-balanced. We swing back and forth between the standpoint of the observer and the observed.

Fifth stage: Tranquillity: Here the experience that the individual sequence of events has no underpinning at all begins to gain ground. Only the momentary is experienced. Only patterns in a constantly changing field are recognized, while the actual center, the true self, is beyond change. Impressions alone keep flowing away, but not contents. Our awareness leaves the individual events behind and remains fixed on the immovable.

We recognize how things come and go. Being born and dying are consecutive events that belong together like the steps of a round dance. Parts exist only in relation to all the other parts. It is important to remain in this stage for as long as possible.

Sixth stage: Dismantling of all ego-activity: Paradoxical pairs—such as arising/passing away, One/Many, subsequent/simultaneous—are resolved in noncausal knowledge. Even fine attentiveness must in the end be set aside, because it is a remnant of ego-activity and disturbs enlightenment. Zen calls enlightenment "pitch-black," meaning that there is no ego-activity or ego-knowledge in it.

The story is told of a disciple of Sakyamuni who had a brilliant memory and knew all his sermons by heart. After the death of Sakyamuni all the enlightened ones gathered together. They would have liked to have this man with them, but because he wasn't enlightened, he remained excluded. He exercised and exercised, trying to get it. Finally, he gave up and lay down in bed to sleep. At the moment he lay down, when his ego-activity had disappeared and all effort dropped off, a profound enlightenment came over him.

Thus even attentiveness can become an obstacle. Enlightenment is not something that can be acquired. We can only create the circumstances that favor the coming of enlightenment, that is, a form of indifference that is no longer dependent on the will. Even our so-called *vasanas* retreat. *Vasanas* are "sunken and concealed wishes, inclinations, and ambitions that can come to the surface at any moment."[18] In Buddhism the term also applies to proclivities, impressions, actions, and thoughts that arise in earlier incarnations.[19] They constitute the character of the person. Also part of the picture are formal powers of the psyche and factual intentions, in other words, first impulses that prompt an action. Transforming these basic structures or basic intentions, which are deeply embedded in our psyche and no doubt go with us into the next existence, is a difficult task.

Seventh stage: Enlightenment: The state of enlightenment is void of any ego-activity. It is the experience of life itself. When we reflect about life, we engage in ego-activity. When we experience life itself, the ego falls silent. At every moment we can experience life in what is. Not until we understand that God can be experienced only in the performance, or execution of the Divine, in other words in the structures, do we understand that all reflecting on these things is only after the fact. But that also means that everything that we customarily call religion is after the fact—thus our theology, our rituals, ceremonies, and dogmas. Religion is not something removed from everyday life, from the moment. Religion is the experience of what is.

Realizing this is enormously difficult. It takes a very long time and requires profound experience before we are prepared to understand religion in this way. This in no way detracts from our religious ceremonies and rituals. On the contrary, it should be the goal of all liturgies and services to lead us to such an experience.

Eckhart has given simple and classic expression to this idea:

Because truly, when people think that they are acquiring more of God in inwardness, in devotion, in sweetness and in varying approaches than they do by the fireside or in the stable, you are acting just as if you took God and muffled his head up in a cloak and pushed him under a bench. Whoever is seeking God by ways is finding ways and losing God, who is hidden in ways. But whoever seeks for God without ways will find him as he is in himself, and that man will live with the Son, and he is life itself. If anyone went on for a thousand years asking of life: "Why are you living?" life, if it could answer, would only say, "I live so that I may live." That is because life lives out of its own ground and springs from its own source, and so it lives without asking why. If anyone asked a truthful man who works out of his own ground: "Why are you performing your works?" and if he were to give a straight answer, he would only say, "I work so that I may work."[20]

It remains an open awareness. Before enlightenment awareness is bound up with mental activity. In the experience of enlightenment, our intellect is silent. But this state, which might be called ecstasy, isn't the last word. We have to come back from the events. The normal space-time experience with its coarse ingredients comes back out on the scene. Normal consciousness continues to unfold in the awakened state. Nevertheless something crucial has happened, the perspective has shifted. For this reason, misperceptions and distorted thinking remain a possibility. First enlightenment must establish itself. In Zen this is actually the hardest thing of all to do: the integration of enlightenment into everyday life. The goal is the "marketplace."

Summary: On every esoteric path there is a progressive dismantling of the view of the world provided by ego-consciousness. Bodily experiences, intellectual activity, gross perception, and time-space experience subside. The dismantling or transformation of these deeply imprinted structures leads to enlightenment.

The actual contribution that we can make is attentiveness—attentiveness to breathing, to the *koan*, to walking, to standing, and so on. Our state of wakefulness is a relatively stable one. Because it can't be easily shattered, we have to devote ourselves to certain exercises. The exercise culminates in attentiveness, which aims at pure awareness without any fixed conscious structure.

We can distinguish three stages of awareness: adherence to the effort (exercise), letting go of the effort, and pure awareness. Putting it in different terms:

- Exercise shatters the momentary state of consciousness.
- In the course of time, exercise has to be let go, and we need only observe until…
- Pure awareness finally arrives.
- Then comes the task of integrating enlightenment into the fabric of everyday life.

Our path is a path of intensive training in attentiveness. It can last a long time and be very hard. Not everyone is ready for it. Those who are ready, however, come to the freedom of life.

In conclusion let me just say that on an esoteric path, we can do nothing. Only by continually letting go of all physical, psychic, and mental structures do we make any progress on the path. In the face of the Ultimate Reality, the only thing left to do is surrender. The Divine unfolds in us if the ego gets out of its way. "God wants you to go out of yourself in creaturely fashion as much as if his blessedness consisted in it. O my dear man, what harm does it do you to allow God to be God in you?"[21]

Transformation of Consciousness

Orthonoia, Paranoia, Metanoia[22]

The problems our world faces today are no longer limited to certain political or cultural questions. As a species, humans have come to a critical point—perhaps the most critical point in our entire history. In fact, our survival is at stake. We are threatened as a race, and the threat is of our own making. Nuclear, biological, and chemical wars; pollution of the rivers, oceans, and air; exploitation of resources; and attacks on the ecosystem: these threats endanger the life of humans on this planet. We know that, but we can no longer make adjustments in our system. It's as if we have programmed ourselves to go under, to self-destruct. Our only chance of being saved is to reach another state of consciousness.

This new state of consciousness is no doubt the next step in the evolution of humanity. Alongside the threats there are signs, in fact, that indicate evolution is mobilizing its forces to work against this downfall. Some people put it this way: the forces of evolution are gathering all their energy for the leap into a new consciousness (a quantum leap). Some of these emerging tendencies seem very confused, indeed perhaps a kind of labyrinth. They announce a new departure, which is beginning simultaneously in many places: physics with its theory of relativity and quantum theory; transpersonal psychology; the esoteric movements in religion; the hunger for a more comprehensive experience of reality; the suspicion that reason and the senses are not the only portals to knowledge.

People have become restless; they are beginning to ask about the meaning of their existence far more insistently than ever before in human history. They are serious about their own psychic and spiritual development. Behind this stands the power of the Divine (for me the power of evolution is precisely that), which mobilizes people, as it were, from within, detaching them from their irrational and self-destructive tendencies, and guiding them in a new direction. This new consciousness seems to be breaking out with much greater forcefulness among young people than in previous generations. But for that very reason, they are often more irritated by this radical new upsurge than their elders.

The break is most sharply visible between those who have already set forth on the path to a new consciousness and those who have gotten stuck in the traditional forms. It's frightening to leave the old riverbank behind to head off on a quest for the new one. Not everyone has the nerve to let go. So this path is like a selection process—a dangerous word when we think back to the Nazi era. In the end, however, that's what it comes down to. This has nothing to do with elitist consciousness. Rather, it refers to the readiness to entrust oneself to a protracted, painful process that will probably not run its course without "martyrdom"—because both spiritual and secular institutions will apply psychological, political, and conscientious pressure, just as they did in the time of Jesus. They have the power and will put it to work. Reform in society and in the Church never went from the top down, but from the bottom up.

This necessary transformation of our consciousness takes place on the path of contemplation in the following three phases:

- orthonoia (*orthos* means straight, upright; *noia* means mind)
- paranoia (confusion, madness)
- metanoia (change of mind)

Orthonoia is characterized by identification with our ego. Here life can run for a long time in supposed order and satisfaction. But appearances are deceptive. Those of us who don't want to grow stagnant in our development have to take upon ourselves a period of inner upheaval. Unless we pass through the stage of paranoia, we cannot enter into metanoia.

Paranoia is a condition in which consciousness is confused and rearranged. Only when the old encrustations break up can fresh patterns be formed. Unfortunately we in the West have all too often viewed this condition as a psychic disease, and not as a transition and process of purification, the way esotericism does. Paranoia is a necessary transition—sometimes even an authentic breakthrough—on the path to our full human existence. It is good to have a companion on such a phase. Otherwise it is easy to get lost in the labyrinth of the psyche. But this condition is often evaluated as an intellectual cul-de-sac, and not understood by spiritual advisers. For that reason John of the Cross vehemently criticizes them, calling them clumsy blacksmiths who can only hammer away blindly.

The esoteric paths understand the human psyche in this situation far better, and they help us recognize the condition of paranoia as a way of salvation. They speak of the dying of the ego, meaning the letting go of caricatures and illusions in which the ego has draped itself. The suffering we experience in doing so is nothing but the destruction of the ego-illusion. The more we can let go and accept, the less we will suffer. Ultimately, this is all about accepting *what is* so that we can submit to the will of God or—as they say in the East—to get into sync with the cosmic law.

Anyone who has read Solzhenitsyn's *Gulag Archipelago*, Shifrin's *In the Fourth Dimension*, or Sologdin's *Notebooks* will be struck by the fact that people in concentration camps go through profoundly transforming experiences. All such authors agree about one paradoxical phenomenon: "Arrest, prison, the camps, in brief, unfreedom, was the most important and significant experience in their life; and not only that, they also assure us that while under the conditions of unfreedom, they did have to suffer the worst psychic and physical torments, at the same time they experienced moments of such perfect happiness that would be unimaginable for people outside the walls of the camps.…Accordingly unfreedom could be defined as the most concentrated and intense form of life."[23]

When we no longer chase after our continuously frustrating fantasies, the sources of anxiety, envy, hatred or—as Zen says—the causes of stupidity, anger, and greed dry up. In turn, we experience the harmony that lies hidden in God's will, the balance of the cosmos, in which there is neither good nor evil, neither up nor down, but only the experience of the moment. The cosmos is always in equilibrium. If we can entrust ourselves to it, which is the same thing as entrusting ourselves to God's will, we come into harmony. The message of Jesus is the proclamation to give ourselves over to the will of the Father and to live like the lilies of the field, that is, to enter the kingdom of heaven by becoming like children.

This kingdom of God is not something that will appear at the end of time. It is here and now, in us. It is the Divine that expresses itself in and through us. If we take the step out of paranoia into metanoia—if we awake from the illusion of ego, from this dreaming condition, as esotericism calls it—and enter the reality of God by transcending space and time, harmony and peace will come to dwell in us. The return (of Jesus) is not to be understood in a temporal sense, as a coming event. It happens when we are able to transcend space and time, reason and logic. In the depth of our being, there is a reality that lies outside time and space.

As we stand on the edge of this abyss, we have to acknowledge that the problems can be solved only through a new consciousness. As Christians, we can call it Christ-consciousness; others may call it Buddha-consciousness, Krishna-consciousness, or simply consciousness of the *perennial philosophy*. Regardless of the label, the solution of the problems takes place first of all in us, and only then in the world around us. The destructive element in the world grows out of our ego's pigheadedness. When we resist the kingdom of God in ourselves, we resist the evolution of humanity and fight against this divine game. In our stubborn egoism we end up struggling against our real happiness. But through our metanoia—through the awakening of Christ-consciousness in us—we can transform ourselves and the whole human race.[24]

FEELINGS AND HOW TO DEAL WITH THEM

Some people think that esoteric paths lead to a lack of feelings. In the course of time, anyone taking such a path would supposedly stiffen into a chunk of ice, as far as the emotions are concerned. Above all, it is said, adherents of Zen are quite unapproachable. They lack warmth and the human touch. The following verse of Angelus Silesius would almost seem to confirm that prejudice:

> Man, where you still are something,
> Still know, love, and hate,
> Then you are, believe me,
> Not free of your burden's weight.

But the poet means something altogether different from stoic contempt for feelings. He's talking about being imprisoned and preoccupied in the realm of the ego.

Every path of spiritual exercise is strict. When we become recollected and look inward, twenty-three may appear to be cold and unfriendly. By contrast, an old Zen master says, "The deeper the enlightenment, the greater the compassion."

Emotions and Feelings

In exercising, the feelings are not repressed or killed, but sorted and purified. If we were to observe ourselves carefully, we would note that there is a difference between emotions and feelings. Emotions are affectively charged, deeply anchored stirrings that prompt us to vehement expression. Feelings, however, are a finer movement in the psyche and hence not subject to this strong reacting and acting out. When released, emotions involve the body much more than feelings do. They take possession of us and force us to uncontrolled activity. They cause karma, Zen tells us. They are completely rooted in the realm of ego.

Emotions belong to the basic structure of our psyche. They sometimes contain an important message from the unconscious and so must not be completely neglected. They can, however, be terrible tyrants. Some therapeutic techniques actually incited the emotions, and the discharge is put to use as a way of healing. But on the path of inner exercise, it is crucial to transform these emotions without repressing the underlying feelings.

Transforming the Emotions

Roberto Assagioli and Viktor Frankl, pioneers in this area, confirm the fact that emotions can be transformed. If we really want to grow and

162

mature, we must make enough progress so as to change our old, well-worn reactions to emotions as they arise. Otherwise we remain trapped on the immanent level, unable to press forward into a transpersonal space.

But transforming emotions mustn't be used as an excuse for running away from troubles that should be treated by a therapist. There are complexes in the psyche that we can resolve only on the pertinent level. Thus in the beginning it may be important to let our emotions out and express them, thus bringing relief, insights, and change. But the time comes when we must learn to have emotions without being owned by them, and where therapy is not only unnecessary but an obstacle to the development of the personality.

When we feel enraged, we should be enraged—but perfectly awake at the same time. Rage must not stifle our consciousness. When we are conscious of our rage, it dissolves and falls away. Thus the rage isn't repressed; it dissolves itself. In the course of time, we sense that it is meaningless to constantly run after our rage and act it out.

The same is true of hatred or greed. We have to learn to look at these emotions, to be awake to them, but not to let ourselves be owned or strangled by them. We are then free and realize that all these emotions are only processes which pass like clouds over the psyche. The resulting power, which was otherwise frittered away in confrontation with emotions, is now available for the actual task at hand: to make our emotions serve our needs. I am continually asked where to find the touchstone for the investment we have to make in the contemplative path. One important criterion seems to me the capacity to transform emotions into positive energy.

Guidelines

The depth of feeling obviously has a decisive power to change our lives. When we are shaken to the depths of our soul, old structures collapse and new life can be born. Feelings bear within themselves the power of transformation.

Sitting is a valuable exercise in the setting free of emotions. *Emovere* in Latin means "move something out." It is more an explosion that liberates, that shatters the old, solidly established patterns that confine us. Hence sitting brings with it a process of purification. Feelings are allowed to surface because they are not concealed by the busy round of everyday activities. But we may not remain hung up by identifying with them. Mourning, anxiety, joy, and aggression, for example, are important sources of energy. But their power is developed *not* by acting them out—a fact often overlooked. Acting out generally means wasting energy. We are afraid of the emotional shock, so we want to get rid of them and throw them out. Rather, we should let such feelings come of their own while we resist identifying with them. We should express feelings—but expressing or showing our feelings and throwing them out are fundamentally different things.

> When the monk experiences a pleasant feeling, he knows: I am having a pleasant feeling; when he experiences a painful feeling, he knows: I am having a painful feeling. When he is having a pleasant secular feeling, he knows: I am having a pleasant secular feeling. When he experiences a pleasant nonsecular feeling, he knows: I am having a pleasant nonsecular feeling.
>
> And so he lingers and practices contemplation of the feelings, internal or external. He lingers, reflecting on the original conditions of the feelings.
>
> Thus his consciousness of the presence of feelings will be developed to the extent necessary for awareness and realization. He lingers unfettered. He clings to nothing in the world.[25]

How do we turn emotions into feelings?

- Recognize your emotions, not for the purpose of repressing them and not to gloss over them.
- Do not evaluate your emotions.
- Take cognizance of the emotions. Admit to yourself that you are, for example, enraged.
- Decide whether to act and react, that is, to express your feelings or not. Deep breathing can help, as can letting things pass, relaxing, going to your exercise. Adults who are forever reacting dramatically to their emerging emotions have remained stuck on a childish level. Deep down these emotions are nothing but reactions to other triggers: feeling accepted, loved, envious, jealous, cheated. We test ourselves to see to what extent we are appreciated, criticized, or rejected by others—a frightening purgatory indeed. The only way to get out of this purgatory is to develop sufficient self-worth to make us independent of other

people's behavior. But feelings of self-worth can't be manufactured; they have to grow. The more we get access to our deeper existence, the more independent we will be from the superficial storms of emotion.

What can help us dismantle these inner patterns in which we constantly find ourselves trapped? Growing in love. Not affective love, but that free, all-determining benevolence for everyone and everything, which doesn't ask about sympathy and antipathy, about friend or foe. This is what Christianity calls *agape*, something that can't be produced. It has to break out.

With every deep experience there is a growth in benevolence toward everything that exists; and it remains even when others meet us in a negative fashion. If we manage to persevere in this communion with our deepest essence, we will not be made insecure, but will react calmly and serenely. Even if we become angry, it will not be obsessive anger, but the anger of love, because something has taken aim against life.

Within our hearts a love can grow that is like an all-consuming fire, a love that transforms negative feelings. This love grows with experience, as the already mentioned Zen saying points out: "The deeper my experience, the greater my compassion."

This love is marked by a double movement: the attraction of an all-engulfing presence, and the outpouring of this love, once kindled within, for everything that exists. Hinayana Buddhism doesn't often speak about love, but it knows love, as does every esoteric path. It speaks more about compassion and sympathy for all living beings, as the following "Sutra of loving kindness" shows:

> So shall he act, he who strives for salvation,
> once he has recognized the place of silence:
> Let him be energetic, upright, unswerving,
> yet gentle, responsive, and without pride.
>
> Let him be frugal and modest,
> not too busy, but clever,
> let him rein in his senses, and be easily satisfied.
>
> Let peace and happiness come down on all creatures,
> may they all be happy!
> Whatever living creatures there may be—

whether they move about or stay put,
small, middle-sized, or tall,
weakly, sturdy or strong,
before our eyes or hidden away,
nearby or at home far away,
already born or still in the womb—
may all creatures be happy!

He should never revile another
and never despise anyone, anywhere;
no one shall seek another's harm
from anger or hostile-mindedness.

Like a mother who protects her son,
her one and only son, with her life,
he shall strive to free his mind from all barriers
towards each and every creature.

His kindness should embrace the whole world,
he should free his mind from barriers,
upwards, downwards, far and wide,
not constrained by hate and enmity, but pure.

Whether standing, walking, sitting, or lying down
he shall beget this frame of mind
and never succumb to indolence.
This is called "divine lingering" in the world.

THE CAVE OF THE HEART

The Cave, a Symbol of the Unconscious

Since time immemorial caves have been a symbol of the unconscious and a place for encounters with God. In the Upanishads the cave is called *guha*, the inner sanctuary, the place that is not accessible to thinking, the dwelling of the Divine. Teresa of Avila called this place "the interior castle," Tauler called it the "ground," Eckhart called it the "spark of the soul." It is the site, or the symbol for the site, of life, from which all phenomena proceed.

The heart is often compared to the cave. Yoga speaks of the heart chakra. It should be the first opened because from this center all frightening appearances can be most easily mastered. P. Lassalle called his

Zen site in Japan *Shinmeikutsu,* "the cave of the divine darkness." The cave is a symbol of our inner being. Those who retreat, those who try to withdraw from their ego-level—to leave behind their concepts, images, and ideas—enter, as it were, the cave of the heart.

The first monks not only went out into the desert, they often lived in burial caves. They entered those caves to snatch the devil's hideouts away from him. It's not easy to understand those who retreat into solitude. In the face of all rational reasons, something ineffable often leads them into stillness and silence. Nevertheless the question can always come up: Why don't they just go on vacation instead of taking this course in silence? Why are they spending the time in solitude staring at the wall? Evidently, they follow an inner call. Their's is a dark faith, an intuitive experience that is sometimes challenged, sometimes not. An inner voice tells them that things are right this way.

Anyone who goes off into solitude, who enters the cave, meets the demons. It is reported of Saint Anthony,[26] for example, that during his stay in a burial cave, he was plagued by such demons. One night a great gang of them came to torment him. The blows they dealt him were so terrible he was convinced that the creatures could not be human. When his friend, who brought him bread and water, came the next day, he saw him lying on the ground as if dead and had him taken to the village church. Many of Anthony's relatives and other people he had helped came to mourn him. But around midnight Anthony woke up. When he saw everyone sleeping and only his friend awake, he begged his friend to help him and to bring him back to the burial cave. When he arrived there, he called out to the demons: "I'm not running away from your blows. Even if you give me still more, nothing will separate me from the love of Christ." And he began to sing: "Even if a whole army fights against me, my heart will not fear."

Macarius, another monastic father, walked one day to Terenuthin, a place in Skytis. Since it was a long way, he spent the night in a burial cave, probably a kind of pyramid with mummies. When the demons saw him take one mummy out and use it as a pillow, they became angry that he was so fearless. They brought a few more mummies and began to shout from within them. To the mummy that he used as a pillow, they cried: "You, over there, come, we're going swimming!" Macarius answered: "Get up, then, if you can swim!" yet he continued to lay with his head on the mummy. When the demons saw Macarius' fearlessness, they left him in peace.

Jesus, too, was led out into the desert to be tempted by the demons. He was surely there for a very long time—forty days is only a symbolic number. Perhaps he lived for years in solitude. After all, we don't know anything about his life between the ages of twelve and thirty. In the Eastern Church, Jesus is often represented in limbo: "Descended into hell," it says in the Creed. The path to resurrection leads through the grave and through death.

In my theology, too, we repeatedly find that we have to go off into solitude and down into the underworld. Thus, for example, Odysseus met the seer Tiresias in the World of Shadows and was told what his future would be. The people of Israel were led into the wilderness before they could enter the promised land. The descent into the underworld was often made into a symbol and celebrated in myths about women, for example, in the Innana myth from the third century B.C. or the Isis-Osiris myth. These are feminine celebrations of life, whose message is "Die and become" (Goethe). In these rites, death was not considered the end of life, but a transforming power. Thus everything that we pass through is a source of power for our life. We're too quick to assume that we have fallen into depression, into a psychic illness. In reality it is often a process of transformation, if only we stick it out.

There is an apocryphal saying about Jesus that goes, "The Jesus Christ who comes in triumph over the dark is the anti-Christ; the Jesus Christ who comes through the darkness is the true Christ." We have to pass through the cave into the resurrection, into the promised land. Caves and solitude are not domains outside of us; rather, they are to be found in the depths of our psyche. They are often elements that we have suppressed, that which couldn't develop or wasn't allowed to develop, that which couldn't be integrated, what we call the shadow material. These are the injuries done to us in childhood and in the harsh experiences from the script of our life. The ancients called them demons; today we speak of depression.

And so those who are taking an inner path will enter the cave of their heart. They will enter the wilderness, the dark night, isolation. There in the cave, they shut themselves off from their thoughts, feelings, decisions, and ideas. Sometimes their temptations aren't at all concrete. Perhaps they express themselves purely as anxiety coming from nowhere, no particular situation. In this very experience of anxiety, the process of purification is carried out. It is often accompanied by confusion and pain. This pain can even become "somatized," that is, made physically perceptible.

Joseph Campbell describes the difference between schizophrenia and the temptations of a person meditating:

> Contemplation is a deliberately induced schizophrenia. You break away from the everyday world and fall into it. The phenomena are the same as in schizophrenia. So what's the difference? The difference is simply the one between a diver who can swim and one who can't swim. The mystic steps down into the water under the guidance of a master and realizes that he can swim, while the schizophrenic goes under.[27]

Thus we have to go through our psychic underworld to clean up and clear away what's there. But this is the path that leads to wholeness. What looks so confusing is in reality a process of purification. Those who hold on, firm in the faith that they are making a breakthrough, will come forth as transformed individuals. All shadow material becomes a new source of power and ultimately leads to resurrection, to wholeness.

It is important that we accept our place in life, which is precisely the site of the process of transformation. Our path is not just therapy in the psychoanalytical sense, even though it is a process of being purified and becoming whole. If we ask our ancestors in mysticism, they will tell us that what's ultimately at stake is abandoning the ego, so that we can find our deepest essence. Everything, even what terrifies us, must be left behind. In the end even control over the ego must be abandoned. But only those who actually have an ego can manage this. People with weak egos have a much harder time. This letting go of the ego is worse than physical death. It's relatively easy to die in the hope that we will be caught up in the Beyond by God. Mystical dying, however, is a death that doesn't know how things will work out in the Beyond. It is a dying that leaves us no sort of hope for "the other world." It is a dying that Jesus has gone through before us when he said, "Father, into thy hands I commend my spirit." There's no wish for heaven here, no hope for being safe and secure with God; only letting go.

Letting go has something to do with humility. We must simply surrender to the flow of life, even in places where this current threatens to drag us into the depths. The word *humility*, like the word *humanity*, comes from the Latin root *humus*, that is, earth, soil, manure. The word *humor* comes from the Latin root *umere*, that is, to be moist; the derivative *umor* means, moisture, fluid. The fluid in any living organism is what gives it life. Perhaps this tells us that there are times when we should meet our demons with a certain inner cheerfulness, with a smile. We shouldn't take ourselves or the demons too seriously. Like Macarius, we should keep our sense of humor (our life) and give ourselves over in humility to the path because humility is the truth about ourselves. We need humble courage to penetrate into the cave of our heart so as to enter this unknown land. It is a journey that leads to other shores, to shores we have never seen. But it is precisely the unknown that we are seeking, the not-knowing in which lies fullness, in which we experience God. We will not find this fullness on well-worn paths.

The monastic fathers place a great deal of emphasis on humility. When Abbot Macarius was on the way home with a bundle of palm leaves under his arm, he ran into a demon on the street. The demon had a sickle in his hand and threatened to attack Macarius. The demon cried out, "I'm suffering enormously from your injuries, Macarius. I do everything you do. When you fast, I don't eat at all. When you keep vigil, I don't sleep at all. But there's one thing in which you simply surpass me." Macarius asked the demon: "What's that?" The demon answered: "Your humility. Because you are humble, I am powerless."

The Allegory of Plato's Cave[28]

Plato puts the following story into Socrates' mouth, as he instructs his disciple Glaucon. People dwell under the earth in cavelike quarters. Upwards toward the daylight there is a long but invisible way out. The men and women in the cave have had their bodies chained to the ground ever since childhood so that they can't turn around. They always have to stay in the same position, and hence they can only look at the rock wall in front of them.

A ray of light falls on this wall, projected by a fire burning behind the backs of the people in chains. Between them and the fire runs a path along a low-lying wall. Thus of everything that passes along this way, one can see only the shadows, and only the upper half of them. Along this wall run people carrying every possible object on their heads: statues, articles for daily use, and all sorts of things.

Plato argues that these prisoners are just like us. They are trapped in themselves, never getting to see anything but shadows cast on the wall of the cave by the glare of the fire.

What they do see prompts them to conversation. They discuss these shadows as though they were really existent things. If one of those people parading behind them were to speak, they would assume that the shadows could talk; and they would understand all the gear being carried on their heads only in their shadow-dimension. This is our ego-consciousness.

Plato now asks, "What would happen if one of the prisoners escaped?" He would turn around and look into the glow of the fire, but that would initially confuse him rather than impart any deep knowledge to him. His eyes would hurt, and he would turn away. He might even assume that the shadows are clearer than what he can see when he looks backward.

But if someone did actually succeed in climbing the steep, rugged path out of the cave, he would come to the light of the sun and would again be full of indignation, blinded by this brilliant light. He would not be capable of seeing even the slightest thing, at least not immediately.

Plato thinks that it's necessary to get acclimatized. One must get used to the light of the sun. The brave escapee would rather begin by taking night walks because the light of the moon isn't so harsh. But later he could see everything and under certain circumstances he could even gaze on the sun itself and not on its reflection in the water and in things.

Plato then asks what would likely happen if one of the prisoners who had climbed up to the light were to come down again and report to the people below what reality looks like. The person would be the target of ridicule; the people in the cave would simply not understand him. They would tell him, "That's what you get! You've ruined your eyes. It really isn't worthwhile to go up." And if they could loosen their chains, they would rather kill the returning messenger than believe him.

In his interpretation, Plato recognizes that we are not automatically prepared to handle reality and truth. In fact, encountering reality and truth often leaves us more confused than anything else.

Acclimatization takes place in a long, tedious process of transformation. In mysticism we call it the path of active and passive purification. The pain of passive purification can be very painful, worse than looking into a bright light, into the flame of fire that hurts our eyes. There has to be a change in the foundations of our personality. This is what Plato means by *paideia*. The usual translation of this word as "education" has a much too intellectual connotation. *Paideia* originally meant a turn-around of the entire person toward his or her deepest essence. Out of this grows a realization based on experience and not on intellectual reflection. Genuine education transforms the person's inmost core by leading him or her into the center, into actual being, out of which action can be determined.

Thus the path presupposes a process of transformation. Becoming free is not enough all by itself. It's not enough to undo our chains because that could just as easily lead to unchecked licentiousness—and licentiousness and lack of restraint are radically opposed to freedom. The bondage, which used to be external, a matter of being tied down to stakes, becomes—when freedom is properly understood—a bond that takes its norms from the deepest essence. It seems that humanity is slowly freeing itself from these stakes, and perhaps one day religion will be acceptable once again.

Until recent times, belief had to be based on knowledge if it didn't want to be branded as overbelief or superstition. Theology was proud to be recognized as a scholarly discipline. True, it has appended to all our articles of faith the statement that God is the wholly Other, but in practice, it has more or less forbidden people to believe in anything but its own tenets.

Today, thanks to atomic physics and the formulations of quantum mechanics, a far-reaching revolution has occurred in our thinking about natural science. Physics and transcendence have moved closer to each other. Granted, this has hardly made a serious dent in the public's consciousness, and word has yet to reach most theologians, among whom the Cartesian-Newtonian world picture, with its mechanistic and positivistic orientation, still predominates. But the pioneers of the new world picture, such as Max Planck, Albert Einstein, Niels Bohr, Pascual Jordan, Friedrich von Weiszäcker, and Werner Heisenberg, leave no room for doubt that mystical experiences and natural science are approaching each other. They are no longer at war, but see themselves in a complementary relationship. Both are necessary for us humans, even for the Church and theologians.

But transcendence is not objectively graspable. Language is always just a symbol and parable for the incomprehensible. Our senses and our reason are constantly imposing a grid on reality that confines and falsifies it. Arthur Eddington has expressed this in an image: the physical world is like waves, which symbolize the underlying sea of transcendence.[29]

Once our thinking has taken the world apart, the world is no longer the one whole world. We can't catapult ourselves out of the picture so as to measure and judge things from a point outside this world. Bohr says that reality is more like a river that is not directly graspable; only certain waves and eddies, which display a relative independence and stability, are comprehensible to our minds.

Thus science has arrived at the frontier of what can no longer be objectified. Mathematical formulas have ceased to explain nature. Instead they come up against a reality they are no longer capable of handling. Like theologians, scientists—with their intellectual concepts—stand baffled in the face of the incomprehensible.

Thus we realize today more than ever that we are sitting in Plato's cave. Perhaps our limbs and our heads will finally be released from the stakes. But then we'll probably be just as confused by the reality we see as were the people in Plato's cave when they looked back into the fire or climbed up into the sunlight.

THE SHADOW

The Meaning of the Shadow

Shadow, devil, monster: we have many names for this psychic complex that we find in all men and women, even in Jesus. We need only read the story of the temptation in the desert to see how Jesus, too, had to integrate his shadow.

The shadow is not just a question for psychology, however; it is a concern for religion as well. All who take the path of contemplation will be confronted by their shadow. Once again, we can see this clearly demonstrated in the life story of Saint Anthony in the desert. When we look at the painting, "The Temptation of Saint Anthony" by Matthias Grünewald, we see that behind the numerous myths about demons and evil spirits stands the lived reality of the human race. These creatures have cast terror into the hearts of people throughout all time and in all cultures. What's more, it seems that our shadow, in the form of devils and demons, meets us once again in the hour of death if we have not made our peace with it.

The shadow is the side of our consciousness turned away from us. That is why we have such a hard time seeing and accepting it. Coming to terms with this partner and antagonist of ours remains one of the most important tasks of our lives. Indeed it is the prerequisite for our process of growth and wholeness. On that point the wisdom of the East and the West, along with contemporary psychology, align: the shadow is a pole of our personality.

In the dreadful images, caricatures, animals, demons, and monsters that emerge from our shadow, we meet our own inner monsters. We meet all the things that we can't accept in ourselves. But it's not enough just to accept our shadow, we also have to affirm it. From negation to affirmation, however, is a difficult step.

Projecting Outward

At first we are inclined to project the shadow outward, onto the opposite sex, the other race, the other culture, the other religion, on Jews, pagans, Nazis, foreigners. That way we demonize in others what we actually should acknowledge as part of ourselves.

Unfortunately this sort of demonization is also possible on the religious level. The distinction between matter and spirit, between body and mind, between man and God, is turned into an unbridgeable cleft. The body, sexuality, joy in nature and in life, are stamped as inferior. This is where religious fanaticism begins. It always comes into existence in a religion where love fails. Faith without love, faith that can't see its own shadow, becomes fanaticism—and we needn't go far to recognize it. We Catholics can think of the way we treat divorced persons and married priests, or of the false images of perfection that have been presented to us as the ideal in our religious education. Many Christians suffer from this unmerciful splitting up of good and evil. In fact, many people seem to be getting in touch with their "church-caused" complexes. Of course there's also fanaticism in the opposite direction. Some people demonize everything intellectual, spiritual, and divine. The fact remains, there can be no growth until we make friends with our shadow.

C.G. Jung says that projecting outward transforms the world around us into our own unknown face, making "others" the bad and evil ones.[30] Thus the first task in befriending our shadow is to withdraw the projections and acknowledge the bad and evil in ourselves. Otherwise the shadow retains its destructive effect.

According to Jung, withdrawing the projection is simply the awakening of the insight that a good many of our prejudices and assumptions about others apply not to them but to ourselves. Thus we have an almost impossible job to accomplish: to look around the corner, as it were, in an attempt to recognize in ourselves the evil that we see outside and in others. For if there were nothing in us corresponding to the shadow outside, we would not be susceptible to its destructive effect. So long as we don't see through ourselves, we deny the modes of behavior that we criticize in others but that are present in our own psyche.

This holds true as well on the religious level. The supposed competence of institutions to stand on the side of truth and to condemn certain activities and opinions of others is to this day a source of great suffering. Granted, no one gets burned at the stake anymore, but the psychic torment inflicted on many people of different convictions is no better. Religious institutions obviously find it even harder to recognize their shadow than the individual person does.

The best way to begin wrestling with our shadow is to ask our dreams how the shadow in us takes on symbolic form. In the Tibetan *Book of the Dead*, we are given examples of how the shadow can show itself in grotesque faces, horrible animals, and demons. When our shadow shows up in a dream, we are typically frightened, feel extremely threatened, and often run away. In reality, we should do exactly the opposite: turn around, look straight at it, and begin a conversation with the shadow figure.

Looking Behind the Mask

The shadow also contains elements that we evaluate positively in everyday life. None of us can live out all our talents and wishes. Much of that falls into the unconscious and shadow side. Some people, for example, have difficulties seeing and accepting their positive features. They may perhaps consider it impossible to display friendship and goodwill, and don't like to admit having such "impulses." There are also positive qualities that we find unacceptable. These, too, we have to acknowledge and integrate into ourselves.

Keep in mind that it is not the shadow itself that does its dirty work in our unconscious, but the fact that we don't realize it. In that unknowing space, the shadow can lead its own life in the dark undergrowth of our psyche. Psychology calls this the splitting off of certain elements. These splits appear as things that aren't part of us, as demons, grotesque

175

faces, black dogs, or simply as a threatening, shapeless mass trying to swallow us up. Our task is to determine what is concealed behind this masquerade—not an easy task because we've denied such threatening elements of our psyche since childhood.

Saying Yes to the Shadow

The more we resist these demons, the harder our task becomes. The more we repress these shadow images, the more power we give them. And although we would like to conceal this shadow side from others, we rarely manage to do so. A good friend can be our best helper here. He or she has a clearer view of our repressions than we ourselves and can uncover their mechanisms.

On our own, we can best "get the number" of our shadow if we ask ourselves: *What would I like to hide from others?* To answer that requires a virtue we don't discuss much these days: humility. Asking the question and applying humility to our struggles to answer it will cause our ego to diminish and, with time, to melt as quickly as a snowman in the sun.

In working with the shadow, there are basically two things we have to do: recognize and accept. It's very important to know that we don't absolutely have to live out the shadow side. It's enough to admit and accept it, which doesn't mean giving in to it. Often, of course, that means setting clear limits for ourselves and saying "no" to our inner tendencies.

Nevertheless it's hard to find the midpoint between admitting and living out on the one hand and putting up fences or saying "no" on the other—because with an absolute "no" we block the flow of life energy. Wilhelm Reich has pointed this out very clearly. With this "no" we build a kind of prison, against whose walls we then continually charge. He speaks of character as a suit of armor that constrains us and hinders the development of our personality. Finding the midpoint between yes and no is a difficult task but one absolutely required for the maturation of our personality.

Coexistence of Shadow and Consciousness

If we recall the Tibetan *Book of the Dead,* we know about the struggle between the terrible and the friendly deities. The responsibility of the dying person accordingly consists in making peace with both of them, that is, to move past both, since remaining trapped by their spell causes rebirth.

Many of us experience this sort of confrontation in our dreams. Some of our dreams involve an endless conflict between persons; other dreams involve the same person, but conflicting feelings of love and rejection. They are opposing forces and tendencies that must reach a state of coexistence if peace is to enter our hearts.

A number of psychologists think we have to befriend these shadow figures or at least learn to harmonize with them. Some are inclined to leave it at coexistence.[31] The shadow is simply that other side that stabilizes our positive side because we have to be constantly alert to the moves of a worthy opponent. We have to be very familiar with that opponent if we don't want to lose the wrestling match. We have to understand its dodges and tricks, otherwise we will constantly get beaten.

How the Shadow Comes About

In his article, "The Inner Enemy," Metzner cites three levels on which the shadow has emerged: developmental psychology, evolution, and theology-mythology.

Psychological level: The experience of conflict comes, at least in part, from our childhood, prompted by sibling rivalry for attention from parents and other adults. This often continues into adulthood and reappears as competitiveness and jealousy in partnerships and careers. Conflict between siblings is richly attested to in literature (Cain and Abel, Jacob and Esau, Cinderella and her sisters, for example). These tensions simply reflect the fact that both the good and the bad brother, like the good and the bad sister, are symbols for processes that take place in our hearts.

William Law, an English disciple of Jakob Böhme, said: "There is only one enemy who has you in his hand, only one imprisonment from which you wish to be saved, and that is the power of your own self [ego]. This self [ego] is the murderer of the divine life within you. It is your own Cain who kills your own Abel."[32]

Evolutionary level: With this, Metzner refers to the long battles between tribes and societies, between the haves and the have-nots. This struggle continues, and it is questionable whether the human race is capable of transforming it into peaceful coexistence in the next few centuries.

Theological-mythological level: Conflict and strife play an important role in cosmogenesis (the creation of the world). In ancient Persian Zoroastrianism (the struggle between light and darkness) is at the core of religion. It is the myth of the battle between Ahura Mazda, the creator of light, and Ahriman, the prince of darkness—a battle that ends with the adversaries taking turns in ruling over the earth as day and night. Behind this lies the notion of a dualism that is evidently a given in all phenomena.

We also have the duality between male and female. Every western movie has its "good guys" and its "bad guys." Both represent types of our psyche, for the vigilant superego constantly sits in judgment over and punishes its victim. The East is familiar with the duality of yin and yang. But as we already know, both halves—the yin and the yang—nestle into each other and form a unit.

In the theistic religions we are inclined to distinguish much more sharply between good and evil, angels and devils, heaven and hell. Both poles stand unreconciled over against each other. Heaven and hell are mutually exclusive. We have eliminated the evil from God. In the East, by contrast, the Ultimate Reality is good *and* evil.

We are constantly presented with an unreachable, perfect image of the saint as our model, and unfortunately, this has contributed to a lot of frustration in personality development. But we don't have to be perfect; the point is to become whole. Failing to harmonize this duality (which is obviously part of the structure of creation) within us, we remain exposed to the destructive forces of the struggle. For transformation to take place we have to become wise judges of ourselves. Inquisitor and accused, judge and executioner—both and all dwell inside us.

The Inner Demons

The demons in the Tibetan *Book of the Dead* are the personification of good and evil forces. At first we project them outward. It will be no different in the process of dying. This inner turbulence often seems beyond our control so that we experience ourselves as a platform where the forces within us do battle. In the Tibetan *Book of the Dead,* they are called *asuras* and *devas.* In reading the book aloud at the hour of death, we should note that our feelings, thoughts, anxieties, and ideas are what bring such structures into being. Here and now we have to confront them; then perhaps when we are dying—and should the superego get on its high horse yet one more time—they will leave us at last in peace.[33]

DEPRESSION OR PROCESS OF TRANSFORMATION?

Human Destiny

From the standpoint of evolution, human beings are still children. We scarcely have a notion of our true potential. The reason for this lies in our deep rootedness in the level of ego-consciousness. Our true identity remains hidden in the depths, and when it tries to unfold, it runs up against the massive resistance of ego-consciousness.

We bear a divine seed within us, a seed that wants to thrust through all the encrustations of the material world, to grow, and to reveal itself. Humans are in a continual process of liberation from the constraints of the ego. Our feverish search for meaning is simply that mysterious evolutionary power of the Divine. We spend a long time refusing to believe that meaning can be found in the deeper levels of consciousness, and that true peace has its home only in the hidden spiritual order of Being.

Our reason is an instrument of our consciousness, no more and no less—an instrument like our senses. It is supposed to show us the way back to our origins, back to our divinity. It's not as if we weren't always from God and in God, but it is our wretched condition that we don't know who we really are. Reason is designed to help us get onto the path to this realization, to lead us through the various stages of consciousness until we recognize our divinity, a divinity that is always there. We actually don't need to search for it at all. We only have to clear away the debris under which it lies buried. Everything is already laid out in us. We have no need to go looking for it outside.

A poem by Kabir gives wonderful expression to this:

I laugh when I hear
that the fish in the water is thirsty:
You don't see
that reality is at home,
and you wander from field to field
—so listlessly!
Truth is here!
Go off wherever you want,
to Benares or Mathura—
if you don't find your own soul,
the world remains unreal.[34]

Or to use another image, the full range of humanity, into which we are supposed to grow, lies like a seed within us, just as the acorn already contains the characteristic features of the oak tree. But it doesn't unfold its dynamic until it is exposed to the darkness, moisture, and weight of the ground. Then it works its way up to the light.

Development always seems to be bound up with resistance. The kinds of resistance that our true essence runs up against in its unfolding often manifest themselves as depression. Hence depression has an important role to play in the developmental process of humanity. What we all too often dismiss is the fact that an obstacle or even a sickness can be our great chance to mature.

Resistance From the Ego

Our life resembles a system of coordinates. The horizontal line has the fatal quality of always pressing for more. The more we have, the more we think we need. We are prisoners of our habits, fears, ambitions, and desires. We begin to defend our possessions at all costs. We work hard, plan, and strive to win happiness and security within these narrow boundaries. But we forget that the world around us is only supposed to help accompany us on the spiritual path, not to interpret the meaning of life. The bad thing is that the walls of our ego-prison often block the view and make us incapable of grasping a thought that could lead us out.

Thus we go through a process that aims to liberate us from the crushing embrace of the physical-psychic-material world. It's a great advantage to be aware of this because all suffering should help us find the way to a quicker realization. It should release us from imprisonment in the ego. Life is a sort of steeplechase in which the hurdles are cut to the exact measure of the individual runners, even if they refuse to see this. We are supposed to mature by means of the resistance we meet, through what Christianity calls "God's will" and the Eastern religions call "cosmic law."

We are proud of the fact that we have free will and are furious if anyone wants to take this "freedom" away from us. But in reality we are slaves to our thoughts, fears, emotions, and desires. This little ego reacts vehemently and bristles when threatened with the loss of its dominating role. It would like to remain in this coarse-grained world of forms and privations, even though that causes it suffering upon suffering. And so we stagger along on the quest for lasting happiness from one provisional satisfaction to the next. We succumb to the basic error of thinking we can find lasting satisfaction for any need. In other words, emotional ties, desires, and anxieties take over us, and we put the blame for our missing happiness on circumstances, fate, or other people.

Esotericism calls this stupidity, pure and simple. People constantly let themselves be led around by the nose. Some recognize that and look for a way out. They pull themselves together and climb out of the cave and away from its shadow images, up into the light of the sun, as Plato put it. But they can't do that without running into resistance. Conflict is as much a part of this development as the encrusted earth is of the unfolding of the seed. They have to ripen and grow on it.

This must be made quite clear at this point: the material and psychic levels are a part of being human, a part of the whole. We must not despise them, we have to experience them as belonging to us without constantly being irritated by them.

The Meaning of Suffering

Suffering has an important function in this process of human development. In suffering the Divine presses us hard to give up, at long last, our state of imprisonment. Suffering, says Meister Eckhart, is the fastest horse to God. We evidently need constant frustration to make us head off on the path.

But our ego does not readily give up the struggle for self-preservation—or rather for ego-preservation. For some of us, in fact, this conflict follows a dramatic and harrowing course. We are so entangled in the threefold level of *physis* (nature), *psyche* (the mind), and *ratio* (reason) that we have a hard time understanding our life as a pilgrimage we have been sent on so that we can mature and grow into our ultimate destiny. The meaning of our existence here on this planet is growth and maturity. We have to learn to distinguish between illusion and reality. Esotericism has a word to express this: *awakening*. We have to wake up to our deepest essence.

The price for spiritual development is high: confusion, pain, fear of madness, and hopelessness. We are fortunate to find a counselor who doesn't immediately refer us to a psychiatrist and who can tell spiritual depression from garden variety ego-disappointment. This phase of spiritual development may also be accompanied by psychosomatic complaints: headaches, stomach trouble, exhaustion, rheumatic pains, to name only a few of the symptoms.

Almost all mystics have gone through similar states at a certain stage of their development. For example, John of the Cross gives a detailed description of this phenomenon in *Dark Night of the Soul*. One great difficulty is that the process has a very slow pace, and nobody can predict when it will begin or end. Spiritual depression is a part of the structure of developing into a mature personality—in contrast to other kinds of depression that are caused by a disappointed ego, that is, by ambition, avarice, or material greed. The more we live out of our deepest inner core, the more anxiety will leave us alone. Our "unknowingness" will be slowly transformed into wisdom.

Of course we may well ask, "Why should we be in this contradictory and pain-laden state in the first place if we have a divine nature? Why did we have to get mixed up in this coarse-grained existence?" I have no definitive answer to that, but I suspect that it does make sense. Ego-consciousness seems to be a necessary transition. What the Bible calls original sin is nothing but the emergence of consciousness from an archaic into a mental form. Original sin is not falling away from God, and not guilt, but the entrance of humans into the rational stage of consciousness, that is, an important new step on the homeward path to our origins. All esoteric paths say that our mode of existence as humans has a special importance in view of our ultimate destiny.

Two Kinds of Depression

One form of depression comes from frustration on the part of the ego, which doesn't get what it unconditionally wants, that is, what we generally understand as happiness: lucky in love, lucky in the lottery, having the material possessions, health, and "eternal youth" that we want. When that doesn't happen, we become unhappy and get depressed. This is where we get expressions such as "Why me?" "How can God be so cruel?" "Why don't I get more loving care?" "Why am I always the Cinderella?"

Not a few of us fall into the other form of depression when we take a spiritual path. This depression makes its appearance when our ego notices that it is being robbed of its dominating power. It then slips into fear, even panic. This depression, in the language of spirituality, is actually a process of purification.

When I am advising someone, and I ask, "What are you anxious about?" I often get the answer, "I don't know!" There are no marital problems, no financial worries, no fears about health. It's pure anxiety. It comes from threats to the ego and is accompanied by a sense of hopelessness, instability, and meaninglessness. John of the Cross has described it in heart-wrenching words:

> Round about the death rattle
> torments of Hell
> cast into the darkness
> plunged into the pool of the lowest depths
> lightless shadows of death
> death shadows
> death groans
> agonies of hell
> suffocating pain
> hanged up in the air unable to breathe,
> the bones must be burnt up in the fire
> the flesh is consumed
> the members are torn apart (Ezekiel 24:10)
> deadly languishing away
> the soul sees Hell yawn before it.[35]

In some cases our thoughts even turn to suicide. On the one hand, the ego level can no longer provide support; on the other hand, the new spiritual level has not been consolidated. It is this level that poses a threat to the ego and becomes a cause of fear. Now what scholars call the numinous element (*numinosum*) is not just "fascinating," but downright terrifying.

At this stage the drive to preserve the ego can once again appear, and with even greater intensity. The ego makes a last tremendous effort, trying to defend itself with all its might, a struggle that often leads to a grueling contest between both levels. The elementary forces of the ego attempt to keep their domain intact, but the power of the deeper levels of consciousness repeatedly calls this into question.

The really difficult thing about this situation is that the cleansing process doesn't spare the realm of religion, so that even there, certainties disappear. As John of the Cross said, there is no longer any support— even in God. The sense of security that religion once supplied melts away. Previously we could feel safe at least in the hand of the "divine Father," but this hand suddenly fails to bear us up. The tide of guilt feelings rises, culminating in the fear that our own failure is responsible for the whole problem.

It is at this point that the process of spiritual evolution has properly begun. What we take to be a psychic illness—or what some therapists define as such—is in reality a process of transformation. But to accept that, when we are totally caught up in it, is enormously difficult. And yet the nature of our condition isn't pitiable now; we find ourselves on the point of departure to a new level of consciousness. We slowly escape the power of the insatiable ego and begin to extricate ourselves from ties to the physical, psychic, and rational world. We see through to the inconstancy of things and realize that clinging to them inevitably leads to frustration.

Ultimately, this is exactly what all the sacred books say. But it was presented to us with a religious gloss that seemed unbelievable because too often it was accompanied by a contempt for and a denial and mortification (killing) of the world. And that is just what we have to avoid. All asceticism has only one justification: to liberate us from the bond to the ego. Things are not good and not bad. The terms *true* and *false, good* and *evil* become irrelevant. The crucial point is to recognize the spiritual destiny of all things, including our own ego-consciousness.

Our ego-consciousness is in fact of great importance. Its existence is a prerequisite for a deeper experience. An animal can't experience what a person does. So the idea is not to kill this ego-consciousness, but to revoke its dominance so that it can be illuminated from the spiritual layer. Passing through the levels of the material and the psychic is part of the process of purification. A complete enlightenment pervades all levels of consciousness, including the physical and psychic. Essentially speaking there is no separation between the higher and lower, between the material and the spiritual. It is the totality that we must experience, and hence our body plays an important role. Without it we can experience nothing, as Kabir says in a poem:

> O friend! This body is his [God's] lyre:
> He tightens the strings and elicits from them the melody
> of Brahma.
> When the strings go slack and the keys are loosened,
> then this instrument of dust becomes dust once again.
> Kabir says, "No one except Brahma can bring forth this
> melody."[36]

In another poem, Kabir writes:

> O Sadhu!
> Cleanse your body in the simple way!
> As the seed is in the fig tree,
> and in the seed are blossoms, fruits and shadows,
> so the sprout is in the body and the body again in the sprout.
> Fire, air, water, earth and aether, you can't have it
> without it.
> O Kazi, O Pandit! Think it over!
> What is there that does not lie within the soul?
> The pitcher full of water under water:
> The water is inside and out.
> One should not name it, so as not to release the error of duality.
> Kabir says: Listen to the word, the truth, that is your
> being.
> HE speaks the word to Himself, and HE Himself is
> the Creator.[37]

Possibilities of Healing

The emotional pain of depression can become so strong that the condition is scarcely distinguishable from a so-called endogenous depression. The desperation and hopelessness seem to be permanent, and there is no predicting how long anyone can remain in such a phase. There is no going back to the old notion of life, but there's also no hope for the future. The symptoms of this condition are sleep disturbances, loss of interest in social and political life, career, and plans for the future. Above all, the feeling of self-worth suffers. This is often combined with childhood deficits, enabling negative features of the total psychic structure to be recharged, so that, for example, aggressiveness and outbursts of anger suddenly appear. There can also be physical symptoms—no surprise there, because a purifying psychophysical force is going through the entire body (*kundalini*).

Worst of all, however, is the fact that we can't understand our own condition, and even well-intentioned encouragement doesn't last long. Gradually, a fear of madness develops, which can be worse than the fear of death and sometimes contributes to thoughts of suicide. Persons who enter analysis at this point will find that their therapists generally find no serious psychic damage, which only increases the fear of going insane. Routine therapeutic efforts don't take hold, drugs are of little help, and there is scarcely any prospect of a lasting cure.

In this situation what possibilities of healing are available?

The first step is to get information. We must be told that we are not suffering from ordinary depression. We must come to recognize that there is a pattern to this "quasi-depression," namely that it constitutes a process of purification, which is the prerequisite for the transition to a new level of consciousness. This is a spiritual development, a process of transformation, and hence a series of positive events.

Next, we have to talk about our condition and feel like we're actually being heard and understood. Such exchanges should be made available frequently because depressive phases come in fits. We must not simply surrender to the depressive mood; we must fight it. The attack offers great opportunities for healing, although just then its crushing embrace feels worst. We must realize that the only way to a breakthrough lies in going forward through the tunnel, not backward. It's up to us, not the counselor, to do the most important work, just by holding on. Thus it takes a lot of courage and self-discipline to profit from this phase.

The next source of help is inner presence in everything we do, the "sacrament of the moment," being "all there" in every moment, in every flick of the wrist. Further help can be derived from physical activity, physical exercise, work, walking, and hobbies.

What makes up the actual drama of the whole process and what ultimately alone brings healing is the encounter with what mysticism calls Nothingness. This Nothingness offers no support and has no end. It refuses every form of demarcation, whether spatial, temporal, or any other kind. At first it isn't easy to endure. This very fact shows that it isn't simply nothing. Instead it creates a compelling impression that cannot, however, be couched in a positive language. But we sense that something crucial lies hidden in it.

In the beginning, this is experienced as meaninglessness and hopelessness, as *horror vacui*. That is the point at which Friedrich Nietzsche stopped short. He has his wise "madman" cry out in the marketplace: "God is dead, we have killed him." Nietzsche was a mystic *manqué*. That is because in Nothingness one track leads to nihilism, and another to the experience of the Ultimate Reality.

Only when we really accept this Nothingness will we discover that it has a quality which leads to the infinite. It is the gateway to religious experience. It is the bright darkness of God.

Christian "negative theology" has characterized God by what he is not. Thus Gregory of Nyssa wrote: "Herein lies the actual knowledge of the One sought, herein lies the seeing in not-seeing, namely that the One sought transcends all knowledge, as cut off on all sides by his incomprehensibility, as if by darkness."

Above all, Meister Eckhart, worked out a lofty metaphysical conceptual scheme in which Nothingness plays an important role. For example, he speaks of a power in the soul "which...does not take God as he is good and does not take him as he is truth. It seeks the ground [of God], continuing to search, and takes God in his oneness and in his solitary wilderness, in his vast wasteland."[38] Thus, in the profoundest desperation, where nothing seems to be left for humans, the transformation takes place: In Nothingness the eternal eye of the Divine looks upon us.

CHAPTER 10

MORAL BEHAVIOR

Everything is connected to everything else. Every part of three-dimensional space is bound up with all the others through basic networking units, so-called wormholes. Through the constantly appearing and disappearing wormhole connection signals move, making possible instant communication through all parts of space. These signals might be visualized as the pulsing of nerve cells in a giant cosmic brain that pervades every part of space.

What happens in any part influences what happens in every other part. "The whole is more than the sum of its parts"—that maxim no longer represents, as it did in the early part of this century, a biological argument against explaining things through physics. Instead it is a law of mathematical systems theory, which for its part has become a solid component of the science of physico-chemical processes.[1]

These statements derive from a science lecture given in 1989 in Alpbach at the European Forum. They are a confession of faith in the holistic world picture, in the interdependence of all life. I would argue that the will of God, properly understood, is connected with this holistic world-view and the interdependence of all being. All being is relatedness. Pascal expressed this with the image of the twig and the tree: a twig cannot grasp the meaning of the tree, but it can be understood in terms of the tree.

In the same way, we can attempt to understand this world in terms of the whole—and from time immemorial this whole has borne the name of God. Today, however, we have to rethink the old tenets of faith and the concept of God. Our life is governed by many circumstances that we cannot change. Hence to know and yet (or just because of them) shape life actively is wisdom.

It is the life of the Divine that unfolds in creation. Anyone resisting this life engenders disharmony that spreads through the entire universe. Perhaps this resistance is the one real sin humans commit. Accordingly, it would probably be better to designate "God's will—karma" in a positive sense, and to call the universe not "interdependent," but "intersupported." In other words, what we have is less mutual dependency and more a shaping influence of everything on everything else. All our energy should be directed at harmonizing with the unfolding of the Divine.

The word *karma* comes from Sanskrit and means "deed." It is the law of cause and effect. Through voluntary actions, we bring about certain events. Depending upon whether our action is shaped by greed, hatred, and delusion or by good will, generosity, and love, we sow seeds that develop differently. We create the preconditions for weal or woe.

It's like the way things are in nature. Once the seed has been sown, nothing can be done to change things. Wheat becomes wheat, rye becomes rye, and we harvest no plums from cherry trees. "He who sows the wind reaps the whirlwind," Scripture says. Thus "God's will—karma" has nothing to do with any pandeterminism. Rather our free will is an integral component in the game of how the Divine unfolds, and the decisive factor is the expression of the will that lies behind our activity. "God's will—karma" has nothing to do with fatalism. Once we realize how much "God's will" has to do with our will, we grasp the enormous responsibility that should shape our actions.

We should, of course, be aware of the motives behind all our activity. When we experience joy and love, we are realizing the fruit of our past actions. And the obverse is true as well: if we are greedy and full of aggression, that, too, is the fruit of previous acts. Undoubtedly, this is an oversimplified presentation of karma; in reality the connections are surely more complicated. But we can recognize from this how crucial positive and negative living is for us, how significant is our good will and ill will. Our life resembles a game of chess. One move leads to another, and none is without meaning for the game as a whole. The game follows its own immanent laws, but we can give direction to these laws with every move of our life. Thus we can also lend the right meaning to the uniqueness and singularity of our existence, in which the Divine expresses itself in this particular way and not another.

Once we realize this, we also know why people develop differently. Granted, there is nothing we can call ego. The ego is only the point of intersection of our psychic activities such as will, expectation, and feelings. They are held together by our memory, which feeds us with the delusion of a certain permanence. Our real activity, however, lies much deeper. But there is something like a "subtle bearer," which goes with us into the next existence.

This subtle bearer is comparable to a billiard ball struck by another. The first ball comes to a halt after making contact with the second, but it transfers something invisible to the ball it hits, which moves on, thanks to the force of the impact. The forces that are passed on are derived from whichever ball came before. In this way patterns and elements are transferred from one existence to the next. Thus a transformation of energy takes place. If we are full of good will, a basic tendency engraves itself in us that generates positive effects here and now and for later on.

To take yet another comparison from the physical world, consider bodybuilding. People who train their bodies acquire a distinct adroitness that continues to be at their disposal. Just as quite specific patterns emerge in the body, so, too, mental patterns imprint themselves and increase their intensity. And just as we can train our body, so we can train our spirit by repeating certain states of mind such as good will, love, and so on.

Thus an act we perform is not over when it stops. It has an aftereffect that strengthens a pattern in us. When we throw a stone into the water, we generate a ring of concentric circles whose waves keep spreading. The same is true of our positive acts. Hence "God's will—karma" is no blind fatalism. Hence, too, perseverance in this form of existence as a person (as opposed to any attempt at euthanasia) has its profound meaning: it is often precisely in times of sickness or in the face of death that a person is prepared for an inner transformation and can exert a positive influence on his or her next form of existence.

Every action, however insignificant, leaves behind impressions on our subtle body. Those who surrender to hatred strengthen the hatred. Those who let themselves be overwhelmed by greed strengthen the greed. At every moment we are shaping the fundamental pattern of our life. Our life is a dynamic process; at any moment we can help determine the direction of the stream of energy. The more consciously and wide-awake we live, the more we will make on-target decisions in every situation. Thus attentiveness plays a significant role in all esoteric paths.

At the end of our life, we will not find a judge who condemns us; rather in the light of ultimate reality we shall recognize the connections that shaped our lives. At the instant of the encounter with the Divine, we shall surely have new, profound realizations of great importance for our future. We can call them grace and forgiveness.

It is highly significant that Buddhism and Christianity advise us not to get hung up on guilt. Guilt feelings easily lead to the development of aversion toward oneself. For this reason belief in forgiveness and participation in rites of forgiveness, which can be found in all religions, have a profound effect. They free us from guilt feelings and lead us to new, positive acts that rescue us from negative attitudes. Hanging on to guilt and the refusal to accept ourselves are negative states of mind that produce a corresponding effect.

The grace of forgiveness consists in our being allowed to recognize the results of our actions. And reconciliation means accepting the consequences of past deeds as a new chance for better action. Given this recognition, people will live more responsibly because they sense that they reap what they sow, and that it is in their power to create better or worse preconditions for their own and other people's future. Thus what we label misfortune can become our greatest opportunity in the maturation process. Grace is the fact that the trouble we have brought upon ourselves can be put to use for our salvation rather than degenerating into punishment.

All we can do is take responsibility for our good and evil deeds and live more wisely. This will be followed by a great readiness to forgive and the recognition that in the final analysis all the wrong that we do to others we do to ourselves. It's like the theater: one act grows out of the previous one.

How Can We Take a Positive Stance Toward God's Will?

Sakyamuni Buddha talked about generosity. We Christians call it "love." Love contains a decisive positive force for our present and future existence and for the existence of all life. Goodness of the heart, as it is often called in Buddhism, awakens the experience of connectedness with all creatures. It guards us from negative acts and makes itself felt as a wonderfully helpful and healing influence on all creatures.

Still more important in Buddhism is the deep insight into the transitoriness of all phenomena. John of the Cross reports a similar insight when he leaves everything behind in his *nada, nada.* Such an experience brings with it nonattachment, and because we realize that our ego-consciousness is a dreamlike condition, we will do our utmost to wake up. This struggle creates a powerful force that leads to liberation and peace. Nonattachment or "letting go," as we usually say, is crucial for a way of life that is in harmony with the core of our being. If we look at Christian asceticism from this standpoint, a number of things make profound sense. Thus nonattachment is practiced because attachment generates a tendency to cling to things and fosters negative basic structures. The Christian expression "accepting God's will" has the same meaning.

Think of it this way: we are taking part in a play whose unfolding action we ourselves constantly influence. This play—God's play—is not determined in advance. It does follow certain ground rules, as all plays and games do. But just as within the framework of a game of chess in which we have the freedom to make a move with this or that piece, so, too, God plays his game by means of our free will. As insignificant as we may be, we act with and influence all the other "members of the cast."

WHAT ARE WE LOOKING FOR?

Rabbi Yehudi told the following story about himself:

> When I was thirteen, difficult passages [in the Torah] disclosed themselves to me in an instant, and when I was eighteen, I was considered a "great one in the Torah." But it dawned on me that a person can't come to fulfillment learning alone. I understood what is said of our father Abraham in the Midrashim, how he investigated the sun, moon, and stars and found God nowhere, and how the presence of God was revealed to him in this nonfinding. Then I explored so long until I too came to the truth of the non-finding.[2]

When a disciple asked the master about the path, the master answered, "If you seek it, you won't find it." The disciple protested: "How am I supposed to find the path if I'm not looking for it?" The master replied, "The path doesn't belong to knowing and not knowing."[3]

So what are we looking for if God himself seeks the path in us, if God wants to unfold in and through us? After all, God's seeking is the process of evolution that manifests itself in us as this seeking.

RETURN TO THE ONE

The essence of God is One. In what we call creation, the One split itself into an unlimited number of phenomenal forms that remain related to one another and yet are a quite individual expression of the Whole.

In the beginning is the One. It is the Holy, the Intact, the Undivided. But our becoming human initiated the primal tragedy of isolation. This is the primordial pain of humanity, a pain of separation that will not let up until the human race has found its way back into the One.

Throughout evolution, we have maintained a dim sense of the Whole that awakens longings in us—we experience homesickness only when we know we have a home. All pain is the pain of separation. All sin is basically nothing but being cut off from our deepest essence. It is the peculiar drive of our ego for autonomy and demarcation. Humans sense the deficit of separation more keenly than other creatures. And so the search for the part that completes us began with our becoming human. Every half needs the other if it is to experience itself as a whole.

THE DRIVING FORCE OF LOVE

Although the splitting up of the One did bring about separation, it also brought something absolutely new: the energy of love. With love there appears in creation a strong new field of energy: the metaphysical yearning for the One. This is the primal force of evolution. For the goal is not regression back into the One, but evolution, which leads forward to the One. In reality this is not a matter of going forward, but of experiencing that the unity is still there, as ever. The goal is not the eye of the hurricane, or eternal rest. The goal is to experience the hurricane of God, who is both eye and storm, rest and dynamism. The goal is the experience of the not-two, the experience of both sides of the coin as One.

Enlightenment is the lighting up of our true self. It pours through our whole being. It brings the moment in which we are granted a touch of that all-pervasive Ultimate Reality. And when we persist on an inner path, we will get at least a glimpse of our own true selves.

Once love has taken possession of us, there is no holding back the impulse for union. The longing to give ourselves away, to the point of sacrificing our life, is characteristic of this passionate love. In fact, it often inclines us toward actions that seem senseless. Only from this perspective can we understand the ascetical exaggerations of some saints. They had no interest in destroying themselves, but measured against love, everything else simply became worthless. This is the compulsion to break through the glass wall of separation and to free ourselves from the burden of individuality. Love shatters the loneliness and redeems us from the prison of egocentricity. It is the actual redeeming force in the universe.

Unfortunately, our ego tends to oppose the fundamental force of Oneness. Yet we get back to the One only through letting go, through laying down our lives, not through holding on and certainly not by conquest. Herein lies the tragedy of those individuals who think they can redeem themselves. The mystical path is not a path of self-redemption.

ETHICS FROM WITHIN

Love has the power to transform. At first the lover thinks the world has changed, but in fact it is the lover who has been transformed from within.

Almost all religious systems work predominantly with moral appeals. Good intentions still play an important role in religious education, but they often have no supportive power. Ethical behavior should not be something forced upon us from the outside or imposed on us from within out of fear of punishment. Fear and punishment are inappropriate means to evoke moral behavior. How sad that the fear of hell has been used as an instrument for raising children, and that the infantile belief in being rewarded or punished after this life leads at best to neuroses. Everything that causes anxiety in them, that gags them, that instills fear in them, flies in the face of a loving, compassionate Divine principle. Above and beyond that, fear of a vengeful God can lead to terrible religious trauma, as the following statements show:

> As a child I had the deepest experience of God. Later I was presented with a threatening monster.

> As a child I loved God, and I knew that I was loved. They took this God away from me. And the worst is, I was convinced that my father would go to hell because he didn't go to church on Sunday. Meanwhile he was love itself and much more honest than my mother. How can one possibly threaten a child that Daddy is going to hell because he didn't go to church on Sunday?

By contrast the ethics of mysticism grow not out of intentions and appeals to the will, but from within and out of deep experience of our own being. In traveling a spiritual path, we are transformed to the core of our personality. This brings with it a transformation of consciousness and a view of the world that transcends the narrow circle of ego-consciousness. In turn, the transformed personality gives rise to different purposes, value judgments, and modes of behavior. We embark upon a life of selflessness, wisdom, and compassion. An incontrovertible inner moral code comes into being, which may occasionally contradict the norms of society or our religious community. It is a code of love. *Ama et fac quod vis* (Love and then do what you want), says Augustine. There are things that those of us who love simply can't do. After all, the more deeply we press forward into our essence, the more we learn that our life is lived from that point outward. Or as one woman put it: "Up till now I thought that I was living. But in reality I am lived by something." Here one thinks of Paul's saying, "It is not I who live, but Christ in me" (Galatians 2:20).

As human beings, our deepest essence contains a power that counteracts and compensates for our egotistical tendencies—if we can learn to trust ourselves to it. If we have truly been transformed, many negative forces that might otherwise block our path will no longer arise. The tension between subject and object, between I and Thou, will be more or less canceled. If this experience pervades the deepest roots of our being, all activities simply can't be taken over by the ego. We will then be led out of our particular individualistic conscious interest into a larger community and finally into the cosmos. During this maturation process, we will develop into individuals whose moral activity is the expression of our inmost essence.

Thus morality is not the cause of a mental attitude where action and conviction agree; rather, it is the effect. In esotericism, this is called *wisdom*, the harmony between God's will and ours.

Hence ethics, rightly understood, is not about fighting certain bad qualities, but about restoring equilibrium. Giovinda uses the image of scales to describe this. When the empty set of scales is out of balance, one doesn't correct this by putting weights in the lighter scale, but by shifting the beam. In the same way, disharmony in the human soul has to be removed by shifting the center of gravity from the I to the not-I.[4]

In the religions of the East, another motive for ethical action plays an important role: there, being human is considered a privileged form of existence. It is valued more highly than that of a heavenly being because in human existence, processes of purification can occur that are impossible in other forms. In addition, enlightenment always brings a profound gratitude for having a body in which the Ultimate Reality can express itself. Those really striving for deep enlightenment, that is, trying to find the meaning of life, will eliminate many factors that impede their path, delay a breakthrough, or make it quite impossible. All those who sense within themselves this urgent love, which is ultimately the mating call of the Divine, have a strong motivation for their action.

Nevertheless the strongest ethical motive in mysticism is the experience of oneness: the fact that we are one with all creatures and that in the final analysis what we do to others we also do to ourselves.

Rabbi Yechiel once asked his father-in-law, "How do they understand 'Thou shalt not steal' around here?" "Well," his father-in-law answered, "One shouldn't rob one's fellows." "There's no longer any need to give us that command," said the rabbi. "Back in Kozk the reading is, 'One shouldn't rob oneself.'"[5]

Like all religions, mysticism is naturally familiar with commandments, for example, to strive in thought, word, and deed not to harm living things; not to take what hasn't been given to us; to live holy lives; not to speak lies and coarse words; not to intoxicate ourselves or cloud our consciousness, and so forth.[6] All these commandments have their actual basis in the experience of unity with all creatures. Loving persons experience for themselves that they cause suffering to others when they don't keep these commandments.

In Buddhism, too, love comes first, even though some Western critics deny this. Dogen Zenji writes in his *Shobogenzo*: "Whatever salutary means there may be in this life for achieving a good rebirth and for making spiritual gain, O monks, all of them together are not worth one-sixteenth of love, of emancipation of heart and mind. Love, emancipation of heart and mind, absorbs them all and shines and glows and beams." And of Sakyamuni Buddha we are told: "This too the sublime one said: Whoever fully consciously awakens boundless love in himself,...for him the chains will become thin."[7]

The following words, ringing with deep wisdom, are ascribed to Laotse:

> Duty without love makes one morose.
> Responsibility without love makes one callous.
> Righteousness without love makes one hard.
> Truth without love makes one hypercritical.
> Upbringing without love makes one inconsistent.
> Cleverness without love makes one cunning.
> Friendliness without love makes one deceitful.
> Order without love makes one petty.
> Expertise without love makes one a know-it-all.
> Power without love makes one violent.
> Honor without love makes one arrogant.
> Property without love makes one stingy.
> Faith without love makes one fanatical.

"If the love for God and the love of the world are mutually exclusive, then, on the very premises of theology, God is a finite thing among other things—for only finite things exclude one another. God is dethroned and un-godded by being put in opposition to nature and the world, becoming an object instead of a continuum in which we 'live and move and have our being.'"[8]

GOD IS LOVE: THE ETHICS OF CHRISTIANITY

In Christianity love plays a still more decisive role. Paul writes:

> If I speak in the tongues of mortals and of angels, but do not have love, I am a noisy gong or a clanging cymbal. And if I have prophetic powers, and understand all mysteries and all knowledge,

and if I have all faith, so as to remove mountains, but do not have love, I am nothing. If I give away all my possessions, and if I hand over my body so that I may boast, but do not have love, I gain nothing.

Love is patient; love is kind; love is not envious or boastful or arrogant or rude. It does not insist on its own way; it is not irritable or resentful; it does not rejoice in wrongdoing, but rejoices in the truth. It bears all things, believes all things, hopes all things, endures all things.

Love never ends (1 Corinthians 13:1-8).

Everyone who loves is born of God and knows God (1 John 4:7).

Whoever does not love does not know God, for God is love (1 John 4:8).

God is love, and those who abide in love abide in God, and God abides in them (1 John 4:16).

Obviously, Scripture doesn't say that "God loves," but that "God is love."

I would like to add a few of my own thoughts here, though I am fully aware that these texts cited above cannot be surpassed.

Love is the law of the universe. In his book *The Mind of Matter,* Charon says that something like love prevails even in the subatomic realm. Electrons can receive and give. And the higher forms of life emerge in taking in and giving out, that is, in communication. Those who cannot love, cannot open themselves and cannot enter into exchange with others. They cannot grow. Love is the prerequisite for growing and maturing.

Psychotherapy tells us that a lack of love and tenderness is the chief sickness of our age. We are perfectly aware of the fact—confirmed by psychosomatic clinics—that those of us who can't love can't become full persons. Love makes human beings of us.

We are responsible for the "signals" we give off—and we are always sending out something: goodwill, aversion, hate, sympathy. Love does not begin with words and embraces; it begins in our thoughts and feelings, even in the thoughts that we have about ourselves. Self-destructive thoughts destroy. Love should be the identifying sign of Christians. "See how they love one another"—so said the bystanders about the first Christians.

Love heals. Love obviously heals more than all other remedies and is in fact the best medicine. This applies beyond the metaphorical sense because sickness is very often a symptom for a lack of loving care.

Unlived love makes us sick. Love must be used up, expressed. Otherwise it becomes pent-up and eventually turns into self-hatred. It degenerates into narcissism. Narcissus, the legendary Greek figure, was so in love with himself that he kept staring into the water to see his own likeness. Because Narcissus was incapable of entering a relationship with another person, he came to grief from his pent-up love.

Only love counts. What we have in our hands at the end of our life will not be our achievements and our work. We won't be asked whether we were Catholic or Protestant or whatever. Reports of near-death experiences tell us that we shall have to face the question of how much we loved.

CHAPTER 11

DEATH OR TRANSFORMATION?

O ur existence is an incredible bustle and brouhaha, and in the course of time, it develops its own set of laws. With time, we can no longer stop; the bustle prevents us from living.

On an esoteric path a good number of people get to the bottom of this empty busyness; to some it gets quite boring; to others it all becomes ridiculous. These are important moments—moments that bring us close to life. They make us ask, "Why are we actually on this earth?"

"THE COUNTLESS WORLDS OF THE UNIVERSE ARE LIKE BUBBLES IN THE OCEAN" (SHODOKA)

Nothing is constant; nothing lasts. Yet we have a hard time coming to terms with this truth. Sooner or later, however, everything dwindles away. When we enter upon an esoteric path, we suddenly sense the transitoriness of everything and in a flash we realize how much we cling to things, chase after ideas, and are plagued by fears. We recognize the blinders that we wear as we go through life.

Life invites us to use things appropriately, to enjoy them, but also to let them go. Transitoriness is just another word for evolution and hence for the perfection of creation. We are not perfect creatures until we experience happiness in the transitoriness of life. For the uninitiated, that sounds masochistic, but it's the truth. I am convinced that we will develop as human beings to the extent that death no longer terrifies us, to

201

the extent that we rejoice at our next existence, to the extent that we can recognize and greet death as the great transformer.

Although we have this fact of transformation constantly before our eyes, we don't want to accept it. Trees blossom and leaves fall; seasons come and go; life blooms from garbage. Without death and destruction there is no new life. Continuous change is the real miracle of life. Being born, living, and dying are the fulfillment of life. Heaven is not a static existence at some point in the distant future. Rather, heaven is to experience for ourselves and accept the perfection of being born and dying as life itself.

Yet our ego resists this with every possible device. The shock of our first gray hair is compensated with dye. After we turn forty, our birthdays become increasingly painful. Eventually, death is the winner in this struggle until one day we can say, "Our brother, death." Then death becomes a symbol for new life.

It may sound strange, but we are objecting to life and life's perfection when we bracket death out of our consciousness, because dying belongs to the perfection of life. We Westerners call God the principle of life. But this ultimate principle reveals itself as life-death-resurrection. That is the message Jesus brought us. That is the message of every religion. Those who object to death object to the resurrection and ultimately to God. They refuse to follow the cosmic law, refuse to accept the truth that lies outspread before their eyes: transformation.

We humans are entangled in a never-ending struggle against everything that doesn't endure. And because this is a hopeless struggle we are full of anxieties. We look for security in other people and in our investments. We look for security in our jobs and plunge into hectic activity thinking we have to leave behind something great when we die. That gives us a feeling of permanence. Perhaps we are also looking for security in a false piety. We believe there must be a God who in the end will guarantee our little ego permanence and eternity in heaven. This ego—as laughable as we sometimes find it—would like to live forever.

Naturally we can't expect the ego to give up its dominance joyfully. But that would be exactly what the order of creation demands of us and what we strive for on every esoteric path: "Die and become! Die on your prayer cushion!" To the extent that our little ego dies—this anxious, desperate, aggressive, opportunistic, manipulative, and all too seldom cheerful conglomerate of psychic processes—trust, true joy, and confidence will unfold. But evidently we have no interest in the evolution of the "Divine principle," in the development of the universe, in the great variety of possibilities. We're interested only in "I" and "mine."

Our exercises should lead us to the realization that all clinging—even to beloved religious ideas and wishes for a specific form of enlighten-ment—runs contrary to our readiness for transformation. Our ego is constantly colliding with what really is.

COORDINATE SYSTEM

We live in something like a "horizontal-vertical" coordinate system, and we can't neglect either of the two coordinates with impunity. Both levels attract each other, so to speak, creating a critical test within us. As a manifestation of the Divine, we have to express this divine principle in our physical-psychic-mental humanness. Hence we're not allowed to lose ourselves either in matter or in pure mind. Mind must increasingly permeate matter, so there can be a harmonization of the two extremes. This is a balancing act that we have to pull off; neither despising nor denying the world is the solution.

THE MEANING OF RESISTANCE

Resistance is necessary for growth. One element in the exercises of the esoteric school is the resistance that the ego offers. Our ego is so constructed that it has to resist. It has to draw us to the material coordi-nate. Without this tendency to cling, to create and achieve, there would be no culture, which would block an important element in evolution. Our ego is the necessary form in which the divine evolution reveals it-self. When the divine One enters multiplicity, this polarity necessarily arises. Thus it doesn't fall under the category of good or evil, true or false. It simply is what it is: an inevitable consequence of the emergence of the Divine into the creaturely domain.

Ultimately, we transform ourselves through these resistances. If there weren't this tendency to create culture, to know joy, to possess earth, we wouldn't be human. Our ego makes us human. It is a perfect expressive form of the Divine Reality. We are geomorphic and theomorphic, that is, we are One. To experience this Oneness is our task in life. And so we don't go forth from this human existence casually because here and now our life is consummated as a divine life in joy and suffering.

Only truly enlightened persons stop resisting. They live because they live, just as the flower blooms because it blooms. They come and go like a flower. But I doubt that there is one person anywhere who reaches this goal completely. In this life we will never come to an end of our path. But no matter; it is the declaration of our goal that counts.

"FOLLOW THE COURSE OF THE WATER"

A monk had gotten lost in the forest. When he came to the hut of a hermit and asked about the way back to his monastery, the hermit advised him, "Follow the course of the water!" Because the monastery lay downriver, the monk followed the course of the mountain stream and arrived safely at his destination. When he told his master about the adventure, the master immediately recognized the wise mountain monk.

"Follow the course of the water!" That means much more than directions for getting back to the monastery; it is advice for life. "Follow the course of the water!" Accept—in summer the heat, the fall the full moon, in winter the snow, and in spring the blossoms!

Some of you are familiar with tarot cards. When players draw card 13, "Death," they take fright. But this card has nothing to do with our own dying or the death of someone related to us. Death harbors the primal knowledge of the order of creation. The card doesn't come at the end, but in the middle of the Arcana. It is the card of transformation. No maturation process can bypass death. Dying means a new beginning. In Christianity we always put death at the end, although Jesus Christ has clearly pointed the way to a new beginning through the Resurrection. When we draw tarot card 13, we come face to face with the invitation to begin learning to die here and now—so as to live here and now. Dying means taking leave of beloved ideas, convictions, and world-views. Only those who can accept dying will be transformed; those who aren't ready for it aren't ready for an esoteric path. Although the path is often difficult, I see this as something positive. If we stay the course, transformation will occur.

All this is easy to say. But when we learn that we have only three months to live, when we are permanently disabled because of a traffic accident, when we lose a child, when we experience the demise of a relationship, it's a lot harder. If we are honest, none of us can say yes with a full heart in all situations. And that's not required. We only have to accept. The actual process of purification and transformation lies in accepting what we cannot change. We may scream and cry and quarrel like Job, but it remains true that singing and dancing are the voice of Dharma. We don't have to rejoice in the suffering, but when there is no longer any separation between ourselves and the momentary situation, we are enlightened.

Of course, we have focused on difficult situations. We could consider some positive or exciting circumstances: you have won a million dollars. With a million dollars in hand, life goes on a lot easier than with a serious illness. The point is to live in the circumstances that life brings. Of course we may try to better the situation. If we're sick, we should do what we can to get healthy. But when things happen to us that we can't change, we can accept them.

Accepting is generally accompanied by hard struggles, at least at first. The ideal, the state of enlightenment, is actually free of struggle and full of the realization that the Divine is unfolding within us, that it is God in us who sees the situation through.

Ultimately, this is nothing different from what we as Christians constantly repeat in the Our Father when we say, "Thy will be done." That is the touchstone of our exercises, the measurable degree of our progress on the spiritual path.

CHAPTER 12

MYSTICISM:
FLIGHT FROM THE WORLD
OR TAKING RESPONSIBILITY FOR IT?

Evolution provides us with several kinds of perception that enable us to manage in the biosphere of our planet and, to a certain extent, to assert ourselves. Although direct access to the essence of Being has been denied us, we didn't need it in the childhood years of the human race. For the human being of that time, it was enough that we feared, felt pain, could run, see, and make ourselves understood in the right way at the right moment. Nothing else had any immediate importance for our survival, so we didn't develop it.

The time when we can be content with such arrangements is past, however. We can no longer afford the luxury of excluding the domain of the Numinous from our humanness. But we are also no longer capable of adopting the religious self-understanding of our ancestors, which is why the esoteric approach in religion seems to be the only one with a future.

We have become human beings so that we might mature and develop our potential. All the miseries and problems, all the difficulties and joys, are designed to help us find the way to our real essence. That is the main task of life; that is life's goal. From this perspective, of course, we have an entirely different orientation in life as compared with the so-called "normal person." I wonder, though, whether mystics aren't the norm, rather than those who block themselves off from the Numinous and thus prevent the full unfolding of their humanity.

We have to experience the dimension from which all things come, and for many thousands of years, we have called this dimension "God." We are bound up with it as if by an umbilical cord. From it we draw life, but we can also press forward toward it, through the umbilical cord, to experience our primal foundation.

Konrad Lorenz is credited with saying that man is the missing link between the animals and the real human beings. We are only halfway to the point where the real *Homo sapiens* lives. Until now our species has been more like a helpless marionette, its strings being pulled by strangers while it waits to be transformed into a complete person. Without this transformation, all rational knowledge and scientific inventions serve our downfall instead of our welfare.

But why do we recognize our actual goal in life so late or not at all?

The path that leads to a real transformation of personality goes through the wilderness, through loneliness, frustration, despair, and the death of the ego. For most of us, this is a dramatic process, and we duck the pain as long as we can. If it comes at all, the insight comes only after a shock, after profound suffering, after something we call misfortune. For many of us, however, these evident pains and tragedies spell salvation.

Some people think they have been condemned to a painfully short span of life on this earth. They don't realize that they have been given a chance to grow and mature—even if this process of becoming whole is bound up with suffering. The path doesn't lead back to paradise, to the Uroboros, but through ego-development, by way of abandoning the ego, to full humanness.

BACK TO THE UROBOROS...OR FORWARD TO THE PLEROMA?

It was always a danger of esotericism that a person might not want to take this "heroic path" of individuation (Ernst Neumann), that he or she might want to flee this world and this body. The state of egolessness is a temptation that not everyone can resist.

The pleroma, the fullness of being human, lies before us. And whether we like it or not, humanity as a whole has to take the path into the age of adulthood. In fairy tales, puberty is often symbolized by the hero's battle with the dragon. In the struggle to become whole, the ego succeeds in overcoming the all-devouring side of the unconscious, the Uroboros mother. Ego-development has driven us out of this childhood paradise of symbiosis, and now the cherubim stand guarding its gates with a flaming sword. No one can go back to this paradise on the path of growing up. Such a return would amount to "Uroboristic incest" (Ernst Neumann). The challenge that everyone faces on the way to adulthood from childhood is what humanity as a whole must overcome on its way to full humanness.

PSEUDOMYSTICISM: THE MYSTICISM OF REFUSAL

, There is an uroboristic pseudomysticism. It is anticosmic and denies—indeed condemns—the world. True mysticism, however, affirms not only the world and human beings but the ego and the historical process in time as well. Mysticism doesn't aim at the beyond or heaven. Rather, it understands that fulfillment lies in the here and now, recognizing that it is just hidden. The beatific vision is the experience of being born and dying as the consummation of the life of God.

The creative element is active and fertile, and hence in its deepest essence, world-affirming. In the mystic, the creative power of God is released. God "reveals himself truly and perfectly and exactly as he is, and thus he fills human beings to overflowing, so much so that they pour out and stream forth from the overflowing fullness of God."[1]

These fundamental realities are the source of our responsibility for the world.

ESOTERICISM'S RESPONSIBILITY FOR OUR EARTH

Harada Dai-un Sogaku Roshi, the father of the Zen school I belong to, reports the following encounter with his Dharma-brother Kato Chodo: "One morning he discovered a chopstick in the trash. He showed me the chopstick and asked me, 'What is that?' I answered, 'A chopstick.' 'Yes, it is a chopstick. Is it unusable?' 'No,' I said, 'it can still be used.' 'Fine,' he cut me off, 'but I found it in the trash along with other worthless stuff. You have taken this chopstick's life. Perhaps you know the proverb: Whoever kills another digs two graves. You have murdered this chopstick, it will murder you.'" Harada Dai-un was seven years old at the time. "From then on," he said, "I was very careful in dealing with all things."

"You have murdered this chopstick. It will murder you." Today we know the truth of this saying much better than that Zen monk did a hundred years ago.

The students at Sophia University in Tokyo once collected into a pile one day's worth of disposable chopsticks. That simple exercise made it clear to everyone that every day in Japan a giant mountain of discarded chopsticks accumulates. To get chopsticks, Japan cuts down the rain forests of Borneo and Southeast Asia. For other "needs," we cut down the rain forests of the Amazon—and enlarge the hole in the ozone layer, even though we know that we're radically altering the climate, that the decertification of Africa is proceeding at a thunderous pace, and so on.

In the esoteric school we believe that everything is an expressive form of the Divine. It's an illusion—a fatal illusion—to think that we experience ourselves separately from everything else. What we do to others we do to ourselves. Whoever murders another is digging two graves.

The mystical path leads back into the world. We don't climb a mountain to stay on top, but to climb back down again. There is an ineradicable bias against mysticism which maintains that it flees, denies, and despises the world—and such a form of mysticism may in fact exist. In fact, the fear of generating negative karma drives some people into a "cave in the Himalayas," into retreat from the world. But that strikes me as a kind of confusion that isn't headed toward full human development.

ORIGINAL SIN OR INDIVIDUATION?

What we commonly call original sin isn't sin at all. It is rather a necessary step in the development of humanity, the step man had to take to leave the paradisiacal state of symbiosis behind. "The basic psychological fact that the ego has become cut off from the true self (and the whole of the psyche) and hence autonomous is projected theologically onto the myth of the Fall of man from God and of the Fall of the world from its primal state."[2]

In reality the evil human ego doesn't fall away from the divine self, but vice versa: God withdraws, as it were, so that we can grow up. Growing up is a painful process, and mysticism knows all about it. It is part of the path of transformation to suffer this tension on the cross.

Hence the unfolding of the mystic's personality, as already mentioned, is not a regressive process of dissolving the ego. The mystical path is always prepared for by strengthening the ego. The ego unfolds along the way. At the end lies not the dissolution of the ego, but a changed consciousness whose center is no longer the ego but the self the ego revolves around.[3]

Because false mysticism cannot accept the abyss of the Numinous, it declares the world fallen, guilty, sunken, seduced, disappointed, and corrupt. It won't acknowledge the fact that life and creation must take place in polarity and tension, and the devil, evil, guilt, sin, and death are all part of that. Ultimately, false mysticism takes creation to be a mistake by God or the work of a second-class demiurge.

The following statements describe the foundation on which true mysticism builds:

> There is an interpretation by the Baal Shem Tov, the founder of the Hassidic movement, of the phrase from Genesis 6:9, "Noah walked with God." At the end of it he says, "So that when the Father went away from him, Noah knew, 'It is so I can learn to walk.'"[4] God had, so to speak, to leave human beings alone so they could walk on their own two feet.

> A Sufi text has God saying, "I was a hidden treasure and wanted to be recognized, therefore I made the world." We have to recognize God in this world. Our human development is the path to this.

> A Jewish saying holds that "God and the world are like twins."[5]

> Eckhart thinks that the world is as old as God: "At one and the same time when God was, when he begot his coeternal Son as God equal to himself in all things, he also created the world."[6] "Also it can be granted that the world has existed from eternity.[7] God and the world belong together. They are only two aspects of the one Reality.

The world is the revelation of the Divine Principle. God can be experienced only through form. That is why every genuine mystic returns to the world. The mystic has a mission there.

Christian, Buddhist, and other redogmatizations paint some mystical experiences as hostile to the world. But authentic mysticism is humanitarian. A Hassidic saying puts it this way: "One man buys himself a fur coat in winter, another buys firewood. And what is the difference between them? The first only wants to warm himself, the second warms others as well." True mysticism understands itself as a path of redemption. The "mystical love-death that does not lead to resurrection is a failure."[8]

THE TRANSFORMATION OF THE WORLD BEGINS WITH US

Fundamental transformation of the world will never be achieved by a new social system, but only by means of the transformation of the individual. We are always crying for the great surgeon to come perform the crucial operation. But those who really want to change the world will not rely on specialists. Only those who leave behind the routines of society—overcoming greed, the mania for possessions, and the hunger for power—will ever change anything.

We wait for the great redeemer in religion as well. Someone will do the job, and we need only hang on to that person's coattails. But true religious leaders should not redeem. Rather, they have to call for conversion, for metanoia, for turning inward to the essential, to our divine nature. But people have preferred raising the founders of religion to the altars and honoring them there rather than carrying out in their own lives the metanoia exemplied by the founders. The path of transformation is long and difficult. It leads us by way of confrontation with our shadow and with the devil.

THE DEVIL, OUR TWIN BROTHER

At the beginning of the Christian religion stands the duality of God and creation, light and darkness, Michael and Lucifer, tempter and tempted. Along with belief in God, we have been given belief in the devil. With this belief we have shifted onto others blame for many a tragedy in world history, instead of looking for the reasons in ourselves and taking responsibility for them. We use the devil to explain the presence of evil in this world. We personalize evil and view it as the countervailing force to the Divine, separated from God. Thus the devil is a figure of projection, blamed for everything bad, standing for our personal and collective shadow.

We have to harmonize in ourselves this duality, which obviously belongs to the order of creation. Otherwise we will remain exposed to the negative forces of this struggle. Inquisitor and accused, judge and executioner, friend and foe, superior and subject: both are found in us. We have to bring them into unison.

Although the hypothesis of the devil must not be maintained, what the devil stands for need not—should not—disappear. We need something that keeps alive our sensitivity to evil. We simply need more up-to-date metaphors for the power of evil that is relevant to every one of us. We need a new language for evil. What Christian tradition calls "demons" are forces that we must not personify. The real evil in our world has different names: religious and political misuse of power, suppression of the weak through exploitative economic systems, destruction of the environment, genetic manipulation, the racial and cultural uprooting of millions by expulsion and flight, hatred of one's neighbor, and fixation on material things.

The devil didn't drop the first atomic bomb; the devil didn't annihilate the Jews under Hitler's and Stalin's opponents in the Soviet Union; the devil didn't terrorized the people of Southeast Asia in World War I; the devil didn't send the Crusaders off on their journey; the devil didn't light the stake for burning the victims of the Inquisition and the persecution of witches; the devil isn't destroying our habitat. It's not the devil's fault that we don't get along with our neighbors. Rather, the evil within us is at work—evil that we have to acknowledge. Once we acknowledge this evil within, we will realize our share in crimes and injustices that are committed everywhere and anywhere in the world.

As individuals we experience ever more forcefully that we are bound up in everything, in good and evil. The devil is the symbol for evil, and thus our twin brother. He is built into our personality and belongs to the structural principle of creation. If we can make our shadow's energies fruitful for the good, we will win him as a helper, who actually does good although he apparently wants evil.

Closely connected with the devil is fear of hell, a fear that comes from an archaic image of God. The God who can impose eternal damnation still haunts people's minds. But the Ultimate Reality can't be explained with a dualistic model of thought. Mystical experience is always an experience of oneness, *unio mystica*, wholeness, the not-two. That, too, is a part of what people call evil.

MYSTICISM: HARMONIZING OR REVOLUTIONARY?

Mysticism with confessional ties is admittedly the best known, but not necessarily the most significant. Mystics who did not subscribe to any religion could express themselves much more freely. Those who were bound to one confession or other came (and still come today) into conflict with the dogmatic fixation of whatever religion or morality they profess. "The authentic basic experience of the Numinous can not avoid being anticonventional, anticollective, and antidogmatic because it is a new experience of the numinous."[9] Mysticism is therefore always revolutionary and is perceived by the institution as disturbing, if not heretical. That often leads mystics into confrontations with the institutionalized religions. Many of them, above all in the theistic religions, were—and are—persecuted, condemned, even executed.

Every mysticism that expresses itself within the framework of the conventional creed is either wishy-washy or camouflaged. It takes refuge in nonreligious terminology or disguises the real meaning of its language. Thus Christian mystics have always adapted their statements to dogmatic theology or camouflaged them so that they were recognizable only to initiates. John of the Cross, for example, who was repeatedly charged before the Inquisition, expressed his experience in poems, above all in love poems. When he expounded these poems, however, he fell afoul of the institution. At the same time, the mystics' confrontations with their religions also promote renewal within the religion.

HUMANS HAVE A FUTURE

Humanity is increasingly experiencing itself as a whole, that is, as a collective personality. This collective personality is based on energies that have not yet been recognized. As human beings we are in a pubertal phase. At this moment we don't know clearly who we are. But the development of this human personality keeps moving ever more speedily forward. At least we realize that friend-foe thinking, nationalism, religious fanaticism, and violence threaten us all and not just within the *cordon sanitaire* where these diseases are especially raging.

214

We can scarcely imagine what the future of the human race will look like. Fortunately, it is announcing itself in a new sensitivity to spiritual values. We are discovering that the universe is mind, and that all physical things are only a condensation of this mind.

What's more, humans are on the way to becoming human. Even if the messengers of disaster on the nightly news don't let up, neither will the Divine Principle let itself be blocked in its unfolding. The world is *not* the failed effort of a second-rate demiurge. It is the work of God who has assured us that everything he made is good. Humanity has a future because it is a future of God.

PART II

TALKS

The holy scriptures of all religions have been written for all men and women, regardless of their level of knowledge. Hence our own Christian Scripture can be read in very different ways. The following talks are primarily concerned with the esoteric interpretation. [The point of departure for some of these talks is the interpretation of the Gospel of Mark by Eugen Drewermann (Olten, 1979).]

"I WILL WRITE MY OWN NAME ON THEM"
Revelation to John 2:17, 3:12

"To everyone who conquers I will give some of the hidden manna, and I will give a white stone, and on the white stone is written a new name that no one knows except the one who receives it" (Revelation 2:17).

"If you conquer, I will make you a pillar in the temple of my God; you will never go out of it. I will write on you the name of my God, and the name of the city of my God...and my own new name" (Revelation 3:12).

A name always means individuality. We are a unique shape of the Divine. We are the self-revelation of God in this quite individual form and are meant by God to be the way we are. Thus the point is to accept ourselves as we are.

"I will write on you...my own new name" (Revelation 3:12). We have a task to perform in this world that is wholly our own. We are the "new name" of our God. In us he goes through this age.

We must have the courage to see this through and not be constantly wishing for a different place, a presumably better situation, more pleasant circumstances.

Our stay here on this earth is only one act of our life. In our current state of consciousness we obviously can't fully recognize where the special importance of that act lies. In any event, the explanation is not to be found in the realm of the ego. We have to press through to our true essence, to the place where we can experience oneness with God. There and only there will our life make sense.

MOSES AND THE GLORY OF THE LORD
Exodus 33:18-23

"Moses said, 'Show me your glory, I pray.' And he said, 'I will make all my goodness pass before you, and will proclaim before you the name....But,' he said, 'you cannot see my face; for no one shall see me and live....See, there is a place by me where you shall stand on the rock; and while my glory passes by I will put you in a cleft of the rock, and I will cover you with my hand until I have passed by; then I will take away my hand, and you shall see my back; but my face shall not be seen'" (Exodus 33:18-23).

God wants to show Moses all his splendor and sovereignty. But to see that, Moses has to enter the dark cleft in the rock while God lays his hand on him, as if pushing him in. We can't grasp the nearness of God with our senses and reason. Only when all representation falls silent can God reveal himself as he is.

God is closest in the very spot where Moses must have the feeling that everything is dark, narrow, oppressive, and empty. Only afterward, when God has passed by, does Moses realize that God was closest to him when everything seemed narrow, dark, and hopeless.

It's the same way in our life. The Divine is always closest to us when we feel desperate and abandoned. It appears as if the transformation process has its own regular patterns, and what we call depression is often the presence of God.

The transformation process is evidently a painful one. It can be understood and endured only if we are able to see it, not as sickness and suffering but as a process of transformation. Suffering is greatly valued in the esoteric school and with good reason. It is the medicine that transforms us and leads us to fulfillment. Those who can see the depths of their own being in this way are lucky indeed.

Lucky, too, are the people who can take their death as God's last affliction, which lets us see his glory when he has passed by. We are afraid of the grave, which allows no way out in any direction and from which there is only one liberation—leaving the body behind. But how otherwise should we rise up out of the grave?

THE CALLING
Mark 1:14-20

There are human goals and enterprises for which it is worthwhile to drop everything. Our career and our position in society constitute one side of life—and finding what we can really live on constitutes the other side. How do we find meaning in life? How do we find our real destiny?

As a rule we are too cowardly to follow our inner calling. We keep finding excuses and allowing others to reinforce our sense to stay where we are. There are far fewer independent men and women than we think. Life is much more comfortable in the herd.

We can't imagine how drastic the situation was when Jesus called his disciples. It took place in a society that did not yet know the possibility of plunging anonymously into the metropolis when one wanted to make a fresh start.

There must have been an incredible fascination emanating from this Jesus. But it wouldn't have worked if there hadn't also been a strong resonance in the disciples, moving them to "bail out." Calling often has to do with bailing out.

Being called can also mean leaving one's family: "And they left their father Zebedee in the boat with the hired men" (Mark 1:20). When young people do this sort of thing nowadays they're lectured for being irresponsible. For most people the insight that leaving one's parents can be necessary is even harder than leaving the external security of a career.

Today, too, an inner departure from the family can be important if a husband or wife takes to an esoteric path, while the other partner refuses to respect the freedom needed for this. Alienation isn't limited to the secular world.

Departing from patterns of childhood and their obsessions is still harder. We are reminded of the traditions, rules, and norms that are supposedly not just dangerous but irresponsible to transgress. But if we want to enter the kingdom of God, says Jesus, we must leave father and mother. As Christians, we have a great deal to learn on this point because we're continually made to feel guilty for walking away from "sacred order"—regardless of how hostile to life it may have become.

As Christians, we are called to freedom, and the gospel should encourage us when the time comes to "walk away" and follow a whole new career.

I am thinking here quite concretely of women whose children are out of the house and who at age forty-five ask themselves, *What now?* I am thinking of men who could retire between fifty and sixty to do something for which they feel a calling and a responsibility. I'm thinking of young people who after their first vocational or professional training realize that they've made a wrong choice and have to begin all over again. And I'm thinking of all those who have set out on a spiritual path, although the people around them reacted by shaking their heads. "And immediately they left their nets and followed him."

The Cornerstone
Mark 12:10

"The stone that the builders rejected / has become the cornerstone" (Mark 12:10).

The depths of religion are expressed in myth, symbol, and parable. These images are anchored deeply in what we call archetypes. Stone or rock is a powerful archetype. It means safety against the surging waters of life. There are many passages in Scripture referring to this.

I would like to interiorize the image. Stone is a symbol for Christ, a symbol for the divine essence in each one of us. He is the only stone on which we can build. Everything else crumbles away.

If we don't have this divine life as our center, we are impeding our maturation process as human beings. God is not a punisher. We are the ones who let the opportunity to build our human house be taken away from us. Those who don't build on the cornerstone of divine life are building on sand. Their life foundation won't bear the weight. God isn't doing anything to them; God isn't executing a sentence. Rather, these people are missing out on a chance. They have chosen a bad site for the house of their life.

We need such symbols and archetypes. Joseph Campbell, the great scholar of mythology, once asked his youngest son, "Why did you go see *Star Wars* twelve times?" The boy answered: "For the same reason you're always reading the Old Testament."

Deep realizations are often nothing more than the return of split-off parts of our consciousness. That doesn't lower the value of such an experience, however; rather, it shows us that the Divine isn't far from us, that it reveals itself to us in images and signs that are built into us at a profound level.

Thus images and realizations that suddenly come to us can be strong motivations for our life. But we shouldn't cling to them. We should dive through them without losing track of their message.

Images from other religions can surface as well. Hence we shouldn't be frightened. I once experienced the downfall and genesis of the cosmos in the dancing Kali, that is, I experienced God, the Ultimate Reality, as emerging and passing away.

The point is, we know that God is not a stone and not a rock; he is not a shepherd and not a king; he is not a father and not a son. If we get hung up on images, we persist in an archaic form of religion. God is what lies behind these images. God is the reality that manifests itself to our ego-consciousness.

In the course of my contemplative path many such images have had an enormous impact on me; they have transformed my life. But I have always known that they were just images behind which lay the Real, which is what they aim to impart to me.

THE IMMACULATE ONE

Today on the Feast of the Immaculate Conception of Mary we celebrate the mystery of the Eternal Feminine: devotion. It seems to me that there is only one kind of prayer befitting a human being: devotion to God, the Ultimate Reality. In this feast we celebrate our fundamental attitude of self-surrender in the presence of God. We celebrate the human race in its pure createdness.

In us, too, there is a place where guilt can't reach, a place where God alone dwells. Here there is no guilt. Here we have done nothing wrong. Here is the "undesecrated countenance" of humanity, as Gertrud von Le Fort says. Here is the "face from before birth," as Zen says. Neither the wickedness of the world nor our own guilt comes here.

But we get to this place only through our own *fiat*, through letting events happen, through receiving and accepting.

In Zen and in Christian contemplation we call this "letting go." We are searching for our feminine dispositions and capacities. Vis-à-vis God we have nothing, but absolutely nothing, to put on the table. Vis-à-vis God, unconditional devotion and receptivity is the only proper stance. But these are the actual feminine elements in us. And only by means of this feminine stance—regardless of what gender we are—can we experience the Divine.

It is the gift of the cosmos for selfless devotion that we celebrate in the form of woman and that we are made aware of in the figure of Mary. Creation itself is feminine. It exists only thanks to the power of God. Our human existence is just the same. Our essence is self-giving, regardless of whether we are man or woman.

We have to be the "virgin" who conceives, that is, we have to be receptive. Only then can we give birth to God. Whether Mary was biologically a virgin makes no difference whatsoever. The myth of virginity proclaims a spiritual truth. Mary sacrificed her ego in the *fiat*. She foreswore any notion of being in charge. "Let it be to me according to your word." Abandoning our ego is what we practice on our mystical path. Mary presents herself to us as pure receptiveness. She can conceive and give birth to God. The "birth of God" can take place in her. Herein, too, lies our role as coredeemers, not in masculine action, but in conceiving and bearing, in bearing the works of God, as Eckhart says.

This feast lets us celebrate an optimistic image of humanity. That feels good amid all the prophecies of doom droning in our ears from literature and the news. The Divine Life is stronger than all of man's power to destroy, and it will prevail if only we learn to be open, to be receptive.

In conclusion a few more lines from Gertrud von Le Fort:

> The man stands, from the cosmic perspective, in the foreground of power, woman lies in the depths. Wherever woman was suppressed, it never happened because she was weak, but because she was recognized as powerful and feared—rightly so. For as soon as the stronger force no longer wishes to be devotion but high-handedness and arrogance, what this naturally gives rise to is catastrophe. In the obscure tidings of the battle over the downfall of matriarchy we can sense a trembling fear of the power of woman.[1]

We are inclined to repress the feminine in us. It is often dark, not clearly graspable. We often don't know what we are pregnant with. Putting up with this uncertainty, waiting until the ripe fruit bears itself, strikes us as very hard to do. And yet everything that is really great isn't something we have made but what has ripened in us.

CHRISTMAS (I)
John 1:1-18

Reality has two aspects: the essence of God and the creaturely. God expresses himself in creatures. We, too, are nothing but this word spoken by God. That is what the Christmas gospel wants to tell us. We are the reflection of his splendor and the image of his nature, as it says in the Letter to the Hebrews (1:3).

Everything has come into being through the Word. Jesus Christ is characterized as the Word through which everything came into existence. "Without him not one thing came into being." We also call this

Christ the cosmic Christ. There is nothing that isn't his shape. We are the shape of God. Everything is made in him. We, too, are his form. We are his son, his daughter.

The Son is the visible shape of the Father. We, too, are the visible shape of God. Father and Son belong together. It is nonsense to speak of the Father unless a Son is there, or to speak of the Son unless a Father is there (Hebrews 1:5). It is nonsense to speak of us without meaning God.

It is also true of us what is said of Jesus Christ: "My son, my daughter, this day I have begotten you," and "I will be a Father to him, and he will be for me Son and Daughter."

This eucharistic feast is the celebration of our status as God's children. In the divine form of this bread, we are to recognize our own divine form.

That is the message of Christmas, which is all about our birth from God. We are meant as Jesus was meant. "Had Christ been born a thousand times in Bethlehem / And not in you, you would still be lost forever" (Angelus Silesius).

Eckhart recognizes no difference between Jesus Christ and us. He says, "In principio, we are thereby given to understand that we are an only son, to whom the Father has given birth eternally out of the hidden darkness."[2]

Christmas (II)

We are celebrating the feast of the birth of a person who later realized that he was the Christ, the Anointed, the Divine. "I and the Father are one," he would later say, "The kingdom of God is within you" and "I am the light of the world."

At his baptism Jesus realized who he really was. Then he heard the voice saying, "This is my beloved Son." At that moment he recognized himself that he was the Christ, the God-man.

Tonight we are not concerned with celebrating a birthday. Anyone who gets bogged down in the story kills the living element in the message of this night. A religious message doesn't refer to historical facts.

Today the Savior is born to you. Not back then, a long time ago. "Had Christ been born a thousand times in Bethlehem / And not in you, you would still be lost forever" (Angelus Silesius). In the feast of Christmas, as in all Christian feasts, we see realized the myth of the unfolding of eternity in time. This myth is realized today in us.

That is why Eckhart preaches: "Whatever holy scripture says of Christ, all that is true of every good and divine man."[3] In the birth of this child, we celebrate our divine birth. This feast of Christmas should teach us about our transcendent origins and thus help us grasp our real dignity. It aims to bring home to us our identity with Jesus Christ so that Jesus Christ can take shape in us, as Paul says (Galatians 4:19) and that we can be other Christs. Recognizing this is the most important task of our lives.

We celebrate this feast so that we, too, may understand that we are God's sons and daughters, that we, too, are "God-men," and that the words spoken at Jesus' baptism were meant for us too: "This is my beloved Son, this is my beloved Daughter." We celebrate this feast so that for all our crassness, earthbound minds, and stupidity, we may notice that our origins are divine.

And only if we realize that will we also act accordingly. Morality comes from the realization of our worth. We do not become worthy because we behave well morally. We *are* worthy, and if we have learned who we are, we will also act accordingly.

We celebrate this feast so that one day it may also dawn on us that, "I and the Father are one," and "The kingdom of God is within us," and "I am the light of the world." This feast shows us the bright side of our existence.

Our humanness is a form in which the Divine resounds like an instrument. But we shouldn't get hung up on the instrument, on our human form. We shouldn't just celebrate our earthly birthday. In earlier days Catholics celebrated their baptismal or saint's day. Then we were told, or at least should have been told, who we are: God's children. As it dawned on Jesus, this promise should dawn on us in the course of our life.

The most important task of the future is to teach people their transcendent identity and thus to lead them to their real worth. That is the true responsibility of all religions, the only important task of our lives, and the profound meaning of this night.

EPIPHANY

On Christmas we celebrate the incarnation of God. The accent lay on "being made flesh." We call tomorrow's feast God's epiphany, in other words, the appearance of the Divine. In the gospel it shines forth to the magi in this child. That is the mythic expression of an event that is constantly being repeated in human life. The Epiphany should also happen in us.

What does the myth have to say here and now?

We are the magi. We come from afar, as the hymn says, out of the darkness of egocentricity. In this darkness the world looks altogether different, "dark" and "overcast," to quote the hymn again. We, too, first went seeking the child at Herod's and in many palaces, until we realized that he's not to be found there. Rather, the child shines forth in the simple things and events of life, in the here and now of everyday life, just as he shone forth to the magi.

But it takes a long time for us to realize that it is in every flower, in every stone, in every person. In order to learn that we celebrate the Eucharist. Hence, as it shines forth in bread and wine, it shines forth in everything, if our eyes have learned how to see.

The divine Child is a symbol for everything that has been created. "All things were made through him," says John. "He is the head of creation," says Paul. The whole body of creation is dependent upon the head. "He is the firstborn" and we are his brothers and sisters.

Nothing exists that doesn't exist in God. There is nothing that doesn't have God's form. There is nothing that isn't *HIS* epiphany.

It takes a long time for us to realize this. But when we do, it changes our world-view in the truest sense of the word. And so it's worthwhile to put all our eggs in one basket, in order to recognize his epiphany in everything.

CULT AND RITUAL

(for the Feast of the Circumcision)

A primeval rite is performed on Jesus. He is circumcised and brought into the Temple. Thus the New Testament bears witness in Jesus' case, as with every other person, that he is born from God, that he belongs to God.

Here, too, we are performing a primeval rite. Here, too, we announce our oneness with the Divine Principle. Cult and ritual are the response to the fact that our origins are divine. They are an expression that goes above and beyond language. Cultic action is a symbolic action that includes far more than a rational confession. Symbol comes from *symballein,* to "throw together." Symbols overcome the cleft between the formal world and the Numinous. Cultic action links the two poles together. Rites are in the truest sense of the word religion, a binding-back of the person to God.

That is why we need rituals and cultic actions. Cult and culture hang together. Cult is the point of departure of every culture. Culture was always connected to the Numinous. The old cultural monuments were temples, cathedrals, and figures of the gods. Today's monuments are skyscrapers, powerplants, television towers, and jumbo jets. Our culture corresponds to our cult. Once again we are dancing around the golden calf in us instead of around God.

Earlier, every stage in life had its own initiation, a quite specific introductory ritual. Biological existence doesn't make the person; at that point he or she is only a highly developed animal. The essence of an initiation was to inform the individual that he has his existence from God. Only when the person realizes this is he or she truly human.

Baptism, for example, means that the person has been born above and beyond his biological birth.

The initiation at the onset of puberty meant that the person had to move out of childhood and into adulthood. A new life begins. But that presupposes the dying of the old life. Anyone who is to be born into a new way of being must make it through this painful process of dying. It is a dying in order to live. But dying is bound up with pain, suffering, sickness, depression, and despair. That is why initiations always involve a symbolic death, with suffering, fear, and danger. In order to grow into a spiritual life, the person must grapple with all these forces. Of course, these are precisely the subjects that the modern person would most like to get rid of: sickness, pain, fear, dying. But only those who go through them will sense behind the fragility of being human absolute and intact Being.

What we perform in the Eucharist is a rite. It is a rite of living, dying, and rising. We are celebrating the structural principle of creation: transformation.

Our world is more like a playground than a serious quest for the meaning of existence. Playing is exactly what we should do. Our life should be shaped by something resembling the lightness of the gospel about the lilies of the field and the birds of the air. But such lightness, which carries everything without clutching it, is becoming increasingly rare. We have forgotten that this playground means time and eternity. In cult and ritual we're reminded of that.

"WHO DO YOU SAY THAT I AM?"
Matthew 16:13

"Who am I?" Jesus asked Peter. "You are the Son of God!" was the answer. I am often asked: What does Jesus mean for you? Do you believe that he was the Son of God? To that I can joyfully answer "Yes!" But I have to say with Eckhart, "How would it help me if I had a brother who was a rich man, while I was a poor man?"[4]

What good would anything be if I couldn't also say, "I am a son, I am a daughter, of God like Jesus?" Eckhart continues: "If you wish to know God, then you must not only be like the Son, you must be the Son himself."[5]

Just read Sermon 35: "See how great the love is that the Father has given us." Eckhart constantly repeats the same point in this sermon:

> God couldn't make me become God's son unless I had the being of the Son of God, no more than God could make me wise unless I had a wise being. How are we God's children? We don't know yet: "It has not yet been revealed us us" (1 John 3:2); we know just this much, that as he said, "We will be like him."[6]

Angelus Silesius writes: "God dwells in eternal light, / to which no road can take you. / Unless you become that light itself, / eternity must forsake you."

Konrad Lorenz was convinced that man was the missing link between the ape and the true human being. We are this missing piece on the path to becoming human. We are on the way to experience who we really are.

There is only *one* life of God. The same life that pulsated through Jesus pulsates through us. Divinity is our hereditary right. Jesus says, "The time is fulfilled, and the kingdom of God has come near; repent, and believe in the good news" (Mark 1:15). But here *repent* means to transcend the usual state of mind. We have to move beyond the ego, which revolves around itself, in order to experience the divine center. They can't be taken apart. To say "man" or "woman" is to say "God"—and vice versa. "One day you will know," says Jesus, "that I and my Father are one."

When Jesus speaks about himself as the Son of man, he takes himself to be human purely and simply. He is the perfected embodiment of the coming of the new humanity. He teaches the higher conscious state of the kingdom of God, of being a child of God, that divine ground of being that is our true essence.

He also teaches about the new species of humans. He doesn't consider himself the only one who can achieve this. When the process of metanoia is concluded, we can say with Jesus, "I and the Father are one." This is the healing of all isolation and alienation.

Jesus is Christ, the Anointed. *Christos* in Greek corresponds to the Aramaic word *M'shekha*. But as Christ, Jesus is the mode of expression for our eternal, transpersonal way of being. Thus we are all Christs; we have all been anointed with this divine way of being. Jesus nowhere says that he is the only one who possesses this life. Like him we have this way of being, which he calls the "kingdom of God" or "eternal life. We shouldn't *become* Christian; rather we have to realize that we *are* Christ. Christ is the name for this new human being.

Our sin is that we do not realize who we really are. We are to realize the Christ-consciousness in us. Jesus' redemptive function in the cross and resurrection consists in leading us to our true essence, to the kingdom of God within us. We don't get to this kingdom by means of some magical action of Jesus; we have to turn within to experience it. We are not only *called* children of God, we *are* children of God. It's time for us to stop looking for a redeemer from the outside. Redemption is within us.

So long as we believe in an unbridgeable chasm between Jesus and us, we have failed to understand him. In this interpretation of Jesus, Christianity doesn't do justice to the religious status of humanity. Religion, too, has to be transformed along with people and their development. So long as we think we need to hold on to Jesus' coattails "to get to heaven," we are living in a way that misses what he really cared about. Only when we learn to look at our Christian religion in this way will we have increased our chances of helping the rest of the world.

It is absolutely crucial which way the pattern of development is headed. We set the course. Thank God, more and more people are recognizing that we can set the course for development into the spiritual domain. We don't yet know who we are; it is not yet evident.

"The blessedness that he brought, that was *ours*."[7] Our family name is God.

JESUS CHRIST (I)
Philippians 2:5-11

Who was Jesus Christ? Jesus called himself the "Son of man"; his followers made him the Son of God. He understood himself as the embodiment of the new person of God's creation, as the person who "will inherit the kingdom." He spoke of the new age of the kingdom of God. Only those who go through metanoia can enter this kingdom. They have to be born into the kingdom of the Father, that is, into that new foundation of being what Jesus called "a child of God" or "eternal life." We are challenged to become other Christs, that is, to press forward to that transpersonal structure of being in which our divine essence dominates. Jesus did not claim this structure only for himself. He did not consider it as booty for himself:

> Let the same mind be in you that was in Christ Jesus,
>> who, though he was in the form of God,
>> did not regard equality with God
>> as something to be exploited,
> but emptied himself,
>> taking the form of a slave,
>> being born in human likeness.
> And being found in human form,
>> he humbled himself
>> and became obedient to the point of death—
>> even death on a cross.
> Therefore God also highly exalted him
>> and gave him the name
>> that is above every name,
> so that at the name of Jesus
>> every knee should bend,
>> in heaven and on earth and under the earth,
> and every tongue should confess
>> that Jesus Christ is Lord.
>
> *Philippians 2:5-11*

Jesus was a historical person. But Christ is a mode of being that is built into all people and is designed to unfold in them. We have to become Christs. We are all called to this. Jesus did not order us to venerate him; there is much more at stake than that. We are supposed to follow him in his realization of God's sonship. We are his brothers and sisters. He is the second Adam, Adam in the sense of human being, the founder of the new race. He is the *cosmic* Christ, a supramental form of being that would like to unfold in every one of us.

The kingdom of God is in us; we are children and heirs. "The time is fulfilled, and the kingdom of God has come near; repent" (Mark 1:14; see Matthew 4:17). Conversion is simply the back-connection (*re-ligio*) to our divine essence. We have forgotten our origins; original sin is forgetting who we really are: children of God. Once we have realized that, we will say, as Jesus did, "I and the Father are one." We are redeemed by recognizing our true essence. Redemption is liberation from our unawareness. Like Jesus Christ, we are called to come forth from alienation. Christ-consciousness is supposed to awaken in us. The true Son of God, brothers and sisters of Jesus Christ, are not striving for self-glorification or a comforting reward in this world or the next, but for knowledge of their true worth.

To find our way to a comprehensive, profound understanding of Christ, we must also constantly question tradition. I am convinced that in the New Testament we have only a selection of the "understandings of Christ" that were accepted in the third or fourth century, when the canon was fixed. There were many other theologians from other communities and approaches to Christ that did not correspond to the views of the Fathers of the Church, who scarcely knew any more about the historical Jesus than we do today. Fortunately, Christianity will continue to exist in the base communities, which are unfolding their up-to-date understanding of Christ. In so doing they know that they are being led by the Holy Spirit just as much as the traditionalists and the fundamentalists.

Jesus Christ (II)

We are living at a very critical point in our history. We realize that what is at stake are not simply economic, material, sociological, political, and cultural issues, but the survival of the human race.

On a deeper level the question is not how are we to survive the threat of chemical and nuclear warfare, of polluted air, contaminated oceans, wasteful exploitation of resources, and irreparable assaults on our ecosystem. For all these threats come from people who have a specific state of consciousness, who show that our behavior is false and no longer changeable. We are manifesting a dangerously irrational conduct, and we can't find anyone to heal us. The crisis in consciousness is perfect. We are sick. Where is the healer?

Who will liberate us from our neuroses? How do we get to a new, higher level of consciousness? Where are the resources we can tap? Evolution always had these resources ready when humanity faced a crisis in its existence, so where are they today? Will there be one of those quantum leaps in consciousness that alone can swing the helm around that seems to be steering our planet into the abyss? It ought to be a great source of hope that so many people have set out on the path to an "expansion of consciousness." Because with our ego-consciousness we have very limited powers for manipulating evolution, which follows completely nonrational laws. Again and again nature has helped itself and produced forces that spared humanity from extinction. That's our hope today as well.

A new species of human is coming. It is not yet organized, but for the time being, is composed only of individuals who don't feel obliged to any existing group, not even religious ones, except for the *perennial philosophy*, which was and is the peak of all religions. It was always carried on by individuals who then became the crystallization point for a group. Even today these base groups transcend all racial, national, ethnic, religious, and gender-specific characteristics. They show great interest in psychological, spiritual, and religious disciplines, without tying themselves down to any one of them. They are the bearers of hope for the future. They arise out of the dying culture of our time, which has been afflicted by the most violent jolts: bloated institutions, governments run by lobbies, insatiable economic giants, aggressive competition, stagnating religious systems, manipulative newspaper chains, dying empty shells that have to struggle to stay on their feet.

The number of people, of those unknown "conspirators," in the base groups of all sorts, is still very small. In fact, from the outside they can scarcely be recognized; their differences lie within. With one foot they still stand in the old era; with the other they're feeling for new paths. We find them in small clusters, not distributing propaganda, but getting results through contagious enthusiasm. Their characteristic feature is a strong and uncompromising love for the collective and for the structures that are anchored in higher dimensions of consciousness.

My experience from the many courses I have taught suggests that breakthroughs to cosmic consciousness are occurring more frequently in recent years than before. This phenomenon justifies the conclusion that psychospiritual evolution is proceeding at a faster pace than people suspect. The birth of the new human being is taking place in our midst. The future is his and hers. It remains only to hope that Christians will recognize their hour and join the ranks of the pioneers.

We have overstressed the divinity of Jesus, who wanted to be our leader into the kingdom of God, as he called this new epoch. As long as it sets up an unbridgeable cleft between Jesus and us, Christianity will never fulfill its true mission. So long as we adore him as God, we will not follow him as our leader. He is the firstborn among brothers and sisters. He told us who we really are: God's children. Being children of God is something that has to be experienced. The Divine would like to make a breakthrough in us.

JESUS CHRIST (III)
Ephesians 1:3, Colossians 1:15

What meaning does Jesus Christ have for someone taking an esoteric path? There is Zen saying, "If you meet the Buddha, kill him." Can a Christian say that about Jesus: "If you meet Jesus, kill him"?

We have to get a firm grasp on two ideas of Jesus: the historical Jesus and the cosmic Christ.

The historical Jesus is the point of departure for our faith. Meditating about him and his words does us all a lot of good. He points the way for our life. He has shown us the way to the "Father."

But I would prefer not discussing the historical Jesus here. If we see Jesus only as a figure, we remain stuck in a retarded religious understanding. This is the Jesus whom we must leave behind. Zen says, "If you meet the Buddha on the way, kill him." If you meet this Jesus in contemplation, kill him. That is, don't cling to the *image* of Jesus because you should *experience* Christ.

The cosmic Christ, on the other hand, as revealed in Ephesians 1:3 and Colossians 1:15, is not a static event or person, not an endpoint in need of no further completion. It is rather an unending process. The revelation of Christ is one way of salvation among many. All mystical teachings have this in common: behind the multiplicity of the phenomenal forms lies a great spirit which expresses itself in everything. Different cultures have given this "great spirit" different names: love, truth, Amida, Krishna, Maitreya. Or they have given it names from nature such as sun, light, bright darkness; or from philosophy, for example, the Absolute, Truth, Consciousness.

In Christianity we use the term *cosmic Christ*. That is how we name this reality of God that expresses itself in the whole cosmos.

We Christians have defined the difference in the reality of God versus creation with great exactitude. In so doing, however, we brought into our religion an unbridgeable dualism. We find similar developments in all religions. Hinduism and Buddhism were the earliest to overcome this dualism. They are familiar with two aspects of reality: essence and form, or Atman and Maya. But these aspects are not separated by a yawning gulf, as in Christianity. They are only two poles of the same reality.

John 1:3 says, "All things came into being through him, and without him not one thing came into being." If we take the Father to be the first principle from whom all things proceed, then the Son (the Word) is what proceeded from him and took on form. The Eastern religions call this first principle "emptiness" or "the void." The void does not mean "nothing," but is only an expression for the first principle. Out of the void comes form. In Christian terms, out of the Father comes the Son. Both belong together, as we say in the Creed. They have the same essence and yet are different. They are one in their nature and yet two. They cannot appear all alone. "Whoever sees me sees the Father," says Jesus. The first principle does not appear alone, but in the Word and in the things that have become. Father and Son are two aspects of reality. That is why Hinduism and Buddhism speak of not-two.

And for the same reason Eckhart says, "At the one and same time when God was, when he begot his coeternal Son as God equal to himself in all things, he also created the world." Or, "It can be granted that the world has existed from eternity."[8]

The cosmic Christ is the aspect of the creaturely in our faith, the aspect of form. He symbolizes the essence of the Divine, which expresses itself in all things that have been made. The cosmic Christ stands for what we call "creation." Just as the Father expressed himself in the human Jesus, so he expresses himself in everything that was made through him. "Without him [the Word] not one thing came into being" (John 1:3). We are made in Jesus Christ, and like him we are the expression of the primal divine principle.

Christianity distinguishes between the divine life of Jesus and our human life. It says that we have by grace what falls to Jesus' share by nature. This theological formula creates a practically insuperable dualism in Christianity.

Why don't we use images like the fountainhead and the brook? The fountainhead is not the brook; the brook is not the fountainhead. The fountainhead brings forth the brook. I can distinguish the two, but they can only appear together. Wherever there is a fountainhead, there is a brook. It makes no sense to speak of a fountainhead that doesn't pour itself out into a brook, and the other way around. The brook is not the source, but it has the same water.

In the same way, the Son is not the Father, but he has the same essence. The creation is not God, but it has the same essence.

Like all mystics, Eckhart leaps over what theology calls the ontological difference between God and man, the notion that God's essence is different from the essence of human beings: "The eternal Father ceaselessly brings his eternal Son…to birth."[9] "Where the Father gives birth to his Son in me, there am I the same Son and not a different one."[10] "The Father gives birth to me as his Son and as the same Son."[11] "Should you be the Son of God, you can't be that, because you have the same Being of God that the Son of God has."[12]

> Now one master says: God has become man, and thereby the whole human race has been elevated and ennobled. We may well rejoice at this, that Christ, our brother, has ascended by his own power over all the choirs of angels and sits at the right hand of the Father. This master has spoken well; but in truth I would not give much for this. What would it help me if I had a brother who was a rich man and meanwhile I was a poor man? What would it help me if I had a brother who was a wise man, and meanwhile I was a fool? I say something different and more penetrating: God did not just become man, rather he took on human nature….All the good that the saints have possessed, and Mary, God's mother, and Christ, in his humanity, that is all mine in this nature. Now you might ask me: Since I have everything in this nature that Christ, in accordance with his humanity, can offer, whence comes it that we exalt Christ and venerate him as our Lord and our God? The reason is that he was a messenger from God to us, who reported our blessedness to us. The blessedness that he reported to us was ours.[13]

236

What would it all help, if we, too, couldn't say, "I am a son, I am a daughter of God"? There is only one life of God. The same life that pulsates through Jesus, the Son of Man, pulsates through us as well.

Eckhart is familiar, of course, with the theological distinction between *imago dei* (image of God) and *ad imaginem dei* (according to God's image), or between *filius per naturam* (son by nature) and *filius per gratiam adoptionis* (son by the grace of adoption). But when he preaches he drops this distinction.

In addition to the passages cited above, here is one more that clearly shows how much Eckhart dissolves the separation between God and man: "Thus is he [man] really the same through grace what God is by nature, and on his part God recognizes no difference between himself and this person."[14] For Eckhart, grace is a boiling over and overflowing of God. Not only does Eckhart's language become blurred, but he is continually going beyond every distinction. One can argue about these things for hours. It very much depends upon whether one takes Eckhart to be a mystic or only a philosopher.

JESUS THE GOOD SHEPHERD
John 10:11

Certain Scriptures show God in the image of a loving shepherd who carries the lambs on his arm and leads his herd to pasture. These texts derive from the period when the Israelites lived as nomads. They speak of the trackless steppe that will be paved with a highway, and of the mountain landscape once so difficult to travel through and that will be made low. This is wishful thinking by nomads for whom it becomes a symbol for the coming of God. They see the city of Jerusalem as a symbol for the glory of God. When they came out of the wilderness into the city, they knew they were safe. Thus we, too, should be full of hope and comfort that it is God who reveals himself in all things, who is crooked in the crooked and straight in the straight.

These texts also tell us that we have nothing to fear, God will prevail. But that is framed in very human terms. God unfolds in what is. God is the inmost principle of this cosmos. The cosmos is his garment. The cosmos is the echo of God. God can give birth only to what is godlike. All our fears of downfall and dying are pointless because God is downfall too. "What do I care about being shipwrecked when God is the ocean?" Where do we think we're falling? God falls in us whichever way we fall. Or, as the *Gita* says, "In rebirth it is only the Lord who is continually reborn." When we die and enter a new existence, it is God who dies in us and enters a new existence. Our reason can't grasp this, but faith gives us hope and confidence because it isn't our life that we're leading, but God's.

Jesus' Transfiguration
Mark 9:2-8

On Mount Tabor the disciples realized for the first time who Jesus really was. He was always transparent to the Divine, only they didn't see it. On Mount Tabor, they recognize him. He is the Son of God. His true essence appears and even gleams through his clothes. The Divine permeates everything unchecked.

But we are not allowed to come to a stop at Jesus. We have to recognize our true shape in Jesus for we, too, are full of God. We, too, are an epiphany of the Divine. Unfortunately our eyes are blocked, just as the eyes of the disciples were blocked the entire time. Life would be so simple if we could always recognize who we are, if we could recognize who others are, if we could experience the radiance that gleams through their clothing.

But our eyes are blocked. We don't see that the whole world is Tabor, that even all suffering is imbued with it. We live in the midst of shining, radiant people, but we haven't progressed far enough to realize it. One day we will have developed enough as persons to recognize ourselves as sons and daughters of God. Eckhart thinks that our first responsibility is to realize who we are: "Now one authority says, 'God became man, and through that all the human race has been ennobled and honored.'...This authority has said well, but really I am not much concerned about this. How would it help me if I had a brother who was a rich man, if I still remained poor? How would it help me if I had a brother who was a wise man, if I still remained a fool?"[15]

Eckhart wants us to understand that this applies to us too. What good would it do me if Jesus were transfigured in this fashion, and I were not? The holiness and divinity of Jesus is ours as well.

And the saints whom we venerate today are not holy because they performed heroic deeds, even if that was supposed to have been confirmed at their canonization trial. They are saints because they are persons in whom the Divine made a breakthrough.

The Divine is always in us. That is why Eckhart goes on to say that the blessedness Jesus told us about is ours. All he wanted was for us to realize that we are children of God, that the kingdom of God is within us, and that we bear eternal life in our hearts.

On the path of contemplation we come to a point where all this seems the most improbable thing in the world. We have to see ourselves in the powerlessness of our ego, so that we go looking for our true essence. Our true essence is hidden from our eyes, but still it shines. Jesus is the promise of that.

We are the dance of the Divine. God dances in us. When we say "in us," that can easily be misread, as though God were in us in some sort of container. Rather, the Divine (and not any human figure) is dancing itself. But as Christians we have a hard time accepting that. We're afraid of moving too close to God. We're afraid that the wall between us might fall, and we could be accused of pantheism. But this is only an intellectual difficulty that vanishes of its own accord in actual experience.

There is an image used in the East that attempts to explicate this problem: the golden lion. Gold can exists only in one form or another, it never exists formlessly. Gold may appear in the form of a lion, but then the gold and the lion can't be separated. But gold isn't lion, and lion isn't gold. Likewise, Divine Reality remains distinct from the human form, and nevertheless *is* that form. The Divine can appear only in one form or another, just as there is gold in this form or that, but no abstract gold-in-itself. God is not comprehensible in himself, but only in some form. Thus God and humanity coexist.

Only from this perspective do the verses of Angelus Silesius make sense.

> Man, if you desire
> and pine away for God,
> then you are still not quite
> wrapped in his embrace.
> I am as great as God,
> He is as small as I.
> He can't be above me,
> I can't be below him.

That God is so blessed
and lives without longing
is something he got from me
as much as I got from him.

The main task of religion is to lead us to the realization of our essence. Religion still speaks of this in many different images: returning "to the bosom of the Father," "to the Father's house," "to the kingdom of God," "to the heavenly city of Jerusalem." But in reality we don't have to go anywhere. We need only give our own divine depths an opportunity to find us.

RESURRECTION

What would happen if the thesis now argued by some writers were proved to be true: "Jesus didn't really die on the cross; he went to India. In fact his grave was found there." What would happen if we could prove historically that Jesus' bones had been recovered? Would Christianity then be just a bad joke?

Easter was an event that took place *in* the disciples. *Resurrection* is not a word for an experience that can be integrated into the categories of time and space. Anyone who removes the Resurrection from the level of symbolism and forces it into the historical domain has misunderstood the message. The message of Easter is attested to by men and women who experienced Jesus as the survivor, as the deathless One. The empty tomb, the angel, the journey to Emmaus, are expressions for this inner experience. The Greek word *ophthe* (reveal) in 1 Corinthians 15:5 suggests that Jesus wasn't simply seen by his disciples. He was revealed or announced to them.

Hence it was not a meeting with a physical interlocutor, even though the gospels describe it that way: Thomas laid his hand in Jesus' side, Jesus ate with them, and so on. Rather, it was an inner experience. "Then their eyes were opened." So we aren't talking about magical, parapsychic, miraculous experiences, but inner certainty. Resurrection is the disciples' experience that this life isn't everything, that, just as Jesus entered a new existence, they, too, would enter a new existence. Life can't die. It will go on.

In the Upanishads we find the saying, "In rebirth it is only the Lord who is born again and again." That is, our superficial ego doesn't enter

240

the new existence. In that existence this life of God emerges once more in a form, but it doesn't have to be the form that we have now. We are so tensed up in our ego that we think we have to save it forever.

But our identity isn't wedded to this ego. We overstress it. Our true identity lies much deeper. We can't comprehend that it's the divine life itself, regardless in what form we rise again. Basically we aren't giving God, this divine life, a chance. We are constantly trying to stem its flow and keep it in check.

These inner experiences are what the accounts of Jesus' appearances aim to express. Paul meets the risen Christ as a persecutor and through his experience becomes a different person. At the same time the risen Christ identifies himself with humans: "Saul, Saul, why do you persecute me?"

In the Resurrection of Jesus the disciples experientially crossed the frontier between death and life. The point is to experience this eternal life, regardless of the form we may emerge in after death. Once we move beyond the circumscribed limits of our ego-consciousness, we enter an experiential space to which many names have been given. These names all designate the same thing, namely that there is no death; dying is only the great transformation into a new existence.

It's hard to understand why people always want to reappear after their deaths only in their current form. And yet I don't know anyone who would really like to live forever in his or her ego.

If the bones of Jesus were to be found today and it could be proven that he had rotted in his grave, my faith in Jesus would not change in the least. The experience of the Resurrection has nothing to do with Jesus' bones. It is an experience that we can have: that our deepest essence is divine and hence cannot die.

The statement is clear: our life does not end with death. We enter into a new existence. And that existence—we hope—is a more comprehensive experience of God than our existence here and now can afford. Which is what we celebrate. We celebrate the death and resurrection of Jesus, and we celebrate our own death and our own resurrection in this mysterious banquet. We celebrate what we are in the profoundest sense: the risen ones, even though it has not yet become apparent.

Resurrection and the Death of Lazarus

When we examine the myths of the ancient peoples, it is clear that in the beginning humans did not know death. They understood the language of the animals and lived, without having to work, in peace. But that is not the description of a place in which man once actually found himself, a sort of uroboristic oneness of a not yet awakened human race. Rather, it is the condition that persons find themselves in when they live at one with God, their origin.

We have been driven out of this childlike oneness by what we as Christians call original sin. But original sin has nothing to do with sin in the actual sense of the word. Instead, we have a description of the emergence of human consciousness from an archaic preconsciousness into personal consciousness.

Our personal consciousness develops a domineering self-promoting activity, which often downright tyrannizes us and which we can't readily shake off. But we sense that there is a place of rest where we can experience the Holy, the Divine undisturbed—a place that can be reached only by passing through suffering and death. *Death* here doesn't mean physical death, but the death of the domineering ego, which bars our way to oneness with God.

For not a few people the path leads through an inner confusion, through a narrow passage symbolized by the grave. Thus it is a kind of initiatory sickness, a return to the original chaos, out of which come transformation and renewal. The key here is the transformation of the "old man" into a new person, as we Christians say, a maturing into the full human form. In most cases the path leads through unbounded loneliness, through despair and psychic distress. It leads through the acceptance of death.

It seems that only suffering can drive us to that insight. Hermann Hesse once said, "Despair is the result of that serious attempt to comprehend and justify human life....On the near side of despair live the children, on the far side the awakened."

The human person dies; that is the realization of every religion, and all religions have developed rites to celebrate this transition. It is not just a transition, but a going home, for what is at stake is not dying, but living. We Christians celebrate this reality on Good Friday and on Easter. And we celebrate this in every liturgy. We celebrate our resurrection, the return to the lost paradise. It's not the paradise that lies behind us, at whose gates stands a cherub with a flaming sword barring the entrance. That is the paradise of children, the paradise of the prepersonal state. Rather, our path into paradise leads through our personal awakening into oneness with the origin, into the pleroma, the fullness. We Christians call it resurrection, heaven, or eternal life; the Buddhists call it *satori*; the Hindus call it *samadh*; other religions have other terms for it. If we compare theological dictionaries, that statement of basic similarities doesn't hold up. But from the standpoint of human experience, in the final analysis all religions are trying to say the same thing: heaven is in us, the kingdom of God is in us, *satori* is here and now, if we manage to cross this frontier of rational consciousness.

That is how I understand the Easter narratives. The accounts of the Resurrection are not historical reports; they are experiences that men and women have had with Jesus Christ.

The message of Lazarus' dying and rising symbolizes our death and resurrection as well. It is a mythical experience, a mythical consummation. The meal is actually a conclusion. In ancient times when one had symbolically acted out the myth by dying and rising, one celebrated a meal. This is what we do today. At every Eucharist we celebrate the dying and rising of Jesus, and our own dying and rising as well.

THE ASCENSION

What are we to make of the Feast of the Ascension? Are we to believe—as we see depicted in countless images—that Jesus rose up with body and soul into heaven? Are we to believe that he is throned there at the right hand of the Father? in a heaven, a sort of Big Rock Candy Mountain? Or should we simply turn away from such an infantile belief and leave it to the naive souls who take their consolation from naive priests?

First of all, it's important to understand that heaven isn't something that's far away. It's not something "up there" to which we have to ascend. It's here and now. The Ascension into heaven does not mean that Christ removed himself from this earth. Heaven is everywhere and always. The Ascension tells us that we are called to enter this heaven with body and soul, that is, to experience God or, to experience who we really are— which amounts to the same thing. We bear this divine core within us. Zen calls it "essential nature"; yoga calls it "atman"; Christians call it "eternal life, the kingdom of God, or heaven."

Christ's Ascension is a term from mythological language. We mustn't take religious statements literally, since religion expresses itself in images and myths. I have already mentioned several times that myth is like a glass window. The glass tells us something about the light that shines behind it, but the window isn't the light. We mustn't stop short at the lines and colors, for they merely point to the light that shines through them.

The Ascension is one such glass window, from which it should be clear to us today that there is a dimension in us that we can't grasp with our intellect and senses, a dimension that we can only experience, to which we can awaken.

This Ascension is about us. We can experience what Jesus Christ experienced. Heaven is always there. What separates us from it is the way we have been taken over by ego-consciousness. If we could cross this frontier of time and space, we would rise up; we would be in heaven. Heaven is the realization that our origins are divine, that we bear divine life within us.

And that is what we celebrate on the Feast of the Ascension under the forms of bread and wine, forms that we can see. Behind them lies concealed that other dimension which we call divine life, heaven, eternity, being a child of God, and so forth—that dimension that we can't see, but that is there.

Heaven is here and now. *Ascension* means experiencing the here and now. That is why we have set out on the path, on a path that is no path, because it's not here, neither up nor down, neither yesterday nor tomorrow, but here and now. In the Ascension of Jesus we celebrate our own ascension. This feast protects us against the flight into a false spirituality, against a retreat from the world.

THE COSMIC CHRIST

Like other founders of religion, Jesus Christ was understood in the West as a personal redeemer. This made Christianity into an absolutely anthropocentric religion. Our world picture, however, has changed so radically that a purely anthropological view of the cosmos is no longer possible. The old pipelines of the anthropocentric, rationalistic, antimystical, and antifeminine understanding of the world and humanity have run dry. Nonetheless, it will be a long time before we revise this one-sided interpretation of the figure of Christ.

Because the historical Jesus was overemphasized, a narcissistic doctrine of redemption evolved. We Christians are more interested in ourselves than in God. We still believe that everything revolves around the earth. We still believe that man is the unsurpassable crown of creation. We still believe that there will be a paradisiacal, static "Sabbath" at the "end of the world."

But the Scriptures of the Old and New Testaments can serve just as well to work out a cosmic, indeed a mystical, theology. What Jesus said about God came from his personal experience, a mystical experience. The words *father* and *child*, which he borrowed from the Jewish understanding of the family, testify to an experience of union that is familiar. "I and the Father are one." However, instead of stressing the union in this family idea, we have postulated that creation is ontologically different from the creator, and thus we have driven a wedge between God and man.

Jesus proclaimed the kingdom of God here and now: "It is within you." But we have shifted it to the future and put people off with promises of an indefinable heaven. Evagrius Ponticus, a fourth-century mystic, writes: "When the spirit has reached the state…of grace, then it sees in prayer its own nature like a sapphire or like the color of the sky. In the Scripture this is called the kingdom of God, which the fathers saw on Mount Sinai."[16]

Instead of feeling ourselves to be the brothers and sisters of the "firstborn," we have made Jesus into the object of veneration and adoration. Instead of seeing ourselves as "other Christs," we have degraded ourselves to sinners and penitents. Instead of using Jesus' teaching to sense our oneness of being with him and the Father, as in the image of the vine and the branches, we have distorted him into the supreme moralist. Instead of recognizing in Jesus our own primal image and likeness of the Father, we have defined him as the "totally other" and moved him far off from us into an unreachable distance. Instead of accepting him as "Emmanuel," as "God-with-us," as he was proclaimed, we have downgraded him to a narrow-minded world judge, hungry for retaliation.

As the cosmic Christ, Jesus Christ has the effect of an archetype who stands for the Divine in creation. He is the archetype for the Divine in us. The Divine, which he called the Father, pulsates through us, just as it pulsated through him. What happened with him has happened with us, only it isn't evident to us.

As this cosmic Christ, Jesus enters Jerusalem and tells us that suffering and dying are also a manifestation of the Divine. We, too, enter Jerusalem with Jesus; with him we go through death and resurrection.

We should learn from this event that life has to pass through many deaths and resurrections. We should learn to unite ourselves with life that knows no death and resurrection. We should learn that death is no more than the process of transformation into a new form of life. Only when we are ready to keep going through death and resurrection into a new form will we do justice to the dynamic Divine Principle.

Whenever we begin to cling to a form, such as this body, we violate the structural principle of creation, which is to be born, to live, to die, and to rise again. Whenever we hold fast, we contravene God, who is not static but dynamic. That is the actual sin of humans: they clutch things. They don't surrender to life; rather, they cling to an idea of life.

Living means going along into an ever new act of evolution by God. *Living* means dancing along and celebrating together, and the rhythm is: being born, living, dying, rising again. Only when we are capable of giving ourselves to life are we risen, regardless of what form this may take. For God is a God of life, not death.

HOLY SPIRITESS

We know that God is neither male nor female. And yet images of God have had a strong influence on us. What would happen to our idea of the Holy Spirit, for example, if we had only heard of the Holy Spiritess? There is no way to imagine what that might have brought about in our understanding of ourselves as Christians, what it would have meant if we hadn't had to project the feminine in God onto Mary, if (instead of their many pictures of Mary Magdalene, for example) our artists could have represented the femininity of God in the figure of a woman, as the Holy Spiritess.

God could have entered our pictorial imagination altogether differently from the way he did. For example, we could have prayed to an archetypal feminine image. Children would not always draw an old man with a beard when asked to do a picture of God with their crayons; it would be perfectly legitimate to depict God as female. In fact, in Jesus' native language of Aramaic (and Hebrew) "spirit" is a feminine noun. And in Jesus' description of God, we often find feminine elements: compassion, motherly care, intimacy, warmth, feeling, beauty, corporeality, eros.

In a little Bavarian village called Urschalling, on the Chiemsee, stands a small Gothic church. In a fresco on the ceiling, there is a painting in which the Holy Spirit emerges as the figure of a woman from the folds of the clothing of the Father and the Son. What would happen today if an artist dared to do that in a church?

Our notion of God and of God's Spirit has been falsified and curtailed because we have made the spirit masculine. Although spirit, breath, and feeling are closely bound together as basic feminine elements, we have turned spirit into something cool and intellectually male. We have masculinized our images of God, and that's sad, for in the final analysis, we must recognize the feminine in God and in ourselves.

Let's just hear how the Pentecost hymn sounds when we address the Spirit as a divine feminine force. Let us open ourselves to the Spirit of God and realize what is said of God's Spirit in ourselves as well:

> Holy Spiritess, Lady of Light,
> From the clear celestial height,
> Thy pure beaming radiance give.
>
> Come, thou Mother of the poor,
> Come with treasures that endure,
> Come, thou Light of all that live!
>
> Thou, of all consolers best,
> Thou, the soul's delightful guest,
> Dost refreshing peace bestow:
>
> Thou in toil art comfort sweet;
> Pleasant coolness in the heat;
> Solace in the midst of woe.
>
> Light immortal, light divine,
> Visit thou these hearts of thine
> And our inmost being fill.
>
> If thou take thy grace away,
> Nothing pure in man will stay;
> And his good is turned to ill.
>
> Heal our wounds, our strength renew;
> On our dryness, pour thy dew;
> Wash the stains of guilt away.

Bend the stubborn heart and will;
Melt the frozen, warm the chill;
Guide the steps that go astray.

Thou, on us who evermore
Thee confess and thee adore,
With thy sevenfold gifts descend:

Give us comfort when we die;
Give us life with thee on high;
Give us joys that never end.
Amen. Alleluia.[17]

ESOTERICISM AND CHRISTIANITY

The goal of esotericism is the experience of union with the Ultimate Reality, which Christians call God, but which has other names in other religions. It is our deepest essence. We can all awaken to this profound experience. That is our actual goal, our actual responsibility. This deepest essence can't be described, it can only be brought about by some sort of exercises. We can only get ready for it to reveal itself to us.

The best way to get there is to sit in attentiveness, which will spread from our posture of prayer throughout our everyday life. Attentiveness helps us empty the heart, so that we can recognize in this emptiness our true essence.

Hence there is no search for a transcendent God, for a God outside. The esoteric paths teach us to look within so as to learn there who we really are. Our true essence is divine. We prepare ourselves for the manifestation of this, our deepest essence.

We have to learn from Jesus that the kingdom of God is in us and that we must turn inward (metanoia). Jesus wanted to lead us to the experience that he had: "I and the Father are one."

This experience of oneness comes by way of the experience of our deepest essence, which is of divine origin. Thus Augustine could say, "*Noverim me, noverim te*" ("If I know me, I know you"). And Confucian philosophy says that when I exhaust all the possibilities of my heart, I know my human nature. Knowing its nature means knowing God.

All that is demanded of us is inward attentiveness in order to experience this presence of the Divine. This doesn't come from thinking nor from clinging to commands, images, and ceremonies—not that I can't use these things, too, on my spiritual path.

The last step in the "imitation of Christ" is not to follow Jesus but, like him, to recognize who we are. Hence he must go away from us. "It is good for you that I go away." We might travel on with the words of Jesus to Mary Magdalene, "Do not hold on to me" (John 20:17). "I still have many things to say to you, but you cannot bear them now. When the Spirit of truth comes, he will guide you into all the truth" (John 16:12-13). "But the hour is coming, and is now here, when the true worshipers will worship the Father in spirit and truth, for the Father seeks such as these to worship him" (John 4:23).

Jesus Christ is no object of contemplation; rather, he is our inmost essence. But that can only be experienced. The prayer of Jesus in solitude, into which he kept withdrawing, was the prayer of the experience of oneness with what he called Father. He was always united in this way with the divine Reality. He was aware that in the depth of his being he shared the divine Nature with his Father. That is exactly what we, too, should realize.

The letting go of external symbols and images in contemplation is common to all esoteric schools. Taoism speaks of the "fasting of the heart," Zen of "making the heart empty," John of the Cross calls it the "dark night of the soul," and Jesus Christ calls it "losing one's life."

John of the Cross argues that the redemption of the world is grounded in this dying of the ego, when a person takes the path of contemplation. In this context it is good to read a bit in his book, *The Ascent of Mount Carmel*, II, 7, 11. Here he says that Jesus achieved the work of redemption in his deepest abasement (*kenosis*):

> At the moment of His death He was likewise annihilated in His soul, and was deprived of any relief and consolation, since His Father left Him in the most intense aridity, according to the lower part of His nature. Wherefore He had perforce to cry out, saying: My God! My God! Why hast Thou forsaken Me? This was the greatest desolation....that He had suffered in His life....This he said that the truly spiritual man may understand the mystery of the gate and of the way of Christ, in order to be united with God.[18]

To become like Jesus Christ in this annihilation is the highest state that the soul can reach. This state consists in experiencing the death on the cross, sensorially and spiritually, inwardly and outwardly. For John of the Cross this *conformatio* with Jesus Christ in his utter abandonment is the precondition for mystical experience. This renunciation of everything also applies to religious experiences, sweet consolations, visions, ecstasies, and other exalted experiences. The goal is not renunciation and emptiness. They are only a transition and prerequisite for the resurrection.

THE SCANDALOUS EXPERIENCE OF ONENESS

We have to live Jesus Christ in his divinity and his humanity. We are another Jesus Christ. Just as he manifested divine life in his humanness, we, too, have to manifest divine life in ours. Since we share in all the mysteries of Christ, we should live them all: being born, growing up, learning, working, being members of a society, suffering, dying, and—like him—rising.

What is at stake here is not an imitation but a "conformation" as sons and daughters of God. We are to love our humanness because our divinity expresses itself in it. We have to find ourselves again in an experience as human and divine.

But there is no longer any human ego in this experience, only that mystical identity that has been continually condemned by theologians as scandalous and that nonetheless finds a voice in all real mystics. Here is an example from Hadewijch of Antwerp:

> I no longer belong to me, there is nothing left to me of myself. He has swallowed up the substance of my spirit. The soul becomes with God exactly what it is. The fire [of love] makes no distinction, it consumes everything it grasps: I assure you....Damnation or bliss is no longer the point, in the fulfillment of love one has become God. Anyone who has understood what a miracle God is in his godliness often appears godless to people who don't realize that or seems unknowing, because of an excess of knowledge.[19]

MYTHS

There are different levels of understanding Jesus Christ, even in the mythical interpretation. Until the fifth century, in fact, there were many more gospels in circulation than we have in the New Testament today. Individual communities also had different understandings of Jesus. In the fifth century, long after Christianity had become the state religion, most of these gospels were burnt by the authority of the Emperor.

Among those that were saved is the Nag Hammadi scripture. In some of these texts the esoteric and mystical element of the life of Jesus is much more forcefully expressed than in the four canonical gospels. At Christmas we have the myth of the virgin birth, at Easter the myth of dying and rising.

The Egyptian path of initiation can show us the carrying out of one such mythical event. From all countries in the Mediterranean Basin people came to Egypt to become acquainted with the mysteries of Isis. Even Plato went there. All those who thought they were up to it could be tested to see whether they should risk the great initiation into the mysteries. It was a path to life or death, that is, the adept was clearly confronted with the dangerousness of the path: "Once you have gone through this door, there is no going back. If you don't get to the goal, you must die." That was clear to everyone. But nobody knew what the test would bring.

The initiate was given an oil lamp. The first passage was a narrow path that got more and more cramped, until the body had to be pressed through a tiny opening. The adept then realized that he had to pass through the element of earth, through matter, as if through a mother's womb, into a new birth.

The second test brought him to a deep pit filled with ice-cold water. There was no going back. With the lamp he could light up only a small field of vision. A flimsy staircase was pointed out. He had to pass through the water in such a way that the lamp didn't go out. There was only one fording point and on the other side only one place at which to come out. If he didn't succeed, he would drown. He had to make his way through the element of water. The path continued, and he found himself in front of a blazing fire. Knowing he couldn't go back, he kept on going. At such a moment, what goes on in a person's mind?

The journey ends in a splendid room. The table is set, music rings out. A very beautiful slave girl comes to serve him. She tells him, "Now that you have all these harsh trials behind you, I am your reward. I am entirely at your disposal." If he went along with the offer, he awoke in the morning to an empty bed. The hierophant stepped out of the background and informed him: "You have not passed the test. You have saved your life, but you are marked for life, and you are forbidden under penalty of death to say anything about the mystery." Those who did pass the test, however, and did not succumb to the sensual allurements, but showed that their longing for the Divine was so great that no need could stem it, were congratulated by the hierophant: "Now I shall lead you into the hall of mysteries and explain to you the mystery of Isis. And for the rest of your life you will be her priest."

How many people would stand up to these trials? Only if a person has gotten to the point that he prefers to die rather than give up the struggle for the Divine should he cross the threshold of an esoteric path.[20]

JESUS CHRIST AS MYTH

In earlier days the myth of Jesus Christ was similarly performed in a number of places. In the Swiss canto of Ticino lies a little village that in a chapel dating from the eighth century, has a baptismal font in the form of a tomb. The person to be baptized climbed from the western side into the tomblike font, ducked under three times, to symbolize the act of dying with Christ, and then climbed out toward the East as if risen from the grave. He was anointed as a sign of his royal state and received the white garment, not to be put off until Whitsunday.

It is important to recognize the metaphorical structure of a religion. If we interpret the metaphors, symbols, and images as facts, we get into great difficulties. When we say to someone, "You're a hard nut to crack," we don't mean that he or she is really a nut. *Nut* is a metaphor. Metaphors in religion are supposed to open up some transcendental meaning to us.

For example, when we read that Jesus went up into heaven, we may not assume that a person rose up to a specific point in the universe. There is no physical heaven. Jesus entered an interior space, an experience that has nothing to do with exterior time and space. We are to rise up with him by going inward to the actual source of our life.

All religions evolve. In the Old Testament God was at first no more than the tribal god of nomads. Then he became the most powerful god among all the other gods. As such he was given supremacy in Hebrew society. During the Babylonian captivity in the sixth century B.C. the idea of a savior became a part of Judaism.

When the world changes, religion changes too. But this is a difficult process. Theology begins by seeing metaphorical statements as historical facts and then absolutizes them. But the metaphorical level is only the mask through which an Ultimate Reality speaks, the *persona* through which this Ultimate reality resounds.

Modern-day religions are caught in the problem of good and evil. They are entangled in moral and social problems. Instead of telling us about the metaphysical experience of reality, they look to an outside solution. Religions have a hard time releasing their adherents from their childhood faith and leading them to youth and adulthood. That's one reason why nowadays so many people are fleeing religion.

Shepherd—or Star Wars?

In the holy Scriptures we are constantly running into mystical images. Consider, for example, the image of the shepherd who pastures his sheep, feeds and waters them, protects them from all dangers, accompanies them through darkness and night.

One of the wretched features of our times is that we no longer have any myths. Few of us have ever met a shepherd. So it's hard for this particular myth to start anything resonating in us. Yet it might increase our trust in the Divine within us. If we give it room, if we can abandon ourselves exclusively to the will of God, we will live this human existence rightly.

The actual purpose of this myth is to show us that at bottom we are at one with the Divine. The myth shows us the way to the Mystery of God. It's the same as with the myth of the virgin birth; it symbolizes the fact that we did not have a mere human birth, but we are born from God and have to find our divine nature in a second birth. It's not enough just to live; we have to live out of the depths of our essence. Hence our physical birth is only half of our being—and it's important to go through the labor pains and the birth canal of this physical birth. But it's still more important to suffer through a second, spiritual birth, to be born again, as the Scripture says.

We no longer have any dominant myths. The question is whether a new myth can arise in our time. Joseph Campbell argues that in our culture things are too short-lived for this to happen. He does point, however, to one possibility: a myth of a planetary society.

The myth of the tribe, of the fatherland, the nation, the language group, the religious community—all have been shattered or are in the process of being shattered. Too many people have been uprooted, and so many political borders strike us as increasingly absurd. Campbell tells us that his youngest son, when asked why he had seen *Star Wars* twelve times, replied, "For the same reason you keep reading the Old Testament."

Perhaps we really are on the way to a planetary society, as *Star Wars* would have us imagine. Perhaps we should feel more like cosmopolitans (citizens of the cosmos), particularly for religious reasons. Whether or not we want science fiction novels and films to sketch in the details, the fact is that our responsibility for nature is moving in a similar direction. The holistic world picture is growing and spreading.

What does that have to do with our spiritual path? What does it have to do with the myth of the shepherd? If we realize that there is only *one* flock and *one* shepherd, we will behave differently in this world because we will also realize that the Divine exists in every one of us. Once we recognize who we are, we can no longer harm one another because we can sense within ourselves the evil we do to others. We can trust the Divine in us. It knows the path; it leads us through all dangers and confusions.

THE PARABLE OF THE TWO SONS
Luke 15:11-32

We can read and interpret Scripture in many ways, and we can question its historicity. Did the things we read about in the Bible actually happen that way?

We can also try to understand the symbols that are continuously used in the Scriptures, for example, water, community meals, covenant. If we understand these symbols in a purely moralizing fashion, we can learn from them what has to be changed in our lives. They can also be understood mystically—above and beyond a conceptual content. What lies beyond the words on the page? What is the Ultimate Reality that all the words point to?

Even the words of Scripture are no more than the finger that points to the moon, and not the moon itself. They are something like a map, but not the landscape through which we intend to travel. A map points beyond itself. Anyone who takes the path of contemplation is warned against confusing the finger with the moon or the map with the landscape.

The mystical meaning of Scripture is hidden in the words, but it's no mystery. We simply have to experience the contents ourselves. Thus the mystical statement is the heart of holy Scripture. The Scriptures are mystical, because they derive from mystical experience. We, too, can have this experience because the hidden capacity for it lies within us. This mystical element in us is the divine life.

The parable of the father and the two sons can be understood as a look within ourselves, with the three characters representing ourselves. The father is our true self, the Divine in us, the essential nature. The younger son symbolizes our ego-consciousness. He is the easiest one to identify with. He acts the way we act before we know who we really are. We think and act dualistically, egocentrically, narcissistically. The older son is likewise our ego-consciousness. He has already experienced his true essence or at least he has an intuition of it. But the experience is imperfect, and he is still trapped in dualistic thinking.

The parable is the story of our own transformation. It shows us the path we have to take, and is a sort of mirror in which we can recognize our own process of transformation.

The three figures show us different levels of our process of transformation. The father, for example, is indifferent, free, full of sympathy and goodwill. Indifferent means nonpartisan. There are no indications that the father wants to deter his son from his adventure. Note that he doesn't give his son any moral prescriptions—and he doesn't chide his older son for being envious. The parable simply says that he divided up the inheritance. The father is free; he shows no dependency on or attachment to his sons. He doesn't use them for his own purposes. The younger son wants to have his legacy, he gets it and can go. The father doesn't ask what it will be used for, and he gives no salutary admonitions. When his younger son returns down and out, the father doesn't ask him reproachfully where he's been, but takes him in. The older son complains, but the father doesn't justify himself nor does he accuse his son of envy.

The father is full of compassion. His indifference and freedom do not mean that he can't feel compassion. He simply doesn't look at himself. His existence is at the disposal of his sons. He doesn't need to stop and think about what he has to do. He acts out of the fullness of a life of experience. He has a clear eye. He possesses *puritas cordis*, the pure eye, of which the Beatitudes tell us. This pure eye is not preoccupied and has no prejudices; it sees reality as it is. The parable says that the father already saw his son coming from afar.

The younger son has a distinct ego-consciousness. Our ego-consciousness swims like a wave on the ocean. The wave may rejoice to be separate from the ocean. Perhaps it even thinks it can live without the ocean. Occasionally it may go so far as to see the ocean as a great obstacle to its freedom and a life of its own. The younger son would like to be "I"; he would like to be independent. He would like to have something exclusively and entirely for himself. His ego-consciousness is something that he hopes to experience separately from everything else. The ego would like to have something all its own. It resists the whole, but that leads to insecurity. The ego thinks it's missing something, and thus it keeps going out searching because what it already has ultimately doesn't satisfy.

This way necessarily leads to misery. Suffering is the natural consequence of cutting ourselves off, of wanting to have things all to ourselves. Yet, this suffering is important because only the pressure of suffering seems to get us on the right road. Suffering is always the distinctive mark of the ego. We may cover up our egoism, but not the effect of the egoism: suffering.

The elder son also represents the ego, but his ego is much more subtle; it lies hidden in the shadows. The elderly son lives close to his father; his ego lives close to the essential nature. He stays home and does everything his father tells him to do. His ego needs his father's recognition, which is the source of security that guards him from obliteration and gives him importance. The elder son has not yet realized that he bears his father within himself and that he must find in himself what he sees outside. His ego-consciousness and his true self are still disconnected.

The elder son thinks of himself as a better person. After all, he hasn't done all the stupid things his younger brother has done. Although he never thought that his happiness could be found out in the world, he sought happiness outside himself, with the father. He is dissatisfied with his father, dissatisfied with his situation. His attitude upon his brother's return shows that he feels threatened. He thought his good behavior was the guarantee of his father's favor, the confirmation of his ego.

As long as we receive loving attention, we feel good. But this caring can become an obstacle. Behaving well out of fear that love may be withheld is not a virtue. This is exactly the situation in which Jesus is continuously confronting the Pharisees. They consider themselves to be the ones who have stayed home, who are closest to God, who do everything that can be done, and therefore hope to be certain of his favor. This is a classic example of how religion can be the crucial obstacle to taking the last step and letting go of the ego completely. However balanced the ego may be in the security of the father, it remains the ego. Precisely when it is in such a state of equilibrium, it often can't take the last step of letting go. That is why Jesus says to the Pharisees, "You cross sea and land to make a single convert, and you make the new convert twice as much a child of hell as yourselves" (Matthew 23: 13).

Thus the parable is the story of our own transformation. We come from God who is "all in all." The journey begins with the search for our identity. Who are we? The younger brother looks for a solution in the pursuit of happiness outside. The elder brother seeks happiness by wanting to command recognition. Along the way, both sons experience the distress caused by their supposed independence; they realize the bankruptcy of their egos. The search for the kingdom of God can finally begin.

It's a lucky person who ends his search in a timely fashion and realizes that he has to be converted. Our journey is like the trajectory of a boomerang returning to its point of departure. But "turning things around" is not enough. We have to be totally absorbed by our true self, by God. We must experience our likeness to God. The father is the source of life for both sons. They have everything from him. They have to acknowledge the fact that independence is an illusion and ends in alienation.

The return home is signaled by the festive garment, the ring, the shoes, and the celebration. Even the elder son goes through a transformation. He recognizes that he has everything that belongs to his father, that there is no separate existence, that he is one with his father. But as long as he keeps hankering after rewards, retribution, and recognition, he lives separated. The feast at the end of the parable is the fulfillment of the transformation. There, all are one: the father, the elder son, and the younger son.

The parable is our own story, our life script. It's designed to help us open ourselves and find our way to oneness above and beyond any rational reflections. Then our real life begins; then we can set off and stay home. Then there is neither outside nor inside. Then we experience everything as an expression of our essence, as a form of God. Then there is no more good and evil, no more above and below, no more rich and poor.

Then we have in ourselves a law that we call love. "Love and do what you want!" Love will be the norm for our behavior.

BREAD
John 6:25-59

Why do we keep celebrating this rite? Along with baptism, it is the oldest recorded Christian ritual. Like Jesus at Emmaus, the first Christians were recognized in the breaking of the bread. Why do most varieties of Christian faith never tire of celebrating this meal?

Rituals interpret reality. They have to be frequently repeated, always using the same words, gestures, and signs, so that the reality behind them may dawn on us. In ritual we awaken a sleeping potential. We awaken forces, simply by repeating words, steps, gestures, and sounds—always the same sign, the same word, the same sound, the same movement that releases a force from the depths.

Rituals are holy, healing, restorative gestures, sounds, and images that give a definite direction to our disordered interior lives. This is not a matter of rational comprehension. Rather we open ourselves to a power that is always there in our center. It is not only there in us, it is the ground of being for everything that exists.

Back to this celebration: immediately after the multiplication of the loaves people came to Jesus. They wanted bread. Jesus indicated to them: "You are looking for me, not because you saw signs, but because you ate your fill of the loaves" (John 6:26). But the food that one fills up on is not the kind Jesus wants to give. When Jesus speaks of bread, he doesn't mean food for the body. For him bread symbolizes a much deeper reality, which in another passage he calls "eternal life": "This is the bread that came down from heaven, not like that which your ancestors ate, and they died. But the one who eats this bread will live forever" (John 6:58).

We are too quick to refer the phrase, "But the one who eats this bread," to the communion host, as if the only thing at stake were that piece of bread. This bread is a sign for the reality of life that hides itself from our bodily eyes. It is supposed to shine forth for us in the bread. And just as it does so, it is to shine forth in everything that exists. There is nothing that the Divine doesn't illumine. Whether or not we realize it makes no difference. All this emphasis is placed on bread so that we can realize how God shines forth in all things. Everything is only the sparkle of the

Eternal. Anyone who experiences that will go through life with great reverence and will deal very reverently with life.

If we can liberate this life in us, we transform ourselves and the world. Then we no longer prevent God from taking form in us and through us. Then we experience him in us and in all things.

"Do not work for the food that perishes," says Jesus, "but for the food that endures for eternal life" (John 6:27). That is, recognize your own deepest essence; recognize your divine primal foundation. At bottom, it's just that simple. First we have to recognize the life in us through simple breathing exercises, in walking, in a flip of the wrist, in the simple things.

We keep celebrating the Eucharist so that we may become aware that just as God exists in this bread, he exists in every one of us, in every step, in every breath. And he exists this way in everything. He hasn't composed a symphony that he plays for himself and perhaps directs from some distant point in space. He *is* the symphony that rings out. And all we have to do is to ring out with him and sound as few discordant notes as possible.

In order to understand that, we keep celebrating this meal.

WATER OF LIFE
John 7:37

The topic today is the streams of living water. Water flows from within us. Water is a symbol for divine being. Our deepest essence is divine being.

At Jacob's well, Jesus likewise spoke about this water of life: "But those who drink of the water that I will give them will never be thirsty. The water that I will give will become in them a spring of water gushing up to eternal life" (John 4:14).

We humans have an existential thirst. We try to quench this thirst at many sources by running after many things. Here Jesus' statement matches statements by the Buddha and other holy books. So long as people thirst only after physical sustenance, pleasures, and superficial things, suffering is inevitable. Although they give in to this instinctual need, it will keep on making itself felt periodically, and they can wear out their lives going off to ever new wells, until they notice that in truth they don't want to quench their bodies' thirst, but the much deeper longing for the water of life, the longing for eternal life.

Dostoevsky thinks that the mystery of the cycle consists in the fact that a person, after drinking earthly water, gets thirsty again and asks, "And what now?" Thus he writes in a book about bread: "Transforming stones into bread, they say, is that really the greatest?" "Not the greatest (answered his interlocutor), great, but second-class; once a person has eaten his fill, he won't think any more about it. On the contrary, he says, so, now I've eaten my fill, and what should I do now? The question remains eternally open."[21]

All our yearning for happiness is latent desperation. We can find rest and security only in our divine core. True thirst can't be quenched with water from an earthly source.

The danger of offering people merely earthly water even in religion is very great, because even in religion one can get caught up in formal matters and forget that only spiritual paths lead to the Real. No authentic guru and no Zen master would accept a disciple who wanted no more from him than fitness and relaxation.

The water of life is the life of God that we all bear in us. It is the Divine Principle that is our true nature. It isn't far from us. Only when we find this water of life will everything else make sense: the joys and experiences of this world.

Both belong together, God and things. But we will be happy with things only if God reveals himself to us in them.

DISCIPLESHIP
Mark 3:31

We are herd animals by nature. Over thousands of years we have lived in groups, clans, castes, parties, clubs, nations, fatherlands. There aren't nearly as many individualists among us as we think. Even the so-called dropouts are still very strongly integrated into society.

Anyone who takes up an esoteric path enters into discipleship. But being disciples of Jesus—or disciples of God, which amounts to the same thing—means bidding farewell to every kind of group identification and, under certain circumstances, even to organized religion.

This is not a demand that one leave the Church; the issue here is completely different. The point is liberation from a bond that lies deep within our unconscious and prevents us from being individuals and living our Christianity without compromise. We become a disciple of Christ—or God—only as an individual.

The only possibility, however, of freeing ourselves from group loyalty, which is one of the most intense connections on earth, is the will to move on to the higher loyalty of God's discipleship. "One's foes will be members of one's own household," says Jesus (Matthew 10:36). "Whoever comes to me and does not hate father and mother, wife and children, brothers and sisters, yes, and even life itself, cannot be my disciple" (Luke 14:26). This has nothing to do with external separation; rather it is a question of becoming a self that is radically involved with God alone.

To become an individual demands separation from every group identification, even religious. This is the "inner hatred" that Jesus calls for. It's not a matter of quarreling with our family or our religious or political superiors. On the contrary, when we become inwardly free, we can build up a creative and positive relationship with our fellow men and women. That is what Jesus demands: "For I have come to set a man against his father, / and a daughter against her mother, / and a daughter-in-law against her mother-in-law" (Matthew 10:35).

When in our dreams we find ourselves battling others, when a young person dreams of rebelling against all authority, when we dream of wrangling with someone we actually love, this confrontation with our unconscious identification becomes visible. At some point we have to stand on our own two feet, protected by no one, to work out our own salvation and follow this inner voice. Just as we have to liberate ourselves from a strangling loyalty to our mother, for example, we have to break free from every sort of entanglement in groups. Before individuality can grow, we have to cut loose. Unconscious ties must be torn apart so that our God-given uniqueness can come to light.

This holds true for every connection that has its roots deep in the unconscious, including our ties to religious institutions, theological systems, and so forth. Let me stress once more that such a breaking off doesn't necessarily mean leaving the Church. Rather it is a step that leads us to the freedom of discipleship with Christ in the Church. Being Christ's disciple means severing all other loyalties in favor of loyalty to Christ or God.

The would-be disciple comes to Jesus and says, "First let me bury my father and attend to the needs of my family piety." The passage doesn't mean that he shouldn't bury his father, but that he still can't undo the deep unconscious ties to his family. He still hangs on.

Too many people in our Church have yet to break off this unconscious tie to their mothers. They are not yet disciples of Jesus Christ, even though some hold high office in the Church. They are still trapped in this mother-bond and thus wear the mask of another person. But when we say to Jesus, "Teacher, I will follow you wherever you go," we are told, "Foxes have holes, and birds of the air have nests; but the Son of man has nowhere to lay his head" (Matthew 8:20).

And don't think that this has something to do with external poverty. It's about the inner daring to live our God-given identity in a community. It's like a balancing act; there has to be an equilibrium between the individual and the community. Finding this balance is not easy. What has to grow above all is that inner freedom that leads us to full human maturity. This act of liberation is accompanied by love, the only ethical element that plays a role here. This is a love that is ready to "hate" father, mother, brother, sister, to separate itself from all unconscious conditioning.

It seems clear to me that it's easy to talk theory about this topic, but that in the individual case it can be extremely difficult when, for example, I have to bring up children—and, in so doing, find the balance between forming their conscience and allowing them freedom. Or I might have to make a life decision, such as whether to remain in or break away from a community or a marriage.

A few years ago I dared to say, "God can lead a person into the monastery, but God can also lead that person out." My remark was highly resented. No doubt there is a virtue of fidelity, which has to consider carefully whether I have to stick with an initial decision or not. On this issue I am most concerned about inner freedom in religion. The fusing of religion and morality was certainly one of the most fateful developments in the history of religion. Religion is not in the first instance ethics. Rather, religion tells us about the transpersonal side of our being that we have to discover. That is also the message of Eastertide; the main topic is not penance and forgiveness, but the realization that we are risen. Out of this realization come conversion and right action.

The karma doctrine of the Eastern religions often provides a stronger motivation for ethics than fear of punishment does. This teaching says that I harm myself and my maturing process when I don't act in accordance with it. Because I would like to break through to a religious experience, I do some things and I don't do other things. Hell and the punishing God are a bad educational device.

But it's no easy path that we take. It is often unprotected, and there's no guarantee that someone will be standing by the wayside to tell us that we're on the right path. It remains a risk. A man's housemates are his enemies. We can only enter the kingdom of God alone, one by one.

Some people have become uncertain because the paths of contemplation or Zen and yoga have been condemned by high Church officials. Listen to your inner voice, and don't let your decision depend on the opinions of others, who may well have a very limited grasp of your spiritual path.

Conformation—Not Imitation

In the esoteric paths the key point is the process of transformation and a process of imitation. Relating that concretely to Christianity means that what took place in Jesus Christ is to take place in men and women. Jesus Christ, who is entirely God and entirely man, is like all of us. Everyone is confronted with the same task that Jesus confronted. We are all called upon to let the Divine express itself freely and unfettered in ourselves. We should become like Jesus in the living out of our own lives.

All too readily we make Jesus Christ into a cult object. But he has been given to us as someone to follow. Jesus Christ is not primarily an object of veneration, he is rather the subject of an internal process, of being filled with the divine fullness (Ephesians 3:19).

Scripture expresses this with images: as way, door, and light, Christ opens up to us an inner access to the divine foundation with whom we want to be one. As bread, as water, and as vine sap, he is to enter us so that we can sense the divine life in us that has been revealed through him.

These Johannine symbols of Christ—I am the bread of life, the living water, the true vine—were not thought up to objectify their message but to interiorize it. They open up the divine center of our life and make it clear that Jesus Christ embodies the figure of our true redeemed being. What we experience in him is what we have to become. He meets us not from outside but awakens in us from within: Christ is a symbol for the awakening divine figure within us.

The major role here is played not by imitation but by "conformation." The point is to uncover the Divine in us, just as it was manifest in Jesus Christ. The redemption process in us aims at becoming Christ, which ultimately means a process of becoming fully human, indeed of becoming God.

The Divine sleeps in every person like a seed. Just as the seed developed in the human Jesus Christ, so it is designed to awaken and enfold in every person. Jesus Christ was completely transparent. God shone through him, lit up in him. The same thing has to happen with us too. God would like to unfold himself in us, to show himself, make himself felt, present himself, as Paul said: "I have been crucified with Christ; and it is no longer I who live, but it is Christ who lives in me" (Galatians 2:19-20).

Jesus came to cure us of the false notion that we live separated from God. His death on the cross struck a fatal blow to this false assumption. If it is granted to us to die with him, we shall also live with him (Romans 6:4). Our path moves through suffering and dying into the experience of unity with God, that is, in the resurrection.

Thus we have to let the Divine come into us, to give it space. Ethical effort serves the unfolding of what lives in us so that human action becomes an "action of God."

HELL OR TRANSFORMATION?

The point of contact with God is here and now. Here and now is also hell. Heaven and hell are separated only by our ego. Whoever can let it go will enter the kingdom of God. There are no magic rituals to lead us up there, only the dying of our superficial ego. And only love has the power to accomplish this. It alone helps us to leave everything to enter into this new order of being, God's order of being.

The transformation runs through several levels. In general we stay on the ego level. The constant identification with the ego level has to become perspicuous. We have to recognize that this ego is only the instrument of our actual, deeper essence. We reach this next level through what Jesus calls metanoia, conversion, rebirth. It is the entrance into a discipleship that lives on the new level, in the kingdom of God.

For many people this means passing through a phase of confusion.[22] Some have a complete breakdown. The offices of psychiatrists are full of such men and women. This is a depressive phase that leads through insecurity and confusion to a new orientation, if the right adviser can be found. It is of the greatest importance for anyone traveling the spiritual path. It's like a labyrinth that winds through many intricate channels into the center of the essence. Here is where the purification process of which mysticism speaks now occurs. If we can accept this process, it leads to a breakthrough, that is, to a new level of consciousness. False self-images and expectations of life can be corrected by transcending the ego. The foundations for anxiety, hatred, and greed disappear. An inner equilibrium, peace, and harmony expand within us.

I have the courage to believe in possibilities and potentials in humans that help them escape from the shattering crises they now find themselves in. If they manage to liberate the healing forces—I'd call this another word for divine forces—they get a chance to survive. With the help of the new level of consciousness, I imagine a world more harmonious and peaceful than the present one. On this level it's possible to develop a global spirituality that is not institutionalized, but represents the unfolding of a human foundation. It is a spirituality oriented not to quantity, but to the quality of life.

This spirituality means looking at the world with different eyes and grasping it in a way that doesn't revolve around the little ego. That's what Jesus meant by metanoia, if I have understood him properly.

ON PRAYER

All religions are focused on an ultimate reality. For some thousands of years, we Westerners have been calling our Ultimate Reality "God"; others call it "Tao," "Nirvana," or "Brahma."

Prayer is communion with this Ultimate Reality. It is the attempt to establish a conscious connection with this Reality which is always flowing through us.

Prayer presupposes a certain polarity, the polarity between man and God, between the finite and the infinite, between the imperfect and the perfect. Prayer arises out of a state of inner tension. Prayer tries to unite something that is badly split, to link our everyday consciousness with our true essence, with the Divine in us. Prayer unifies two aspects of reality that have fallen apart in us humans.

People have both personal and transpersonal qualities or, as we say in religious language, the human and the Divine. This is a coordinate system made up of nature and supernature. Only when we stand in the center of this system can we be fully human. When we neglect or even deny the Divine in our existence, we remain blocked in the growth process. We remain half-human.

People should pray to open themselves to the Divine within so that it can, so to speak, pray in them. That's what Paul thinks at any rate: "And because you are children, God has sent the Spirit of his Son into our hearts, crying, 'Abba! Father!'" (Galatians 4:6).

Real prayer asks for nothing. Real prayer is pure self-surrender. To the mystic school, petitionary prayer is the lowest way of approaching God. Strictly speaking, mysticism doesn't even acknowledge petitionary prayer. Thus Angelus Silesius writes:

> Man, as long as you are wont
> to thank God for this and that,
> Then you are still trapped
> in the barriers of your frailty.
>
> God loves and praises himself,
> as much as ever he can,
> He kneels and bows,
> and adores his very self.

Eckhart speaks of people who hinder themselves in prayer by paying too much attention to externals.

> Then again there are "good" people who impede themselves by fixating all too much on repentance and expiation. They stop at the sign instead of striving to come to the purer truth.[23]

> But the prayer of the mouth is something that holy Christendom instituted so that the soul could be recollected from the external senses into which it had scattered itself, to the diversity of transitory things. Then when it has been concentrated into the higher powers (reason, will, and memory), it becomes spirit. And now if the spirit fastens upon God with its will completely agreed, then it becomes godlike. Then for the very first time the spirit stands in true adoration, when it has come to the goal for which he was created. But we have been created solely for God and accordingly are modeled after him. Anyone who does not succeed in uniting the spirit with God is not a truly spiritual person.[24]

With this you will note well that all multiplicity must be eliminated, even the humanity of our Lord as something particularly
present. As Christ himself said to his disciples, "It is to your advantage that I go away, for if I do not go away, the Counselor will not
come to you, the Spirit of Truth, whom the Father will send in my
name!" But here "good" spiritual people prevent themselves from
reaching true perfection by fastening with a lust of the spirit onto
the image of the humanity of our Lord Jesus Christ. In so doing
they only lose themselves in visions, since they see, even though in
an image, things in their mind, be it men or angels or our Lord
Jesus Christ's human form....And so he was thinking not just of
his disciples in the narrow sense, but of all those who from thence-
forth would be his disciples and wish to follow him to high perfection: to whom his human side is an obstacle, insofar as they fasten
on it with pleasure.[25]

Those who think that praying is concerned with reason and verbal
formulas alone are beginners in prayer. A Sufi thinks quite differently
about the matter.

> "Ask them," the abbé begged me once more, "how they prepare to
> come before God. By fasting?"
> "Oh no," answered a young dervish, laughing. "We eat and drink
> and praise God who has given man eating and drinking."
> "Dancing," answered the oldest dervish with a long white beard.
> "Dancing?" asked the abbé. "Why?"
> "Because dancing extinguishes the ego," said the old dervish.
> "When the ego has died away, there is no obstacle to union with
> God."

BENEDICT

"Benedict, the man of God, got up even before the nightly prayer
time, while the brothers were still sleeping peacefully. He stood at the
window and prayed....As he was thus looking out around midnight, he
suddenly saw a light that spread from on high and all at once scattered
the darkness of the night. It streamed with such brilliance that as it shone
in the darkness, the night was even brighter than the day. As he himself
later said, the entire world was gathered together as if in a single sunbeam and shown to him."[26]

Benedict was a mystic. The episode described above shows this quite clearly. There is a metareality that we can't see with our physical eyes. It is experienced from within as light, the light being only a symbol for what is experienced.

The crucial sentence in this description of Benedict's vision is "...the entire world was shown to him as in a sunbeam." This metareality, which we Christians call "God" is, to use the current term, a holistic reality. Benedict experienced God in his cosmic oneness.

We have built-in possibilities that transcend everything we can cognitively know. In our practice of contemplative prayer we are basically to do nothing but open ourselves to this holistic reality. We strive to enter this fine-grained conscious space, which is normally covered over by coarse-grained spaces that are a prison. But it takes a long time before people even notice that, and still longer before they really want out. They look for a path like the one we are taking here.

What happens to us in all this doesn't necessarily have to happen on our prayer cushion. Benedict got up before daybreak in the tower and looked out on the landscape. A deep mystical experience is not dependent on time, place, or our religious creed, but solely on the strength of our devotion and our determination to let nothing take precedence over this metareality—or God, as Benedict formulates it. Everything that is can be the gateway to the experience of this reality. Only when we have realized that religion is literally an everyday affair, that the Divine occurs right now, and that we have only to break through here and now, will we understand and live our life as a sacred pilgrimage.

Benedict described his way with three important phrases:

Vacare Deo: being free for God; having time for God. What we do in the exercise of contemplation is take time to come to ourselves and thus to this metareality: having time for God.

Habitare secum: living with oneself; staying home. But this is precisely what we find very hard—staying home, not tearing off.

Ora et labora: pray and work. There is no dividing line between religion and the everyday routine. Until we understand that, we won't be truly religious. Benedict explains further: "Handle all things like holy altar implements." This means a sacralization of our lives.

Many people who come into this house have been damaged by the Church. They have a Church neurosis. Nothing gets on their nerves more than this religious terminology. But Benedict meant to say no more than Bodhidharma when he declared to the Emperor Wu, "Nothing is holy" (see Hekiganroku 1 1). Everything is the way it is. And thus, as things stand, everything is "holy altar implements," but not because we use them for religious purposes. It is "holy" in itself. Everything is an expression of the Divine. Religion is everyday life, and everyday life is religion—that is just how the Divine plays itself out. Until we have understood that, we are not religious.

VISIONS
Luke 2:36-51

In today's gospel we meet a prophetess, Anna. She had been married and was widowed at a very young age. That evidently got her to take the inward path. She no longer left the Temple, it says. It's always distress that gets us to set off on the inward path. And when this distress turns into torment, there often comes a deep experience, an experience that can have enormous importance for our life and perhaps for the lives of others as well. We suddenly recognize our own essence, our true form. A vision such as the one Anna had is an act of knowledge that culminates in the conviction that despite everything, life makes profound sense.

Only a few people have such realizations while taking a course on contemplative prayer. I don't want to label them visions right off, although they can certainly approach that. Here, too, the depth can vary tremendously. Practically everyone has the experience, at least once, of suddenly getting absolute clarity about some issue he or she had been wrestling with for ages. This clarity often appears in some sort of image. The realization blends with a symbolic structure or figure: "She spoke of him to all who were looking for the redemption of Jerusalem." She recognizes in the child salvation for herself and for her people. Such realizations are often simply the return of split-off portions of our consciousness. That doesn't lessen the value of the experience, but it does show us that the Divine isn't far from us, that it reveals itself in such signs and images coming from our deepest essence. We can say yes to ourselves and go on living.

Thus visions and realizations that suddenly occur to us can be a strong motivating force for our lives. But we shouldn't cling to them; rather, we should simply acknowledge their message.

For Anna the vision was a profound religious experience. And with her experience she gave others courage.

WISDOM

For us, wisdom is an abstract concept; we don't connect it with any specific shape. And yet *hochma* (Hebrew for "wisdom") was originally a female deity, a mythical figure, later characterized in Judaism as an abstract, masculine, divine force.

Wisdom is first of all the wise conduct of life, the art of waiting, accepting, and maturing. It is very close to growing and to wholeness. In biblical wisdom literature, Wisdom speaks only to sons, not daughters. It's as though our feminine half were speaking to the masculine half. We're not talking about men and women here, but about the fundamental masculine and feminine attitudes in every one of us.

It is said of Wisdom, "Before the ages, in the beginning, he created me, / and for all the ages I shall not cease to be" (Sirach 24:9). Wisdom is a feminine principle that pervades the entire cosmos and reaches beyond death:

> For whoever finds me finds life
> and obtains favors from the LORD;
> but those who miss me injure themselves;
> all who hate me love death
> *Proverbs 8:35-36*

The teaching of Wisdom is an "anima-upbringing." The feminine speaks to the masculine. The feminine is the more comprehensive. It is the creative element that was present in the making of the world, and the primal source of life in us.

Those of us in the West have developed a mentality in which deeds and achievements—and being—count. Ruling, directing, ordering, and producing stand at the top. Only logic and intellectual knowledge are taught and carry weight in our society.

But Wisdom is not intellectual knowledge; it is insight into the true nature of things. It is the ordering principle of the cosmos and in hu-

mans. While the masculine principle in its autocratic way readily vio-
lates and rebels against the order of the cosmos, the feminine principle is
identical with the basic order of the world and hence with the will of God
as well. Indeed, it is the basic order of the world; it is the will of God.

The patriarchal element created the commandments, which demand
unconditional, often senseless obedience. The commandments can be
so absolutized, in fact, that they go against nature. But Wisdom is not
oriented toward a patriarchal, masculine, or authoritarian will of God.
Rather, Wisdom is oriented toward the cosmic order that we experience
when we turn to our inner self. What is at stake here is our real life. This
is not thinking in contraries, but experiencing unity and wholeness. The
images of wisdom are the tree of life that grows and unfolds from within,
and the source of life from which all things flow.

Hence it is Wisdom, too, that stamps the perfect human being. Our goal
is to become wise. At the end of the esoteric path stands the sage.

The figure of Wisdom is unequivocally a strand of matriarchal tradition that is in conflict with the patriarchal Jahwist tradition in the Bible.
The figure of Wisdom surely comes from matriarchal religion. Thus she
is a necessary completion of our patriarchal image of God and man.

But she represents a side of us that must be admitted and developed.[27]

THE APOCRYPHAL GOSPEL OF MARY:
THE FEMININE IN HUMANITY

Every religion gives us a visionary anticipation of the goal. But evidently not everyone is granted the gift of looking upon this goal because
the organ that views the new goal can't be the old consciousness. It has to
be part of the new person, the person who has gone through the initiation of rebirth, of metanoia. Only those who come from the truth can hear
the voice of truth. "Only in his light do we see the light." Even if this new
consciousness—I might call it Christ-consciousness—is still rudimen-
tary, it is the prerequisite for a resonance of the new life awakening in us.[28]

Most people who get a glimpse of this new life, this new possible
existence, instinctively fight it off. They sense that it will unsettle their
old life, and they don't want to expose themselves to this disturbing influence. We see this very clearly in the apocryphal Gospel of Mary. It
wants to tell us that we can't recognize and pursue our goal with purely
natural effort, reason, and will. In fact, there is no point in trying to

distance ourselves with intellect, will, and natural longing from the forces of the past because these forces are themselves part of the past. That's hard for the Christian who has been trained to rely on good intentions, on keeping the commandments, and on exercising legalistic piety. Entering Christ-consciousness is possible only when the imperishable within us awakens and comes to our aid. This light, which exists in all of us, even if hidden, has to illuminate the dubious region of darkness so that we may really set off on the path.

Only the feminine element, the receptive and listening part in us, can sense and adumbrate the new consciousness, as the Gospel of Mary tells us. The feminine is represented by Mary. Passion, understanding, and will are represented by the masculine figures of Peter, Andrew, and James.

The first great obstacle, symbolized by Peter, is the human passion and longing to take control of the new consciousness. Longing is clever. It says to Mary (the soul), "You're deceiving yourself. Your search for eternity is only a compensation for unfulfilled and disappointed wishes. You think your longing is from above and is aimed at something imperishable. In reality these are regressive patterns from childhood, feelings of abandonment and disappointment. You can't stand the uncertainty of existence and so you flee to a false sense of security." In this way some psychologists try to throw out all religious tendencies, branding them as pure regression.

The second great obstacle, represented by the figure of Andrew, is reason. It reproaches the new consciousness with ignorance. After all, reason is the authority we use to orient ourselves. This applies to religion as well.

"Why do you think you know more?" says reason to this inner realization. "You have no criteria for your inner experience. Where are you going to get your security? Is your realization truly authentic? Aren't you chasing a phantom?" First of all it takes courage to rely on this inner tendency, until it's strong enough not to let itself be condemned and dissuaded by reason.

The third force, symbolized by James, is the will. It tells the soul that it, and not she, is in charge of the path to God. In the final analysis, will believes it can provide the motivation for the return home with energy and strenuous endeavor.

But the soul, in the figure of Mary, has to tell the will that it's on an ego trip unawares because it believes it can reach salvation with good behavior, right methods, hard work, planning and striving, and keeping the commandments. But in reality it's just the old ego that wants to maintain its sphere of influence in the new world.

The forces of the old consciousness try to drag us back into their orbit. They can't accept the fact that rest, silent attentiveness, looking inward, and receptivity are the only attitudes by which we can recognize our true essence, the Divine in us. They still think that even in religion, activity, plans, intellectual truths, and good intentions should be taught as the main instruments to pave the way to the new consciousness.

Mary is the symbol of the feminine in humans, for the new person of the kingdom of God. Thus in the Gospel of Mary, it's not a question of Mary versus Peter, Andrew, and James. Rather, the feminine, the receptive element, is better suited for experiencing the Divine than the active, masculine element. The feminine gives us access to our deepest essence. It has an affinity with God that reason and will don't.

Hieros Gamos—Sacred Marriage
Talk at a Wedding

This room is familiar to the two of you. You have repeatedly come here for days of self-examination and reflection. Today not only does the room have a completely different character; you, too, are here for a completely different reason. You have opted for this ceremony. Why? Some of our acquaintances may be shaking their heads and saying, "Well, let them have their *idée fixe*. It's still one of our social forms." Your being here is more than an act with religious trimmings that society wishes or still accepts.

What takes place in a marriage is the initiation into a community *in via*, into a way of life, still more into a way of salvation. Marriage is not a try-your-luck booth at a fair, but a way of salvation. Anyone who is looking for nothing but narcissistic masturbatory pleasure in marriage will come to grief, as every therapist who counsels married couples is well aware.

Two people do not find each other by accident. They find each other because they are to approach and ripen toward their definitive destiny together. I would like to take a little digression to explain this.

The essence of God is One. In creation the One divided itself into an unlimited number of possibilities, manifesting itself in the many. It divided itself into a boundless number of manifestations, which remain related to one another and yet are an altogether individual expression of the One.

Thus in the beginning is the One. The One is the Holy, the Intact, the Undivided. All pain is pain of separation. All redemptive pain is a drive toward completeness, the longing of the part for the Whole, a longing to overcome the primal suffering of isolation.[29]

We still have an inkling of the Whole, and it awakens yearning in us. We feel homesickness only because we know that we have a home. All love is the entrance to, and the beginning of, the path to home, that is, to God, to the One.

The One must step outside itself. Unless it does so and thus becomes two and many, there is no creation. But with creation there comes about the splitting up of the One and hence unrest. All creatures sense that they are no longer whole. And so what has been split up presses back toward Oneness. Oneness is also our deepest essence.

As humans we sense this deficit caused by division more than other creatures do. That is why once human beings emerged, the search for the completing part had to begin. Each half needs the other in order to experience itself as a Whole. For our deepest essence is not masculine and not feminine, but One.

We have given this longing for Oneness a name—the name is love. Love shatters the limits of loneliness in which each one of us is trapped, and liberates him or her for the Whole. Love is longing for lost oneness, for our original condition.

When we became human, the "primal tragedy of isolation" began. It is the primeval pain of humanity, a pain of separation that will not let up until it has found its way back into the One. What we call sin is basically nothing but isolation from our deepest essence. It is a peculiar drive for autonomy, individuality, and demarcation.

Our true identity lies much deeper. We will find it only when we leave behind this superficial ego. Marriage is the initiation for the common attempt to find this foundation where all oneness can be experienced.

Love is another word for homesickness. The splitting up of the One brought a separation, but it also brought something absolutely new: the energy of love. Love is far more than the reproductive drive. It is the centripetal force powerfully urging us back to the One. It is especially strong between the sexes. Just as the power of attraction arises between two magnetic poles, so love arises between a man and a woman.

With that we see appearing in creation a strong field of energy that is far more than the sum of its parts. Love is something that can't be explained because it goes far beyond the physical and psychic structure of humans. It is the metaphysical longing that once again represents the primal power of evolution. It leads to the incomprehensible demarcation of the ego that is necessary so that we can find our way back to the One.

But our ego tends to oppose the basic force leading to fusion with the One. It is different from the mystical drive toward Oneness in that it wants to cling and have things for itself. But we come back to the One only through self-surrender, not through the desire for ownership or conquest. That is where the tragedy of humans lies and above all the tragedy of men who try again and again to make oneness and wholeness all by themselves.

The ego tends to use others to enrich itself and to profit from them. It wants to have something and thereby to raise itself, but it doesn't seek the higher oneness in union with others. It wants to remain the central point of its little world. It turns the other into a tool for its personal goals and pleasures.

It debases its partner into a commodity that can be used and abused at will. It drains its partner and then throws him or her away. This sort of love is only an extension of selfishness. No one has given this a more dismal, loveless definition than Kant, who wrote that marriage is a "contract for the reciprocal use of sexual qualities." The danger every marriage runs is that it may press the partners not toward oneness but toward the will to possess another person.

Your common path is therefore a process of growth, which is painful. Love and suffering are closely connected. And it seems that love even needs suffering in order to ripen. So be prepared for hours in which you will have doubts, when you will want to run away from each other. These are important hours of growing and maturing.

The mystic and the true lover have a lot in common. The way of the wilderness and the night is well known to mysticism. This darkness is also found in human relationships. The point is to complete the sensory with the supersensory, and that is evidently impossible without suffering.

Spiritual tradition calls what binds man and woman together *hieros gamos* (sacred marriage). Love becomes a communion, a symbol of the oneness of the Divine with the human.

Many passages in holy Scripture appropriate this symbol. Thus, for example, in Hosea: "And I will take you for my wife, forever; I will take you for my wife in righteousness and in justice, in steadfast love, and in mercy. I will take you for my wife in faithfulness; and you shall know the LORD" (2:19-20). Isaiah says, "For your Maker is your husband, / the LORD of hosts is his name; / the Holy One of Israel is your Redeemer, / For the LORD has called you / like a wife forsaken and grieved in spirit,... / For a brief moment I abandoned you, / but with great compassion I will gather you" (54:5-7).

The true human essence is the couple, a man and a woman. That is what the Priestly account of creation says: "Male and female he created them." The true human being is the Godman, the person who knows that the divine dimension is part of his or her wholeness.

Your final goal is not the other person. Your common goal is this divine dimension that you are to find each other. And that is the real reason why you have found one another and why you are to set off together on your journey. Your love is the departure from loneliness toward returning home to God's wholeness. Your wedding is the initiation, the sacred commencement, of this road to home.

WHERE DO WE COME FROM?

A reading from the *Gospel of Thomas:*

> Jesus said, "The Kingdom is inside of you, and it is outside of you. When you come to know it yourselves, then you will become known, and you will realize that it is you who are the sons of the living Father. But if you will not know yourselves, you dwell in (spiritual) poverty" (3).

> Jesus said, "If they say to you, 'Where did you come from?' say to them, 'We came from the light, the place where the light came into being on its own accord.' If they say to you, 'Who are you?' say, 'We are its children, and we are the elect of the living Father.' If they ask you, 'What is the sign of your Father in you?' say to them, 'It is movement and repose.'" (50)

> His disciples said to him, "When will the repose of the dead come about, and when will the new world come?" He said to them, "What you look forward to has already come, but you do not recognize it" (51).

Religion should tell us who we are and what the meaning of our existence is. It should not frighten us with a vengeful God who passes judgment on us at the end of our life. It's not right that this primitive image of God should still haunt people's minds and strike fear into their hearts.

By contrast, if we stay with the consoling images shown us in this reading, we won't die in fear of a judge. We are his sons and daughters, and we are the chosen ones of the living Father.

We belong in this family. God is, so to speak, our last name. And when asked, "Where do you come from?" we can answer, "We have come from the light." And it is the light that looks through these eyes of ours—often darkened and distorted, but it is the divine light.

And we shall return there. I hope and wish that the path we take will transform us so that we can be free from fear when we cross the threshold that separates us from the next existence. It is only a threshold. In our religion we have talked too much about death and the Last Judgment. We have spoken too little about eternal life, although the Scriptures are filled with it.

Our identity is the life of God, which is characterized as light in the gospel. If we could realize our true identity, we wouldn't be afraid.

"His disciples said to him, 'When will the repose of the dead come about?' Jesus said to them, 'What you look forward to has already come, but you do not recognize it.'" Eternal life is there, but we don't recognize it. And so we are afraid.

The path of contemplation involves working out our fear of death. That is why the dying of the ego is a basic theme of all mysticism, both Eastern and Western. "One who dies before he dies does not die when he dies" (Abraham a Santa Clara).

Death is an intermediate goal of all mystical experience. The new birth that follows it is the final goal. The path to true life passes straight through death.

In the face of death there is fear. Every transformation is blocked off by fear. If often swells when we sit down to meditate. All anxiety is ultimately the ego's fear of death. Our exercise is the best preparation for dying. All we have to do is let go so that what we really are can shine forth.

I hope that despite fear and pain, some sense of this light remains in us all, even in the dark hours. That light suffers in us, as it suffered in Jesus all the way to his cry on the cross, "My God, my God, why have thou forsaken me?" But this was not the last word. I hope that all our lives can end, like his, with "Father, into your hands I commend my spirit."

THE LAST DAYS
Mark 13:24-37

What are we to make of this gospel? We know that we can't take it literally. What does its mythical statement mean? We have to elevate it to the level of subjectivity. To put it in another way, we have to ask ourselves what horizons must come crashing down in us? What in us must go under? What sun in us must be darkened? What stars must fall from heaven so that the Son of man in us can rise and fulfillment can begin?

What is at stake here is a series of inner events. We are to step outside our narrow consciousness. Jesus used the word "rebirth" for this. This has nothing to do with a physical rebirth, but with the expansion of our consciousness through the dimension of the Divine.

Actually we are always in this state of rebirth, in this dimension of the Divine. It's just that we don't perceive it. With our everyday consciousness, it feels as if we were in an aquarium (Drewermann), thinking that the cosmos ends at the glass walls around us. And then we get frustrated and depressed because this confinement makes no sense.

We have chronic defense mechanisms that prevent us from looking through the panes of glass. That's what original sin is. We don't know who we are, and so we do all sorts of stupid things that we call "sin." We think we are trapped in a miniworld. We turn around at the glass wall and don't bother to look out.

This miniworld must set so that God's world can rise. These false stars that we cling to must fall from heaven. This false sun of our little ego must be darkened. We must go through personal fears and distress and through social and political upheavals, perhaps even through revolutions.

The Son of Man will come with power and glory. I understand this to mean not the return of an historical Jesus but the appearance of the true human being in us, the blossoming of the Divine in us, which in the language of Christianity we call "being a child of God."

The new heaven and the new earth are not places somewhere in the universe, they are here and now, right behind the glass of the aquarium walls where we find ourselves. Some day we will notice that these walls never existed.

This generation will not pass away until all this takes place. That has nothing to do with time. It can happen at any moment. The return of Christ is a timeless phenomenon. The Son of man, the new human being, the divine person, is in us. We just can't recognize him yet.

And what does all that have to do with this liturgy? Today we celebrate the coming of the Son (and Daughter) of man. Today we celebrate what we really are, but don't yet realize. Today we celebrate the new heaven and the new earth and the new human being. Today we celebrate the Divine, which not only pervades all universes but manifests itself in all universes. We are not those poor, miserable fish that go on mindlessly bumping against the glass walls. We are bound up with everything by this divine life, whether we realize it or not. Here and now we celebrate that.

ETERNAL LIFE

We often use religious terms without asking ourselves what they really mean. For example, what does "eternal life" actually mean? Every age needs to reinterpret the meaning of eternal life because what the phrase says changes.

If we compress the history of the universe into one year, with every month corresponding to more than a billion years, we glean an interesting picture. Through the impetus of the mysterious Big Bang, primordial matter expands, pushing out against its own gravitational force and cooling off. In a tiny fraction of the first second of January 1, matter comes into existence: the elementary particles and immediately thereafter the simplest atomic nuclei, hydrogen and helium. By the end of January, radiation and matter are already decoupled, and the galaxies come into being.

In mid-August our solar system originates from a collapsing cloud of gas and soot. Complicated chemical, and then biological structures, develop on the earth's surface. Rocks form by the middle of September, and by the beginning of October, we find fossil algae. Over the course of the next two months a tremendous variety of plant and animal species emerges.

On December 19, plants colonize the continents. By the twentieth, the land masses are covered with forests, and life makes for itself an atmosphere rich in oxygen. On the twenty-second and twenty-third, fish evolve into four-footed amphibians and conquer wet *terra firma.* On the twenty-fourth, reptiles develop from these creatures and settle the dry land. The first warm-blooded animals arrive on the twenty-fifth, but the first mammals do not appear alongside the saurians until late that evening. On the night of the thirtieth, the Alps begin to fold upward. On the night of the thirty-first, in other words on the last day, humans branch off from the apes. At five minutes to twelve, the Neanderthals are alive, and Jesus Christ is born fifteen seconds before midnight. At one-half second before twelve the age of technology begins.[30]

We cannot act as if religion began with the history of revelation in Israel around six thousand years ago. Where and what was God before that? What we call the human soul came forth from the animal kingdom, and unfolded from it as our bodies did. It is simply unimaginable that at one moment man was still an animal and at the next moment, man was a human being.

Thus we have no alternative to accepting that, as human beings on this dust particle of earth, we are a part of cosmic evolution. We act as if the universe had been waiting for seventeen billion years so that at long last this species (which for a few hundred thousand years has been capable of self-reflection) might arrive on the scene.

Science tells us that galaxies continuously arise and pass away, yet we consider ourselves so important that we make the universe revolve around us and see ourselves as the absolute culminating point of creation. When will we finally dispatch our exaggerated anthropocentrism in favor of a cosmological perspective? Are we humans really the main concern of the evolving galaxies and worlds of which we have practically no idea? If the theologians would look through the microscope and telescope, they would speak differently about God and man. We still don't understand ourselves as a part of an enormous cosmic evolution that ultimately is nothing but the evolution of the Divine Principle itself. The anthropological point of departure of Western thought must be corrected by cosmic thinking.

This will also have consequences for our belief in the resurrection. Humans have been in existence for two to three million years, and we have no reason to doubt that they will exist for less than two million more years. The difference separating us from our future descendants will at that point be as great as that now separating apes and humans. In what body will we rise?

God's life is the structural principle of all complex systems. What prevents us from equating mind and the life of God? That would mean that everything is animated by God's life and that all structures are simply the unfolding of the Divine Principle. It is the dance of the Divine itself, which we call the "cosmos." And we humans are dancing along. We are a dance step, an individual and indispensable dance step of God, now and in our next existence, and in the one after that and the one after that and...

What does that have to do with some of our age-old rituals, rituals that are as old as the human race itself? The sacred meal, for example, celebrates both aspects of reality: the visible and the invisible. That is why we prepare bread and wine. We see the bread and wine, as we light candles and burn incense, bow and sing. In that ceremony we celebrate both aspects of reality. And all our efforts at contemplation mean just this: we are trying to experience both aspects as one, so as finally to experience ourselves, too, as the expression of the Divine. Therein lies our unique significance.

THE NEW JERUSALEM
Revelation 21:1ff

Religion expresses itself in images, parables, and myths. Abstract dogmas are an invention of reason and at bottom can't completely satisfy us. Nevertheless many people have a very hard time abandoning this apparently solid foundation of their intellect and trusting themselves to a deeper experience. In the West, reason has become the supreme authority for the comprehension of reality. With it, Western man imagines he can understand everything. But behind reason lies another, entirely different dimension of knowing.

Today's text tries to lead us into this dimension of understanding. Two images are called into consciousness: the "New Jerusalem" and "God's tent" among us.

The "New Jerusalem" is not a place, but an image for a state of consciousness that can come about here and now. In Scripture it is also called "eternal life" or the "kingdom of God." The "New Jerusalem" is not something to come. It is here and now. Only a cognitive barrier separates us from it. If we can pass through it, we learn that we bear within us this divine spark that all religions speak of. In this state of consciousness there are no tears because even tears reveal the Divine.

There will be no more death. Those who experience life in their depths know that being born and dying are the consummation of the Divine.

They experience oneness with life. They dwell in the New Jerusalem. The New Jerusalem is the experience of the Divine.

That is also what the image "God's tent among us" is supposed to mean. Like all images of our inner life, this one is archetypal, that is, it goes far back into the human past, to the imaginative world of the nomads. Tents were their accommodations, their home. And hence this image tells us that the Divine can be experienced as our home, as our true nature. God is at home with us, and we are at home with God.

Now there is no more crying or mourning, for death is understood as a transition to a new form of existence. It is the great transformer. What is divine and eternal in us remains the same in all forms of existence.

What does this have to do with the ritual that we celebrate here, with the Eucharist? We celebrate our passing over into the new existence that we Christians call resurrection. We celebrate the "New Jerusalem." We celebrate this new reality, even though it often seems to be so far from us. We believe in it and by believing in it we receive motivation for the path that is to lead us to the experience of this reality.

Jesus Christ is the type in whom we recognize our own path. He has passed over through suffering and death into the Resurrection. That is exactly what is granted to us. We celebrate what we already are in our inmost depths but do not experience. We already live in this New Jerusalem without noticing it. The Omega Point is distant from us, not in time, but only in experience. The new heaven and the new earth have arrived. God has pitched his tent among us.

PART III

PERSONAL ACCOUNTS

NOTE

The following accounts are highly personal experiences that describe how people become aware of a more comprehensive reality. They are best read with the understanding that John of the Cross recommends for the perusal of such experiences:

> It would be ignorance to think that sayings of love understood mystically, such as those of the present stanzas, can be fairly explained by words of any kind....And it is for this reason that, by means of figures, comparisons, and similitudes, they allow something of that which they feel to overflow and utter secret mysteries from the abundance of the Spirit rather than explain these things rationally. These similitudes, if they be not read with the simplicity of the spirit of love and under-standing embodied in them, appear to be nonsense rather than the expression of reason, as may be seen in the divine Songs of Solomon and in other books of the Divine Scripture.[1]

We have to avoid looking for mystical experience only in the domain of religion or in the language of denominations. The Ultimate Reality cannot be fenced in, not even by religion. It happens to people at a time when they aren't thinking about it. In fact, they are often totally unprepared for it. It comes over them suddenly in ways they did not foresee. I have known religious who were disappointed that their experience had nothing to do with Christianity, and I have known agnostics who were surprised by a deeply Christian experience.

Mystical experience has quite different modes of expression. Sometimes it's an experience of "light" and "oneness." But it's not the usual light, and it's not one with something, but only oneness.

A second form of experience is solidarity with everything that lives, out of which grows a deep caring and love for all creatures. The "opposite number" disappears. What remains is a tree, a bird call, the sight of a flower, or a simple utensil.

We tend to assume blasphemy when we hear someone say, "I am God" after a profound personal experience. But it is the experience—not, to be sure, of the superficial ego, which would in fact be blasphemy; it is the experience of the true self, of the divine core in human beings. It is the experience of God with himself.

This experience is often highly unspecific and enters our consciousness as a strong jolt of energy, which can be felt as very painful. Generally it is connected with the process of purification. The person feels handed over, lonely, and abandoned. It is the dark night that knows not a moment of comfort. After such an experience, everyday life can long be altered until the usual routines again get the upper hand.

The following section contains a few of the many personal accounts I have come across.

...EVERYTHING IS LIGHT...

Fear, doubts whether there is truth, whether there is a God, and if there is truth, whether I can ever recognize it. And at the same time the knowledge that I can't live without truth, without meaning, without eternity. This conflict leads to unbearable tension. With this conflict inside me, I go into the woods. All of a sudden the tension dissolves. Everything *is* light—not *full of* light—everything vibrates and pulsates, but quite gently. Not only the trees, but the air as well. No I and Thou; only light, one.

When the experience leaves me, I find myself sitting on a tree stump again. Everything is easy; the tension is gone. But shortly afterwards, the questions begin: Who is God? Who am I? Is the ego only an illusion? Does the ego have free will?

No formula fits. They say, "God dwells in the heart" or "God dwells in the center of your essence"—as if there were that sort of personal district, that sort of boundary line!

...THERE IS NO DEATH...

I am confronting dying and I feel that it's going well, although I know that deep down there is no death, only the external decay of matter. Immortality is here and now, or else it doesn't exist at all. I feel at bottom a deep oneness, and I can't fall out of this oneness—not even in death. There are no limits except the ones set by man.

...WE CHOP UP THE NOW...

Midnight. When is yesterday? When is tomorrow? We try to chop the now into pieces, so as to record it, but it's indivisible.

Eternity isn't composed of time like a straight line made up of an infinite series of individual points. Eternity, infinity, heaven, is a pulsating now. "This day I have begotten you."

...I HAVE EXPERIENCED THE "FEAR NOT"...

I was breathing, when suddenly it crossed my mind: *Am I breathing or is someone breathing in me? Am I in God or is God in me?*

287

Then the first doubt: Inside? outside? What is inside? What is outside? I experienced it as one and told myself: *Breathe or let it breathe in you!*

It went on like this for a while, then the second doubt popped up: God in me, time, eternity. That, too, I experienced as one and noticed that there is no yesterday and no tomorrow, only a today.

The third doubt frightened me: Am I God? Is God me? And I told myself: *I believe in my Lord Jesus Christ, who died and rose from the dead. Am I taking to pantheism?* (I had to think of the brook and the fountainhead, and I noticed that in a certain sense I have always been in God.) I went on breathing, but with a feeling as if it were the whole universe that was breathing. I experienced a deep oneness with all people, and that filled me with deep joy and at the same time with great sadness at the thought of so many people who don't have that experience, and I wished that they all could.

In all this I was afraid—afraid I might not be on the right track. It gave me a great sense of peace when Fr. W. told me, "Don't be afraid! That's how reality is, neither inside nor outside, neither yesterday nor tomorrow." I experienced the "fear not" that's repeated so often in the Bible, and a great peace and silent joy remained with me.

...NO ROOM, NO PEOPLE, NO BOUNDARY...

I meditate together with two other people. As I breathe out I say inwardly, *Letting go.* A tear—a harsh light—heat emanating from my heart—there's no room, no people, no boundary, "letting go of oneself." Connected to everything, even with the things I don't know at all. Total silence. They ask: "How long?"—"No time!"

I sat until the end. We ate together in the evening, went to the evening worship, and then I went home. I listened to the silence and went to bed. Everything as usual. For the first time I have been able to see and listen to people. I felt myself close to them and to things—for weeks and months.

...ALL AT ONCE I WAS WITHOUT FEAR...

During a course in the garden: Suddenly everything was filled up and altogether dense. I had a feeling that I was bound up into something that reaches from the garden to the stars. Everything around me was familiar and connected to me in a new way I had not known before. Something like an infinitely deep peace, like a boundless joy, swept over me.

After the course and during a conversation: All at once my experience of space and of the people in it has changed. The distance in me vis-à-vis others suddenly changed into a feeling of intimacy, into a nearness and solidarity that I experienced as warmth and vitality.

All at once I was without fear. As I looked through the large window, the landscape was filled as if with something invisible, on the one hand, transparent and yet sharply outlined, and, on the other hand, quite close, as if it were a part of me. Over it all lay something like a brightness, a radiance, that made everything appear clearer, more colorful, more intense.

...NO MORE QUESTIONS...

This afternoon the events all came in a rush. More than rest and peace; everything is good, no more questions. It's indescribable. Then the feeling that streams of light were flowing around me, that I was being empowered. In the evening at the Eucharist I suddenly had the sense of being bound up with everything in love, in suffering with one another. When I last had a similar experience to this, I was unwilling to suffer. Tears, gratitude for the ability to sympathize.

...IN FACT, I WAS IN HIM...

On Good Friday I took part in the services and had the following experience. There were around twenty-five teenagers in a retreat house. When the liturgy began, I forgot everything. I simply did what had to be done. Another priest was the celebrant. After the liturgy I realized that I simply was with the other priest, in fact I was in him. The experience was so gentle, more like the curling of the waves on a pond. If I hadn't reflected on it, I never would have noticed it.

It seems to me that the more ego-consciousness falls away, the more one is present in this inner reality, in this "Nothingness."

...THERE WAS NO BREAK BETWEEN SITTING AND WALKING...

On the fourth or fifth day of the course it was simply there. It was a sound and yet not a sound. I didn't have to make it anymore. It was simply there. I didn't have to breathe it anymore. The tears flowed, and I kept stammering, "Why me? I'm so unworthy. Why me of all people?" There was no break anymore between sitting and walking. It all went very simply. In the courtyard, when I looked at the grass, I could have gone on crying incessantly. Everything was transformed. It was no longer me here and the grass there. It was so close to me, a heart-felt solidarity. Happy-sad and full of goodwill and tenderness for everyone and everything, that was, I think, my basic mood.

So that was it. I can't render it any better, although I haven't quite hit the nail on the head in describing how it was. It was just that everything was transformed, although it was the same as before.

...WHO'S GOING UP THE STAIRS?...

I tried to live everyday life, attentive in my actions, aware of what was happening. And all of a sudden there they were, the questions: Who's going up the stairs? Who's rinsing the vegetables? Who hears the telephone ring and then picks it up? Who makes the notes sound on my violin? What is looking in me, when I look? What is it that makes the people and cars pour through the streets? What touches the earth there, as the snowflakes fall? What drives the first green sprouts up from the ground? Whence comes the power that sounds the penetrating call in the little blackbird's throat? And behind everything again and again: Who am I, at the deepest level, primordially, at long last? What *is*, anyway? It gives me no peace, as if my whole life depended on an answer to it. Somehow my picture of the world has turned upside down, a spinning, bubbling tohu-wa-bohu.

...JUST A SPOON...

I am seventy years old, but today I saw a spoon for the first time in my life...just a spoon...it's enough to make you laugh...just a spoon...only a spoon!

...YES, THAT'S IT, THE RADISH ON THE PLATE...

I could no longer stop exercising. I felt an enormous strain. And suddenly I was there. But there was no more "I" to be "there." No more confinement and no more longing to get to some place or other. I was aware of my breath, which was simply there—the way the clock ticked—without any boundaries.

I couldn't express it, couldn't say it. I didn't want to mutilate the experience with words. Even now the words are wooden.

When I was at supper...yes, that's it! The radish on the plate, that's it. Joy! Bowing! Biting into the radish! Crying, laughing. That's it. How beautiful!

...THE RAINDROPS WERE FALLING INTO THE WATER...

I stood by the pond and saw how the raindrops were falling into the water. Actually it was all contained in that: this constant changing of outward form, an eternal being-lost-in-oneself. And then when I passed by the compost heap: the certainty that everything can only lose itself in itself. And later while sitting: everything whatsoever lives out of the same thing and there is nothing at all that could be outside.

...INTERTWINED IN THE TURNED-UP FINGERS OF GOD...

Today I was out for a long walk through the countryside. The earth is blooming: the first green shoots, anemones, birds building their nests, farmers working in their fields. And in all this busy activity, the same fullness pressing inexhaustibly toward life. I know that I am intertwined in these millions and millions of God's turned-up fingers.

...SEEING AS THOUGH I COULDN'T SEE...

The early morning hour lures me out into the fields and lets me take part in a miracle of creation: sunrise on a clear day. As I linger in the perfect silence, my whole existence suddenly feels gripped by a shudder, as if I had been struck by lightning. But there is nothing to hold onto, nothing concretely known or comprehensible. I am struck, as if scorched, branded, as if I had been flung by a lightning bolt into the void of unknowing. It's seeing as though I couldn't see, hearing as if I couldn't hear, knowing as if I couldn't know. The ringing of the monastery bells announces the moment of consecration during Mass. Visualization of the divine Essence—mystery out in the wheat field. All truth is simple.

...WHEN I LOOK MORE CLOSELY, IT'S GONE...

For some time now I can no longer agree with this notion of a personal God, this brother, partner, friend who is always there for us and who waits for us. Right now I experience God as dark, faceless, nonpersonal; not the God-man Jesus Christ on this earth, but the godhead in the things of this earth, in me also, as power, as intensity, as the existence (*Da-sein*, literally being there) of everything. And I can no longer share the Christians' glib certainty of salvation, the jubilant cry of those who have been saved once and for all. Because my experience of God is so new, so vulnerable, bound up with so much upheaval and pain. And when I try to look more closely at what I have experienced, it's gone. It takes time and silence to grow in me, not verbose religious services. And one more thing occurs to me: my powers of speech fail me. How am I to talk to people—and about what—without their declaring me insane?

...BOUNDARIES CEASE TO EXIST...

The dog barking outside was in me; the door to the hall was a door within me. I was in the room, and the room was in me. There was nothing outside me. The boundaries ceased to exist. I was filled with a deep feeling of happiness....My view of things was suddenly straightened out, and I sensed in myself the norm that is the origin of all norms.

During the walk the trees were my beloved and venerated brothers. I kissed them and pressed the dark, moist earth to my lips. The morning was like an act of birth. Creation had been made for me, and I spoke with the trees, the lake, and the mountain.

...EVERYTHING IS GOD...

During a cross-country run I suddenly sensed, I knew, I saw that everything that is life in me, that makes me a living creature, is God. He himself *is* my life. I can't express how powerful that was! And all the trees and bushes around me—all that is God!

In the winter I also once had a profound experience of God with a tree. And once in the spring I woke up and sensed so powerfully the pulsating life, his life, in me and outside in nature, and exultant, insane joy! After the course I spent many weeks in tremendous joy, pure joy over life, because I am allowed to exist.

...WHERE EVERYTHING IS THE WAY IT IS...

> Where the rhythm of time ends,
> and the boundaries of place.
> Where no stream of thoughts can reach,
> Where feelings no longer spin about.
> Where nothing is added to things
> in meaning, intention, difference.
> Where everything is the way it is, pure.
> And everything in essence equal.
> Where I go walking with God,
> in essence equal.

...WHY DID I STUDY THEOLOGY?...

> In the tree you are the tree,
> there you fly in the bird,
> before he wept in the child,
> and now you laugh in the woman living nearby.
> Why did I study theology?
> When I had forgotten it all over again,
> you were there.

...IT'S A MAGNIFICENT GAME...

Is it blasphemous to see an evolution of God? Nowadays I think of creator and creation as totally, radically identical. That means that I no longer have any use at all for this terminology. Completely identical— totally. And I can no longer see this identity as it is represented in the figure of the dancing Shiva. It's a magnificent game. Thus suffering and joy, death and life—everything, everything, everything, is one together with everything else. I no longer see creator and creation over against one another. And so even the destruction of nature is a component of this game. Can I say that love is somehow, nonetheless, a moving force here too? May I also think of myself in this sense as identical with God? That's how it seems to me.

...IN ALL THINGS GOD IS LOOKING AT ME...

During a week of exercises, it was on the second evening in my room, when a great serenity came over me, such as I had never experienced before.

And in all things God was looking at me—and I was God. It was so wonderful and yet so completely self-evident. And then I drifted off to sleep. The next morning everything was just as usual, and yet everything was completely different.

...SIMPLY SITTING...

While sitting today I again became aware of my unrest in the shoulder area and of my tendency to contract and shut myself off there. I consciously made my shoulders sink. All at once it felt as if my whole chest had burst open and I was flung out of myself. A single outward impulse. Seconds without ego, empty and vast without beginning or end. I found myself again, simply sitting.

...NO MORALITY, NO CONSCIENCE...

I'm standing in the bookstore, I pull a book off the shelf, something on the meaning of art. I page through it and read a sentence, which I can't remember anymore now, and I'm thunderstruck: *That's it.* A wave is set in motion. Everything becomes clear to me, everything. I'm in remarkably high spirits, and I run out of the bookstore. One realization came hot on the heels of the next. Total knowing without an object of knowledge. I am completely beside myself with happiness and enthusiasm. I know what it's all about. It's as if I were floating. I feel myself enveloped in a warm whirlwind. I know that I'm extremely close to it. Everything is clear. And then the feeling—I am free, completely free. East and West, I'm free to choose. I now have absolutely no ties to anything, not to any ethics, any morality, any conscience; there's nothing there anymore, nothing whatsoever. I run down the street. The whole thing is simply unreal. I am perfectly relaxed and bursting with energy. I feel superhuman. At the same time I know that I belong to something much greater. It is gigantically great, indescribably great, much greater than the earth, unimaginable. It is as if I stood in the middle of a giant whirlwind, like a hurricane, exactly in the middle. All around me is unimaginable energy, but I feel secure, secure precisely because of this energy. One could also call it God. He shatters every nameable dimension.

...I'M STILL LOOKING. CAN THIS BE ME?...

What I experienced was like dying: Often enough I had stood in front of the door to the void, to the foggy, bottomless Nothingness. I'm familiar with the "undertow," with the feeling that I have to go through it, and at the same time I know the fear that I won't be able to cope with the tremendous intensity that awaits me there. Indeed I have a deathly fear of being extinguished in everything that I was before, in the face of a reality alongside which there is nothing left. Up till now my "solution" was to turn back in time. But what if the void suddenly rushed like a tidal wave at me and over and under and around me? I can't describe it more specifically, only this: it's not a catastrophe, not annihilation. Only looking. I'm still looking. Can this be me?

...I WAS NEVER SO AWAKE BEFORE...WITHOUT ANY TIME...

It's like walking in fire, for weeks. The old blacksmith in our village did it this way: when the iron was at white heat, he fit the horseshoe to the form of the hoof. Something is happening with me like what happened to the iron. And I can only let it happen because the whole thing isn't about me. Bidding farewell and letting go are no achievement of mine, my clutching hands *get* opened. Things I had come to love lose their power of attraction all by themselves, ideas fall away, interests, ways of living; actually everything is undergoing change. But the comparison with the blacksmith limps on one point: in the end—and yesterday evening as I was sitting was one such end—there is no last hammer blow and then a transformed piece of iron. Instead, there was something like a fiery blast that melted down everything, and no "then," no iron. Only fire. I was fire, everything was fire. Formless, soundless. A glowing force that has no origin, that doesn't die down. I was never so awake as in this moment without any time. It's not hard for me to put the whole in religious contexts as an experience of godhead, of being God, so long as the traditional concepts can remain transparent for what is altogether different from anything a concept could express.

...IT WAS GOD AS THE "TOTALLY OTHER"...

On the third day of the course I was continually entering the void of consciousness after a very short time. Each time it was as if I were being pulled by a kind of suction into nothingness, into total silence and motionlessness. Then I was completely at one in myself and was in a deep state of absorption where I could stay without effort. Still I didn't feel liberated and light, but rather spellbound and rooted to the spot. The only thing that I saw was every stirring of my being. That wasn't enough for me. I didn't want merely to look at my own being. Father W. said I should very carefully open myself to God, in a very gentle movement toward him. I tried it, and then something indescribably great happened: a thick, red, warm stream flowed out of my heart toward "Him"...That was the real "prayer of silence." A flow of love, trust, and peace...It wouldn't stop. It continued even when I went to bed. Whether I was sitting or lying down it was the same. Despite this I was fresh and well-rested in the morning.

Then came the first sitting in the morning. I told myself, *Open yourself carefully to God!* The thought had scarcely crossed my mind when "something" arrived, an incomprehensible, powerful reality, a presence, or the deity. (What should I call it?) It was God as the "totally other." I didn't see Him, but I sensed Him, and it was so powerful and almost uncanny. I can't exactly express it in words. And at that very moment I knew: Nothingness, the Void, that's what He is!

...I BEGAN TO SEE "NOTHINGNESS." IT WAS UNFENCED REALITY...

A few days ago I read about contemplation....When you look at God, you see nothing, and that is precisely the point: when you look at nothing, there's nothing there. That isn't any sort of experience or a kind of realization. In fact, it is what God is. God is "Nothingness." Immediately after that I began to see "Nothingness." It was unfenced reality, reality without edge or fringe, and all my dependency seemed to have disappeared in this seeing. A great wave of relaxation came over me; nothing needed to be done. Shortly before this experience there was a time of about two weeks when I was almost constantly on the point of crying. There was no reason for this crying; it was just a gentle touch within me, a tenderness that did not keep me from my duties.

...EVERYTHING WAS SO RIGHT...

The pillow on which I sit forms a wafer-thin boundary between the body that I am and an unfathomable transcendence, which keeps opening more and more to a boundless expanse....The power of this boundlessness broke in over me during a nightly meditation session and made me see that beyond my capacity to experience and perceive only *BEING* existed, collected energy without any discharge of power. I found myself in a condition without ego-consciousness, without sexual awareness, incapable of love, incapable of sin, without fear, without ecstasy. Everything was just so right. Nothing would have been more absurd than to try to analyze this experience or give it a name.

...ONLY THIS NAMELESS THING...

Then came the times when as I was sitting I had the impression that I was stepping out of the woman who was sitting there, and that from far outside her I was watching a play, with myself and the whole world as the theater. What was it that stepped out? And who remained sitting there? Where was "I"? "My" consciousness no longer had any individual coloration, and in the moments of experiencing God, there was no longer even any experience of...but only this Nameless thing. In such states— I believe, as I look back at it now—it's just spiritual existence.

...IT IS A RADICAL GOING MAD...

At the end of the last course I had gotten more absorbed in sitting than ever before, as if I no longer existed, free from myself. And for the first time the perception of this state and the perception of my everyday consciousness (the fact that I'm sitting here and breathing, that my neighbor is swallowing his food, someone else is walking around in the meditation room, and so on) took place at the same time. Such overlapping of two conscious states is something that happens to me often now. Sometimes both states seem to be freely available for my use. I no longer recognize myself—it's an altogether radical, elementary going mad.

...IT RAN...

During the cross-country run something became undone in me after we had run for an hour. Suddenly I was in a state of effortlessness and lightness—I wasn't the one who was running anymore—"it" was running. It was a wonderful experience.

...DON'T TAKE A *SINGLE* STEP...

I notice: I myself don't have to do anything at all. I am only one of the ingredients of which life is fashioned, the thread from which the cosmic carpet is woven. This dimension of life is neither rationally comprehensible nor fathomable—only discoverable and experiential, beyond all foundations. You yourself are opened up for this foundation; you can't summon up anything for it—except that you let go of everything and add nothing by your action. Not even the letting go takes place voluntarily; it's a matter of submission, an event that you can neither prompt nor hinder, you can only perceive it, admit it, "endure" it.

Going by this path is more like being pulled. One must not take a *single* step oneself. "Let yourself go"—how easy it sounds, how hard it is.

...IT PRAYS WITHIN, IT BREATHES WITHIN...

I live in a state of incapacity, of inner powerlessness, of sickness—without being organically sick—of intensive, inward pain. It is the subtlest and at the same time the most massive form of abandonment that I have ever experienced.

My real life increasingly goes on within me. It prays within me, it breathes within me, it laughs within me, it weeps within me—and for some days now there has been nothing but loving weeping or weeping love. This pain can't be described with words. It is as if all inclinations that are still impure had to be consumed...as if transformation could occur only through wounding and extinction... Without any action on my part, I am drawn into a kind of cauterization. As it proceeds, nothing in me offers any resistance, nothing runs away, nor asks why, nor understands what is actually going on here.

...IT'S A GOING UNDER TO LIFE AND DEATH...

With increasing pain and growing frequency I am experiencing my senses as useless for the perception of being. They distort and darken the truth more than they illuminate it. They need a thorough purification in the form of an elimination of their peculiar experience, so as to receive the truth nakedly and genuinely, in order to become transparent to the light.

Still I sense a painful inability to contribute something active to this process. Together with my senses, I have to plunge into an ocean of emptiness, of nothingness. It's a going under to life and death—and I'm afraid to let go of myself. There are still many supposed "treasures" that my ego tries to cling to. How far is the way?

...WHY DOES THE DIVINE PATH HAVE SO MANY INHUMAN FEATURES?...

God completely withdraws himself. Wanting to grasp at him means holding an empty shell in your hands. My heart becomes incapable of longing; all at once I no longer sense any thirst for God. Eating his bread or not eating it is all one—as if being full of God or empty of God were the same thing. Overnight I have lost the taste for God and for things. Suddenly I can no longer sing the praises of creation. My former enthusiasm has disappeared and given way to an indifference that I find terrifying.

I become aware of a change in my senses: my ears seem to be deaf, my eyes blind, my taste deadened, my mouth struck dumb, because words trying to take shape turn empty and hollow.

I'm often seized by a constricting fear of the unpredictability of this development, which threatens to cut off completely any initiative of my own. The share that I can bring becomes increasingly smaller. The things that made up my humanness, my own distinctive features, shrivel into insignificance. Something or other in the core is disintegrating, and it's as if I didn't have the strength to preserve it. The current condition, which holds my whole being in its painful grip, is comparable to the desperate situation of a drowning man whose cry for help is stifled in his mouth. Because of this despair, doubts arise about whether I can continue the path in anything like the old manner. I have never sensed such fear of falling into a profoundly depressive state of mind like the last time, when every activity was taken away from me, and one layer of skin after the other seemed to be stripped off. But that can't be the meaning of the process of becoming whole, that you become human only through losing and forfeiting your potential. Why does the divine path have so many inhuman features?

...GOD, WHY ARE YOU LURING ME?...

The question keeps posing itself more urgently: could my love, my devotion, my intensity, my presence, have been directed to a God who wasn't God at all?

Could I have so drastically mistaken this truly divine God up to now thanks to my human imagination and mode of experience? God, why do you lure me so vehemently, so unconditionally, so entirely onto this path—and now you deprive my steps of your presence, which means joy, hope, and courage to me?

Why is it so hard for me to understand that the path evidently has to go by way of the total abandonment of all my thoughts and images and wishes before it can ripen into a path of becoming one with the God-man?

I fumble in the darkness. I have to leave behind every seeming security that my consciousness and my senses pretend to provide, in order to put one foot in front of another as I enter a condition of not-knowing, not-being-able-to, and no-longer-wanting. Oh how my nature balks, still balks at this time now, which seems to be the only possible one for the divine path.

All things are so empty, so boundlessly empty. The sunlit treetops are empty, the tree is empty, the song of the birds is empty. Friends who meet me are empty. God is empty, my heart is empty. Back in the past, didn't this same heart have enough profound experiences of how everything was saturated with God's fullness? Is this experience, like that one, only a different testimony to one and the same unnameable reality?

...I HAVE APPARENTLY BECOME GODLESS...

"My God": it's a familiar, well-rehearsed formula, but now there is no divine conversation partner to whom the heart can turn. If I were to pray to God now as I used to in my distress, it would be a sin—separation. My erstwhile faith is topsy-turvy.

A sob bursts out. My heart has long been crying within itself. Finally there is only the great clarity: the No is at bottom Yes. Everything is Yes that has its roots in this depth and is born out of it as love. Everything is an absolute Yes.

Many hours afterwards an "Abba" takes shape. But not anymore the way it used to, as a salutation for "God." Instead, out of the primordial *A* something finds its voice, stammers *b,b*...(that stands for all the silent signs of the alphabet, for all the expressions of what can be perceived though not articulated)—and presses, flows, sinks back into the *A*.

Abba is the same word, backward or forward; there is no difference. The primal image and the mirror image, expanding out and turning back, before and after, it is not-two. Can a godless person pray?

Abba! A!

...EVEN THE MOST LIFE-THREATENING ILLNESS LOSES ALL MEANING...

When I got home, I again experienced what life is and what it means to be allowed to live. Above all I experienced the immeasurable power, the inexpressible joy that every moment contains. (And now I feel the great poverty of my vocabulary, because there's no way I can express what I really experienced.) If we were to grasp the moment in its brightness and its greatness, it would shatter us. My soul exulted and thought: *every moment is so precious—and if I had only a few left, but lived them attentively and consciously, that would be fullness enough*. Now I saw it clearly: in view of this precious fullness of the moment, even the most life-threatening disease loses all meaning, and all fears are naught.

...ONLY OLIVE TREES, ONLY CICADAS...

When I get out of the airplane, something strange happens: the olive trees are no longer symbol-laden natural creatures that immediately prompt my brain to make metaphors; they're quite simply "just" olive trees.

I have sat every morning. Today I noticed a change: there was no more me, there were only cicadas, then a door that opened and shut. And these sounds weren't the same as usual; they were a work of art; perfect!

...ONLY THIS STEP, THIS MOVEMENT...

I'm going to get something, to make a phone call, to write, etc.—but that's only this step, this movement, this number, this book, this bill...It's a miracle and yet quite banal. There is no room for ifs, ands, or buts.

...WITHOUT A WHY...

I sit because I sit;
I walk because I walk;
I eat because I eat;
I sleep because I sleep.
Empty. Without a why.
Valley is valley and mountain is mountain.
There is only breathing, there is only walking,
       there is only sitting.
Otherwise nothing; nothing more.
I drink the clear water of the moment—spring water.
       Now I know how Now tastes.

...EVERY LEAF AND EVERY PAVEMENT...*HE* WAS EVERYTHING...

Early in the morning I went on a long run. Instead of praying the rosary along the way as I usually do, I was completely taken up only in what is, and I was suddenly overwhelmed by his presence in all things. Every sound and every movement, every leaf and the pavement beneath my feet was filled with divine life. Everything was *HIM*. I was ecstatically lifted out of myself and yet bound up with everything. The experience lasted for several days. I was overpowered by his omnipresence.

...I LOVE SO LITTLE...

Lunch. Washed the dishes. I'm lying out on the bench. I want to go in. I pass by a little tree, and then it happens; I sense how it radiates love, how everything that I see wraps me round with love. Tears keep coming, I experience love and I can love—and I love so little. I sense that this is the beginning of something that goes much deeper.

At some point or other I return to everyday life. I see differently, hear differently, walk differently. I open the door differently. I see the birch, its white trunk, and suddenly feel that while I'm looking at it I experience everything.

...FOR A MOMENT I WAS THIS SOUND...

The dog stormed through the room; he had snatched up a piece of paper from somewhere. It made a scratchy sound. For a moment I was that sound.

Out walking the dog all of a sudden I realize: if I'm nothing, then I'm everything. If I'm nothing and everything, you're nothing and everything, then we two alone are everything. And together we're everything too. Thus we are one and the same...and that's what I wanted to say to the world back when I was a baby. Because that alone would "save" everyone and "heal" everyone. Communicating that to everybody is what loving your neighbor means—nothing else will do. I wanted to keep this knowledge and save all beings, but I forgot it again. This desire to help and save lodged itself in me as an urge to go to the Third World, so as to help all men and women. All my life this illusion has plagued me, especially since it never got fulfilled.

Suddenly I realized that I didn't have to go to the Third World because I have once again recognized what "brings salvation." What could I have ever managed to bring the people there? Nothing, nothing that could have contributed to their salvation. I need only to persevere sitting on my pillow and set an example to others by my inner transformation; that is my gift. Free from illusion I laughed out loud. I laughed out loud for hours, I cried and I laughed.

...That's what I wanted to tell the world back when I was a baby.

...THE PAPER IS WHITE, THE INK BLUE...

Rest and confusion; joy and pain—often both simultaneously. In everything something has changed, everything is one. Words fail me. Everything is changed; everything is the same. The paper is white, the ink blue, the fountain pen black.

...EVERYTHING IS THE SAME...GOD-REALITY...

God has become reality, and the great question, "Do You exist?" has fallen silent. I am all tied up in this and can't get away anymore. Again and again God, life, fullness. The world has become different. There are no longer such great differences between work and free time because everything is the same: "God-Reality."

...THERE'S NO MORE OPPOSITE NUMBER...

The experience of nature takes place on an entirely new level. Nothing is looking at me, speaking to me, has anything to do with me—because nothing is not the object of my experience. There is no more opposite number, no duality of subject and object. What is looked at fuses with the one who is looking into a single essence. I am the tree, the tree is I.

...CAN YOU HEAR HOW EVERYTHING OUTSIDE IS GETTING GREEN?...

Today I wrote in a letter: "Can you hear how everything outside is getting green?"—and only afterwards did I notice what I had written there.

...IN THIS I AM AT ONCE IMPORTANT AND UNIMPORTANT...

There flows through you what I, in my limited way of expressing things, characterize as light. I recognize this light in me, and yet it doesn't remain in me; others will be able to get a glimpse of it through me, and so on it will go. In this I am at once important and unimportant. In this "ego" I can know, see, hear, sense, smell, and taste—and again let go. It's not "me," but it finds in me space, time, and a home, and I lose in it space and time, and find a home.

I thank you so much for what I am experiencing. There is no "true," no "false," and no stage or goal to be reached, only a continuous effort, which is actually no effort at all, but an opening and a liberation, in other words, just life. That counts, and in this everyone and everything all have the same chance. It's not the state of liberation, but the readiness for liberation.

...THAT I HAD SPENT MY WHOLE LIFE RUNNING PAST IT...

When I got back home, my whole nature was changed. I was thoroughly pervaded with tenderness. After many years of darkness, my heart began to live again. One morning I suddenly broke out into tears. For a moment I felt or saw what my heart had been longing for my whole life long. I sensed that actually it's all there, but that I had spent my whole life running past it. What hurt me most of all was that I have loved so little and have always been trapped in my own madness, and that I can never again make up for this lack of love.

My ego couldn't get anything at all out of this moment. But slowly I am sensing that some far-reaching things *have* happened to me.

...I ALWAYS STAYED "WITHIN" THE GATE...

At first I sit quite relaxed and calm, I have no concerns or responsibilities. I sit and try to become "empty."

In the Dokusan I am given the task: "Who am I if I am not driven?"

Up until this moment nothing had been driving me—I protested inwardly against the assignment: "Who am I if I am not driven?"

I move on to the next conversation: "Everything is in order: your thoughts, your experience. Ask a question anyway!"

Now, I am sitting again with the old assignment: "Let your prayer be self-surrender." What happens now is really indescribable. It happened in an instant. I'll try to describe it in somewhat comprehensible terms. I sit down on my cushion and say to myself once again, what W. had shortly before assigned me in the Dokusan: *self-surrender, self-surrender....* After a short time I was hit by an enormous wave of force, called love, like the wave of an explosion, and at the same time by an immense burst of light. This light and the love struck me with gigantic power. I am immersed in light, indescribably bright, and in love. Before me I see a great golden gate in radiant light. I hear music and I feel myself pushed forward through the gate. It's as if behind the gate lay a city with many people who are all merry and content. Everything is immersed and enveloped in an enormous fountain of light. The heavenly Jerusalem occurred to me apropos of this, as an example, though I basically don't like this Christian terminology. I felt as if the voice was about to say, "Go through the gate."

I am shaken by what happens to me, and at the same time I am horribly afraid. Something in me says: *When the people inside the gate see you in all this bright light, they'll notice that you don't belong there. If you go through the gate, they'll throw you out.* A dispute flares up inside me. I start crying and leave my place; I walk into the garden. I am desperate. By the next round of sitting I have got a grip on myself. I'm sad that I didn't dare go through the gate. Now I sit striving to find the gate again. I want to take a second run at it, to venture through the gate so full of promises.

With all my goodwill and all the great efforts that I make I don't succeed in finding the gate, much less in going through it. I recall my prayer exercise: "Let your prayer be self-sacrifice." Just that. I committed myself to what was happening in my body. Again the recollection, "self-surrender." Again I commit myself to what is happening. I feel a fusion with the pressure. When the pressure meets counter-presssure, power and energy arise. Driven by the pressure, a great lily unfolds in my breast. I think, *my heart chakra has opened.*

It's like a dam bursting. The world has totally changed, although, of course, it's still the same. A jolt of energy shoots through me, as if with one hundred thousand volts. I feel the power, energy, and joy of life. Everything about me is living and vital. It's as if I'd been immersed and drenched with love—from the very beginning. I no longer have to find the gate, I don't need to pass through it, because I have always been "inside" the gate, and I always will be. What separates me from the state of being "inside the gate" is actually just my thought-world. Thoughts and the feelings resulting from them generate a fictive world.

It makes no difference what I do, wherever I turn, I am enveloped and surrounded by love. All being *is* love. There is only one single authentic reality, namely love. This love embodies becoming and passing away, but also everything that we find here in life and, beyond that, death too. It is a satisfied, rich love, exuding all things. It's no gaunt, petty-calculating love. I sense joy—joy, sun, and love. Aren't we all children playing the great game of life? Only don't we do it with too much deadly earnest and with all too absurd realities?

I feel as if a veil had been torn from my eyes. I see the world differently than I did before. I understand what's meant by "sleeping humanity." With my reason I had grasped this by reading; I knew what it was all about. Now I feel and experience it.

...NOTHING BUT THE GREAT SILENCE...

Lord, I am afraid of letting go, of being and having nothing, of the void, of the invisible and ungraspable, of loneliness, paleness, of springing into this world devoid of time and space. I can hear nothing but the great silence. Suddenly it breathes me—I sense it quite clearly.

Lord, today I rejoice at the prospect of having to be nothing. I work and don't reflect on what I'm working for; it's simply that way. Today it's light and animated; tomorrow, when the ego makes its claims, it will be more burdensome. I work and rejoice that I am.

Lord, sometimes it's so strenuous on the way. Suddenly my path goes through the thicket, and my pace comes to a standstill. Lord, just this one step and then the next one.

...WHERE COULD I LOSE MYSELF?...

Lord, you are no top and no bottom; you are no inside and no outside, no small and no big, no full and no empty. Lord, you are everything. All our concepts and systems are rooted in you. Everything begins and ends with you. Where can I lose myself in there forever?

...I AM...AND YOU ARE ME...

Lord, I am. I don't know what for or why. I don't have to know, because since you are everything, it's unimportant to ask about the What and the Why. I am because I am. Melted down into the universe, into the micro and macro. Lord, you are the center, and you embrace everything. You are in all directions. You are round and drawn-out. You are my neighbor, and you are me.

Lord, when I let go and throw myself in blind trust upon you, I have the feeling, even in the wildest rush of everyday life, of lying warm and secure in your "bosom." I work and rejoice that I work; I read and rejoice that I read. Lord, I don't look into the distance or to tomorrow; I see and sense only what's in the moment now, and again in the moment now. Now is rest, now is pain, now is excitement, now is tension, now is silence, now is listening.

...WHEN WILL THE LAST CORDS BREAK?...

I'm standing in space and speaking to what has no space; I'm standing in time and speaking to what has no time. At the moment I'm dangling between space and spacelessness, and sick to the point of vomiting.

Lord, when will the last cords break? I wish I were allowed to close my eyes and to fall far and deep. In falling, I'll be transformed.

Lord, after days of inward struggle and pain, today I feel liberated. I know nothing about this inner event. Perhaps you wanted to clean up, and I held on tight.

Lord, although I wish to get away from myself, I'm mad about the way you do it.

I feel weak and pathetic, and that's exactly what I don't like. It's hard for me to leave my ideal vision of myself behind and to accept myself for who I am.

Lord, what language do you speak? I can't hear you. Lord, all I hear is silence, not the calming silence but the all-consuming kind.

Lord, I'm falling deeper than the deepest depth. In this profound darkness, I no longer see whether I'm walking. I see and feel nothing but darkness. My movements are staggering for sheer weakness and nausea.

My present leave-taking is a farewell to wishes and ideas, well-worn traditions, and certainties. A departure from the broad, straight path where everything is loud, colorful, hasty, and bright. It leads by way of a path that is narrow, full of rocks and pebbles, dark, and silent.

Lord, man is silent, nature is silent, and you are silent; now it's deepest night.

Lord, I didn't know that I can become active in compassion. Becoming silent, sticking it out, standing firm with you, in you, for you, and hence for others, and vice versa.

I feel a great and painful sense of loss, which I'm barely able to articulate. It pains me. I *am* pain, everything is pain.

Lord, who are you, to whom do I speak? Everything is as if it's been let go in me—I'm speechless. And all around me a tidal wave, chaos, a whirlwind. Standing in the middle of the whirlwind, I feel untouched by it all. I feel like a stopped clock surrounded by clocks that are loudly ticking away.

Lord, all my darkness is myself. The way to undivided life is a long one, especially for me, since I have an iron will and a strong temperament.

Lord, in the dark I am nearest to you and to myself. There my true essence is set free. In this darkness, however, I can also recognize faces that disappear in the harsh light of day. They lie in ambush for me and try to seize me—now that I have let go—and carry me off.

Lord, you are everything: the mountain of garbage and the manicured city park, the wide and the narrow street, the judge and the condemned man, the fence and the freedom.

Lord, my dependency on people and things cries to heaven. The reversal of polarity causes me such difficulties in withdrawal that I'm scarcely capable of moving my body.

Lord, the whole evil is clinging to matter.

Lord, I am neither good nor bad; I'm just the way I am.

Lord, I feel like the atom: split, scattered, and poured back into the melting pot. I'm no longer myself.

Lord, I feel your methods of sanctification and your bitter medicine; still I beg you to intervene, if it is needed.

Lord, if I get rid of everything that is mine, then I am a homeless person. I have neither parents nor siblings, neither husband nor children, neither house nor tradition, neither religion nor laws. I have no good opinions and words of advice. I am abandoned, a stranger.

...WHAT IS MY ESSENCE?...

God is my deepest essence? Overflowing light and love. God is light! God is love!—Looking on and being looked on. My deepest essence is unchangeable.

To see the world as if one were opening one's eyes for the first time. Every moment the first moment. The tree rustles and the wind cools my face...and my index finger penetrates the entire universe. The things have no name. I have blown out the match, and yet it goes on burning. For hours, the powerful deep laughter that shakes everything.

All things come out of the Void and go back into the Void. gong...gong...gong—click...click...click!

...MIRROR, MY EYES, RECOGNIZE IT THERE—
I, YOU, GOD, EVERYTHING...

Arrived home on my pillow. Crying inwardly for joy. I didn't know that everything is so simple. My whole life I've been looking for the "big blue ribbon," and yet all I had to do was open my hands and accept it.

Christ stands for life, for everything. Christ is the ruler—today and forever. I wrote it on the wall of a Doric temple. It will remain there until the winter rains wash it away.

I understand, I understand, only I didn't know it. That is the path: all the detours, then you get lost, impossible to go on, and now seeing the well, seeing the tree. The camel has long passed through the eye of the needle, and I sit there and ponder how it could happen. There is no eye of the needle anywhere. I am afraid, deathly afraid. What if I die here?

Kyrie eleison for me and for all.—Earlier I prayed for strength; now I pray for weakness so that I can sense my neediness.

Will I find God? Will I be found?—Evening. There's nothing to look for or to find. Clarity. Clarity. My hands know it, my shoulder knows it, but my head?

I am afraid to look into the mirror, for I see *HIM* there. In my eyes I see *HIM*. My feet know it, my hands, my knees. They pray the *Kyrie*. And now my eyes have seen it too.

The girl that went in front of me, I wanted to touch her, lay my hands on her shoulder, and embrace her; yet I was afraid of seeing her face.

Fear! When I recognize you and you recognize me, be careful with me, so that I don't have to be terrified of you in the darkness.

I sense your love in me so strongly that I would like to embrace my patients. Your love is like fire.—Freedom. I don't have to do anything, just simply be as you are. Neither good nor evil, neither wise nor foolish, neither strong nor weak—no, simply the way it is. When the wind blows through the willow blossoms, the seeds fly off. The wind is everywhere. I am everywhere. What if I now lose myself completely in your presence? Treat me like a seriously ill patient, very lovingly. Speak kindly to me; forbid me to reflect on everything.

I have the feeling it's Easter. The earth smells of death and resurrection. I hear the birds singing a new song. Form is Void, Void is Form.— The circle closes. Christ—an interchangeable form of the Divine— Mother Mary, Athene, God, Father, Son. I can only stammer: My God, there are no words anymore.

I ran out into the garden and saw everything for the first time. The girl at the pond. We fed the tadpoles and made up names for them.

Eucharist. I am afraid of your nearness in the symbols of bread and wine. Afraid you may come too near to me, that I might lose myself in you. I hold fast to the voice of the young man kneeling next to me. He looks at me in surprise, when afterwards I thank him.

I sit on the staircase and cry. I no longer know who I am, where I am. I dissolve in the sounds. I look in the mirror, look in my eyes, I don't know how long. I look and seek and seek and look. Then I see it: "Moon of truth." The mirror, my eyes, in them I recognize *IT-I, YOU, GOD, EVERYTHING*.

On the trip back home I write Hallelujah on the notices stapled to the telegraph poles.

...THE DOOR IS OPENED, I DIDN'T KNOW IT...

The door is opened, I didn't know it.
The door is right by me, I didn't see it.
The door is for entering, didn't I want to?!

NOTES

PART I: LECTURES

INTRODUCTION
1. Daio Kokushi.
2. From G. Börner, "Die Entstehung der Welt aus astronomischer Sicht" (lecture), Alpbach, 1989.
3. Gary Zukav, *The Dancing Wu Li Masters* (New York, NY: William Morrow Company, 1979), 327.

1. SEARCH FOR THE MEANING OF LIFE
1. Rabbi Nachmann of Brazlar.
2. Josef Quint and Harow Shapley, ed. *Meister Eckhart* (Munich, 1979), 34.
3. Al-Halladsch, "O Leute, rettet mich vor Gott," *Texte zum Nachdenken*, Herder TB 1240, 26.
4. C.G. Jung, *Gesammelte Werke* (Stuttgart, 1963), 362.
5. John of the Cross, Translator E. Allison Peers, *The Complete Works of Saint John of the Cross*, 3 Volumes (Westminster, MD: Newman Press, 1949), *Living Flame of Love* (hereafter "LF"), iii, 9 (III, 211). All subsequent quotations from John of the Cross will be taken from this edition, with volume and page number cited in parentheses.
6. John of the Cross, *The Ascent of Mount Carmel* (hereafter "AMC"), iii, 12 (I, 248).
7. Quint, 353, l. 23.

8. Quint, 308, l. 6.
9. Quint, 60.
10. LF, iv, 5 (III, 209).

2. SCIENCE AND MYSTICISM
   1. See C. Lilly, *Das Zentrum des Zyklons,* Fischer TB 1768.
   2. See Harold Burr, "Elektrische Felder des Lebens," in *Lesebuch zu bedrängenden Fragen unserer Zeit* II/85, ed. E. Naudascher, Karlsruhe.
   3. Rupert Sheldrake, *Das Schöpferische Universum,* Goldmann TB 14014, Foreword.

3. TRANSPERSONAL EXPERIENCE
   1. See Ken Wilber, *Halbzeit der Evolution* (Munich, 1984).
   2. Quint, 29.
   3. Quint, 180.
   4. Quint, 355.
   5. John of the Cross, AMC iii, 12, 1 (I, 247-48).
   6. Kabir, *Im Garten der Gottesliebe* (Heidelberg, 1984), 1.
   7. Gesänge des tanzenden Gottesfreundes, *Texte zum Nachdenken,* Herderbücherei 679, 67.
   8. LF, iv, 9 (III, 211).
   9. Ibid., iv, 10 (III, 212).
   10. See Z. Shibayama, *Zen in Gleichnis und Bild* (Munich, 1979), 82.
   11. Quint, 102, l.12.
   12. *Up from Eden,* (New York, NY: Doubleday, 1981), 297.
   13. Quint, 358, ll. 21.
   14. Quint, 397.
   15. Garma C.C. Chang, *Mahamudra-Fibel* (Vienna: Octopus Verlag, 1979).
   16. Quint, 61, l. 16.

4. RELIGION OR ESOTERICISM?
   1. Esotericism comes from the Greek word *esoteros* = inside, within. Exotericism comes from *exoteros* = popular, understandable to the laity. The word *esotericism,* however, is not used here in the sense of something strictly for initiates, that

is, people who belong to an esoteric group; and the word *exotericism* is not used in the sense of something for noninitiates or outsiders. Rather the word *esotericism* is meant to characterize a spirituality whose goal is experience and that sees in this goal the meaning of religion as well.

2. Quint, 450, l.3.
3. Ibid.
4. See Nicholas of Cusa, "Verteidigung der wissenden Unwissenheit," *Philosophisch-theologische Schriften I* (Vienna, 1962).
5. Whatever is in the world and takes place there receives its meaning and becomes intelligible from the standpoint of what was always present in "primordial time" and happened as a divine event, as duplicated in myth and cult. Thus myth is a form of religion. *Der Große Henker VI,* 851.
6. See Thorwald Dethlefsen, "Das Ostermysterium," lecture.
7. See Joseph Campbell, *Living Myth.*
8. See T. Dethlefsen, "Gedanken zum Ostermysterium," lecture.

5. Christian Mysticism and the Eastern Esoteric Paths

1. See Michael B. Green, in *Spektrum der Wissenschaft,* November 1986, 54.
2. Zukav, 330.
3. Ibid.
4. Nicholas of Cusa, *Studienausgabe III,* 133.
5. The Gospel of Thomas, Nr. 22, cited in *The Other Bible,* Editor Willis Barnstone (San Francisco, CA: Harper & Row, 1984), 300.
6. Quint, 436, ll. 9.
7. C.G. Jung, *Zur Psychologie westlicher und östlicher Religion* (Olten, 1971), 116.

6. Contemplative Prayer: An Old Christian Tradition

1. See AMC, ii, 15 (I, 128-29).
2. Ibid., iii, 14 (I, 255-56).
3. Ibid., and John of the Cross, *The Dark Night* (hereafter "DN"), Vol. I, Collected Works (335-486).

4. See M. Guyon, *Kurzer und sehr leichter Weg zum inneren Gebet*, Editor E. Jungclaussen (Freiburg, 1988), 51.

5. DN, I, 1,1 (I, 350).

6. F. de Osuna, *Versenkung*, Herderbücherei 938, 30.

7. AMC, ii, 14, 2 (I, 118-19).

8. Ibid., ii, 13, 7 (I, 117).

9. See Hugh of St. Victor, *De sacramentis I*, 10, 2.

10. See Bonaventura, *Itinerarium* (Munich, 1961), 41.

11. *The Cloud of Unknowing*, Editor James Walsh, SJ (Mahwah, NJ: Paulist Press, 1981).

12. See E. Jungclaussen, *Suche Gott in dir* (Freiburg, 1986), 51.

13. AMC, Introduction (I, 11-15).

14. Claudio Naranjo, Robert E. Ornstein, *Psychologie de Meditation* (Frankfurt, 1988) Fischer TB 42298.

15. See Ken Wilber, *Halbzeit der Evolution* (Munich, 1981).

16. See *Writings From the Philokalia*, Translator E. Kadloubovsky and G.E.H. Palmer (London: Faber and Faber, 1979), 194.

17. John Cassian, *Conferences*, Translator Colm Luibheid (Mahwah, NJ: Paulist Press, 1985), Conference X, 137.

18. Demetrias V. Nagel, "Puritas Cordis," in G. Stachel, *Ungegenständliche Meditation* (Mainz, 1978), 140.

19. Ibid., 195.

20. *The Cloud of Unknowing*, 130-31.

21. Ibid., 131-32.

22. J.E. Berendt, *Nada Brahma, Die Welt ist Klang*, rororo 7949, 38.

23. See *Aufrichtige Erzählungen eines russischen Pilgers*, Editor E. Jungclaussen (Freiburg, 1968), 25.

24. See Berendt, *Nada Brahma*, 102.

25. Ibid., 152.

26. Ibid., 55.

7. Great Mystics' Paths of Prayer

1. J. Cassian, *Conferences*, Prologue.

2. Ibid., I, 4.

3. Ibid.

4. Demetrias V. Nagel, "In munen muso," *Ungegenständliche Meditation*, Editor G. Stachel (Mainz, 1978), 140.

5. Ibid., 141.

6. Evagrius Ponticus, *Praktikos* (Münsterschwarzach, 1989), Nr. 64.

7. Ibid., 146.

8. Ibid., 149.

9. Ibid., 152.

10. John Cassian, *Conferences*, 137.

11. Nagel, "In munen muso," 154.

12. Meister Eckehart: *Die lateinischen Werke*, Editor J. Quint, IV, 198, 11.

13. Meister Eckhart, *Die deutschen Werke*, Editor J. Quint, I, 253, 6 (hereafter "DW").

14. *Mumonkan* 19.

15. Meister Eckhart, *Deutsche Predigten und Traktate*, Editor J. Quint (Munich, 1977), 436, ll. 9 (hereafter "DPT").

16. DW, V, 403, 4-5.

17. DPT, 438, 4-5.

18. DW, III, 485, 10-11.

19. Ibid., V, 209, 1.

20. Ibid., I, 52, 9-10.

21. DPT, 433, ll. 22.

22. DW, III, 196, l. 14.

23. Ibid., III, 19, ll.2-3.

24. DPT, 420, 24.

25. DW, I, 312, ll. 8-9.

26. Ibid., III, 240, ll. 3.

27. Ibid., I, 351, ll. 8-9.

28. Ibid., 170, l. 1.

29. Ibid., 203, ll. 3-4.

30. Ibid., 284, ll. 1-2.

31. Kabir, *Im Garten der Gottesliebe*, 6.

32. DW, Sermon 53.

33. D. Mieth, *Meister Eckhart* (Freiburg, 1979), 96.

34. Ibid., 92.

35. DW, V, 203.

36. Ibid., 275, l. 10.

37. Ibid., 277, ll. 1-2.
38. On this point see Gottwald Wolz, "Übung und Gnade," in *Zeitschrift für Philosophie und Theologie*, Vol. 34 (1987), 1-2, 147.
39. LF, iii, 33 (III, 177-78).
40. See LF, iii, 34 (III, 178-79).
41. Ibid.
42. Ibid., 12 (III, 123-24).
43. Ibid., 41 (III, 182).
44. Ibid., 55 (III, 190-91).
45. AMC, ii, 4, 2 (I. 74).
46. Ibid., 13, 7 (I, 117).
47. Ibid., 14, 9 (I, 122-23).
48. Ibid., 14, 1 (I, 117-18).
49. Ibid., 14, 2-3 (I, 118-19).
50. Ibid., 15 (I, 127-30).
51. Ibid., 14, 2 (I, 118-19).
52. Ibid., 14, 2-3 (I, 118-19).
53. Gerald Brenan, *St. John of the Cross* (London: 1950), 43, 47-48, 53, 55.
54. See DN, i, 5, 2 (I, 364).
55. See Gerald May, *Will and Spirit* (San Francisco, CA: Harper & Row, 1982), 108.
56. DN, i, 10, 2 (I, 379).
57. Ibid., 10, 4 (379-80).
58. AMC Prologue 3 (I, 12).
59. See LF, iii, paragraphs 53 to 66 (III, 189-98).
60. Ibid., iii, 60 (III, 193).
61. Ibid., 43 (III, 183).
62. Ibid., 52 (III, 189).
63. Ibid., 62 (III. 194).
64. Ibid., 30 (III, 176).
65. Johannes Tauler, *Predigten* (Einsiedeln, 1979), I, 204.
66. Ibid., I, 201.
67. LF, iii, 30 (III, 176).
68. Ibid., 46 (III, 184-85).
69. AMC, ii, 22 (I, 172-184).
70. E. Jungclaussen, *Suche Gott in dir*, 55, 73 (hereafter "SGID").

71. GS, 12. (GS evidently = The Writings of Madame Guyon, ed. P. Poiret, but no such reference is provided—tr.).
72. Ibid., 13.
73. Ibid., 19.
74. Ibid., 24.
75. Ibid., 21.
76. Ibid., 23.
77. Ibid., 19.
78. Ibid., 280.
79. Ibid., 26.
80. SGID, 112.
81. Ibid., 191.
82. Ibid., 90.
83. Ibid., 86.
84. Ibid., 85.
85. Ibid., 45.
86. Ibid., 46.
87. Ibid., 50.
88. Ibid., 81.
89. Ibid., 109.
90. Ibid., 108.
91. Ibid., 86.
92. Ibid., 100.
93. Ibid., 102.
94. Ibid., 51.
95. Thomas Keating, *Das Gebet der Sammlung* (Münsterschwarzach, 1987), 43.
96. Ibid., 44.
97. Ibid., 45.
98. E. Lorenz, *Der nahe Gott* (Freiburg, 1985), 122.
99. Ibid., 15.
100. Ibid., 109.
101. Georg Denzler, *Die verbotene Lust* (Piper, 1988), 252.
102. I. Behn, *Spanische Mystik* (Düsseldorf, 1957), 265.
103. Zukav, 327.

8. JESUS CHRIST IN CONTEMPLATION
   1. AMC, ii, 11, 7 (I, 105-06).
   2. Ibid., 11, 12 (I, 108).
   3. S. Kirkegaard, *Einübung im Christentum*, XII, 102.
   4. Painadath, In: *Christ in der Gegenwart*, Nr. 47, (Freiburg: Herder).
   5. AMC, ii, 7, 11 (I, 92-93).
   6. Ibid., 12, 5 (I, 111-12).
   7. Ibid., 7, 12 (I, 93).
   8. See *Apokryphe Evangelien aus Nag Hammadi*, Editor K. Dietzfelbinger (Andechs: Dingfelder Verlag, 1988).

9. PSYCHOLOGICAL ASPECTS OF THE INNER PATH
   1. From Zenso Mondo—*Dialoge von Zenmeistern*.
   2. See Ken Wilber, *Wege zum Selbst* (Munich, 1984), 1.74-75.
   3. Ibid., 170 -71.
   4. LF, iv, 9 (III, 211).
   5. Shibayama, *Zen in Gleichnis und Bild*, Barthverlag, 82.
   6. Jean Père de Caussade, *Hingabe an Gottes Vorsehung* (Zürich, 1981), 146
   7. Ibid., 68-69.
   8. Ibid., 147.
   9. Ibid., 153.
   10. Ibid., 30.
   11. Ibid., 33.
   12. From the Sanskrit.
   13. Quint, 63.
   14. Meister Eckhart: *The Essential Sermons, Commentaries, Treatises, and Defense,* Translators Edmund Colledge and Bernard McGinn (Mahwah, NJ: Paulist Press, 1981), 251-52 (hereafter referred to as "ME").
   15. Quint, 324.
   16. ME, 253.
   17. Ibid.
   18. See *Lexikon der östlichen Weisheitslehren* (Munich, 1986), 425.
   19. Ibid., 317.
   20. Quint, 180, l. 9.

21. Ibid., 181, l. 38. Cf. also Ken Wilber, *Psychologie der Befreiung* (Munich: Scherz-Verlag, 1988), article by Brown, 229.
22. These comments follow J. White and his article in the book by S. Grof, *Die Chance der Menschheit* (Munich, 1988), 234.
23. Mihajlo Mihajlov in: *Lesebuch zu bedrängenden Fragen unserer Zeit*, Editor E. Naudascher, II, 83.
24. On this section see also Chapter IX, "Depression oder Transformationsprozeß?"
25. See Maha-Satibatthana-Sutta = Teaching on the awakening of attentiveness in Hinayana Buddhism.
26. See *Weisung der Väter*, Editor B. Miller (Freiburg, 1965).
27. Joseph Campbell, *The Power of Myth* (New York, NY: Doubleday, 1988).
28. See Plato, *The Republic*, Translator Francis M. Cornford (New York, NY: Oxford University Press, 1977), 227-31.
29. See H. Dürr, *Physik und Transzendenz* (Munich, 1986), 14.
30. C.G. Jung, *Gesammelte Werke IX*, 2nd. half-binding (Olten, 1976), 18.
31. See R. Metzner, "Der innere Feind," in S. Grof, *Die Chance der Menschheit*, 78.
32. Ibid., 79.
33. Ibid., 64.
34. Kabir, *Im Garten der Gottesliebe*, 55.
35. See Willigis Jäger, *Kontemplatives Beten*, (Münsterschwarzach, 1985), 15.
36. Kabir, 51.
37. Ibid., 58.
38. *Meister Eckhart: Teacher and Preacher*, Editor Bernard McGinn (Mahwah, NJ: Paulist Press, 1986), 265.

10. Moral Behavior

1. B. Toban, *Raumzeit und erweitertes Bewußtsein* (Synthesis Verlag), 134.
2. Martin Buber, *Die Geschichten der Chassidim* (Zürich, 1949). 715.
3. *Mumonkan* 19.

4. See L. Govinda, *Lebendiger Buddhismus im Abendland,* (Munich, 1986), 96.
5. Buber, *Die Erzählungen der Chassidim.*
6. Govinda, 102.
7. Ibid. 107.
8. Alan Watts, *This Is It* (New York, NY: Random House), 120.

12. MYSTICISM: FLIGHT FROM THE WORLD OR TAKING RESPONSIBILITY FOR IT?
   1. Quint, 277, l. 25.
   2. Ernst Neumann, *Kulturentwicklung und Religion* (Frankfurt am Main, 1981), 178.
   3. Ibid., 182-83
   4. Ibid., 178.
   5. Ibid., 169.
   6. ME, 78.
   7. Quint, 450, l. 2.
   8. See G. Schmid, *Die Mystik der Weltreligionen.*
   9. See E. Neumann.

PART II: TALKS
   1. Gertrud von Le Fort, *Die ewige Frau* (Munich, 1962), 21.
   2. Quint, 258, l. 13.
   3. ME, 78.
   4. Quint, 178, l. 16.
   5. Ibid., 227, l. 23.
   6. Ibid., 317, l. 30.
   7. Ibid., 178, l. 31.
   8. ME, 78.
   9. Ibid., 179.
  10. *Meister Eckhart: Teacher and Preacher,* 251.
  11. Quint, 185, l. 21.
  12. Ibid., 317, ll. 19, 30; 318, l. 12; 319, l. 10; 319, l. 30.
  13. Ibid., 180, ll. 16.
  14. Ibid., 317, l. 24.
  15. ME, 182.
  16. Evagrius, Ponticus, *Praktikos,* 18.

17. The Missal in Latin and English, Translators J.O'Connell and H.P.R. Finberg (London: Burns Oates and Washburne, 1958), 488-90.
18. AMC, ii, 7, 11 (I, 92-93).
19. See Bäumer-Despeigne, *Hadewijch von Antwerpen*, Copr.: Bannhalde 25, CH-8500 Frauenfeld, 16. (the address, but not the name, of the publisher—tr.)
20. See Schuré E., *Die großen Eingeweihten* (Munich, 1986).
21. Fyodor Dostoevsky, *A Raw Youth*, as interpreted by E. D Drewermann in *Tiefenpsychologie*, 691.
22. See Grof Stanislav, *Spirituelle Krisen* (Munich, 1990), 234.
23. F. Pfeiffer, *Meister Eckhart* (Aalen, 1962) 239, 17.
24. Ibid., 249, 8-18.
25. Ibid., 240, 19-35.
26. Gregory the Great, *Life of St. Benedict.*
27. See Christa Mulack, *Die Weiblichkeit Gottes* (Stuttgart, 1984), 178.
28. See K. Dietzfelbinger, *Apokryphe Evangelien aus Nag Hammadi* (Andechs, 1988), 256.
29. Walter Schubart, *Religion und Eros* (Munich, 1966), 93.
30. G. Börner, "Die Entstehung der Welt aus astronomischer Sicht," a lecture given in Alpbach in 1989.

PART III. PERSONAL ACCOUNTS

1. See E. Lorenz, "Ins Dunkel geschrieben," Herder TB 1505, 65.

INDEX

About the Author

Willigis Jäger, a Benedictine monk, entered Müensterschwarzach Abbey in Germany in 1946. After studying philosophy and theology, he was ordained a priest. For several years he taught at the abbey boarding school and then worked many more years with the church groups Missio and Misereor.

Following this, Father Jäger spent six years in Japan training with Zen Master Koun Yamada. Returning to Germany as a Zen teacher of the Sanbo Kyodan school of Zen, he opened a meditation center in Würzburg where he holds both Zen *sesshin* and courses in Christian contemplation.

Through his publications and his lectures at various congresses, Willigis Jäger has become one of Germany's best-known teachers in the area of Christian and Eastern esoterics. His most recent American books are *The Way to Contemplation: Encountering God Today* (Mahwah, NJ: Paulist Press, 1987) and *Contemplation: A Christian Path* (Liguori, MO: Liguori Publications/Triumph™ Books, 1994).